The Doctoral E

Donna Lee Brien
Craig Batty • Elizabeth Ellison
Alison Owens
Editors

The Doctoral Experience

Student Stories from the Creative Arts
and Humanities

Editors
Donna Lee Brien
School of Education and the Arts
Central Queensland University
Noosaville, QLD, Australia

Craig Batty
School of Communication
University of Technology Sydney
Sydney, NSW, Australia

Elizabeth Ellison
School of Education and the Arts
Central Queensland University
Noosaville, QLD, Australia

Alison Owens
Learning and Teaching Centre
Australian Catholic University
North Sydney, NSW, Australia

ISBN 978-3-030-18198-7   ISBN 978-3-030-18199-4   (eBook)
https://doi.org/10.1007/978-3-030-18199-4

This Palgrave Macmillan imprint is published by the registered company Springer Nature Switzerland AG.
The registered company address is: Gewerbestrasse 11, 6330 Cham, Switzerland

This book is dedicated to all creative and hard-working doctoral students and their supervisors.

Foreword

Doctoral learning journeys have, as their expressed aim, the completion of the highest form of education: the doctorate; and yet they are so much more than cognitive, intellectual journeys completing a significant project and producing a thesis or series of connected publications. These journeys are also life and identity journeys, and it is refreshing and insightful that this book intertwines the several strands—personal, ontological, learning, cognitive and intellectual—because at the heart of every doctoral journey there is always a person learning and changing, and there is often a range of supportive (one hopes) invested others circling the seemingly lone intellectual traveller. Recognition of the unique intertwining of people and learning, community and the individual, new learning and knowledge construction in the discipline or inter-discipline, lies at the heart of this rich and diverse collation of stories from the doctoral candidates themselves, and their supportive others. As Chinua Achebe comments, 'storytellers are powerful' (1987), and the construction of one's own doctoral learning journey as a story is clearly evidenced in this book as powerful, challenging and enabling for the candidates who have been invited to intertwine the strands of their physical, intellectual, emotional and imaginary lived experience as they journeyed through the doctorate.

A unique contribution of this book is its focus on the student voice, more commonly written about and researched in empowerment terms among school students and undergraduates. Here the doctoral candidates are telling their own stories, and this offers an authenticity often missing from research articles which thematise and select what the authors deem important. Personal, creative, critical views are often themselves formed through the process of that writing. The students here interweave strands of importance, and the editors explore, theorise, contextualise and offer guidance on the journey in its broader context of institutions, supervision, discipline orientations and the processes of the doctorate. The felt, lived experience in the doctoral student voice is both personal and intellectually oriented, located in self; in struggling, facing challenges and systematically working forwards, occasionally recovering from a backward slip, and breaking through with new discoveries and revelations. This is formed here into their own work and their own writing. Bringing together the student voices is enabling and very rich; they empower themselves as they express their experiences, in their own way and their own words about their own journeys.

However, this book is not just a concatenation of competing voices—it is a carefully curated live piece. The authors have drawn the student stories and voices together into well considered sections which emerged from those stories, so that rather than the more familiar doctoral study piece which offers a clarification of the research process—of methods of data collection and analysis—the students' voices and the stories lead.

In earlier work on doctoral learning journeys (Morris et al. 2011), we discovered those vital interconnections between the personal, learning and institutional dimensions of the doctoral journey, finding, for example, that the personal, domestic dimensions could so influence the progress on the learning journey that sometimes it completely halted. Latterly, working with creative doctoral students and particularly students from Indigenous origins (specifically a Maori and an Aboriginal student whose work I examined), and an Aboriginal graduate who I interviewed, in those interviews the supportive role of family and community emerged as essential to that journey. Much recent work has surfaced issues which show the relationships between wellbeing, mental health, the emotional damage or support provided by supervisors, and successful doctoral student journeys (Johansson et al. 2013; Wisker and Robinson 2012, 2015). While research on academic identities and work on impostor syndrome often concentrate on the emerging and sometimes stultified academic identities of doctoral candidates as they meet challenges and face hurdles, some of the positive, as well as some negative, interactions between personal worlds and learning worlds are also acknowledged by doctoral students (Wisker et al. 2017).

For some students undertaking creative doctorates in particular, the intertwining of the creative, the personal and the intellectual lies at the very core of their work. This can be a further element of complexity leading to potential paralyses in the work, or struggles with institutional requirements while pursuing something highly creative, or/and a rich intertwining of the intellectual development alongside the creative and the personal. Latterly, workshops I have facilitated have focused on the intertwining of ontology and epistemology, and more straightforwardly, a concern that the doctoral candidates' creative questioning, confusions, contestations, changes, risk taking, intrigue and questioning are inextricably intertwined with the research journey. In these workshops, candidates and supervisors remembering their own journeys have told of the breakthroughs into new understanding which lead to valuable contributions to knowledge and, much more, breakthroughs in ways of learning and understanding which fundamentally affect and enrich the learning journey through, and beyond, the doctoral project.

The student voices in this book's curated stories articulate such intertwining at all stages of the doctoral learning journeys. This is a very valuable, essential companion piece to journal articles and handbooks, and the book's focus on humanities and arts students offers a particularly rich and in-depth look at those intertexts between the personal, the learning, the creative, experiencing the researcher self, the development and contribution of research, new knowledge and understandings, and the invaluable new changes in both the intellectual and the personal journeys.

References

Achebe, C. 1987. *Anthills of the Savannah*. London: Heinemann.

Johansson, T., G. Wisker, S. Claesson, O. Strandler, and E. Saalman. 2013. "PhD supervision as an emotional process—Critical situations and emotional boundary work." *Pertanika: Journal of Social Science and Humanities* 22 (2): 605–620.

Morris, C., and G. Wisker. 2011. "Troublesome encounters: Strategies for managing the wellbeing of masters and doctoral education students during their learning processes." *HEA ESCalate Subject Centre Report.* http://escalate.ac.uk/6828.

Wisker, G., and G. Robinson. 2012. "Picking up the pieces: Supervisors and doctoral 'orphans'." *International Journal for Researcher Development* 3: 39–153.

Wisker, G., and G. Robinson. 2015. "Experiences of the creative doctorate: Minstrels and white lines." *Critical Studies in Teaching and Learning* 2 (2): 49–67.

Wisker, G., G. Robinson, and S. E. Bengtsen. 2017. "Penumbra: Doctoral support as drama: From the 'lightside' to the 'darkside'. From front of house to trapdoors and recesses." *Innovations in Education and Teaching International* 54 (6): 527–538.

Centre for Teaching and Learning,   Gina Wisker
University of Brighton, Brighton, UK

What is most personal is most universal.
—*Carl R. Rogers,* On Becoming a Person: A Therapist's View of
Psychotherapy

Acknowledgements

This book, on the doctoral journey, has been a journey of its own. Coordinating the work and energies of four editors, not to mention our significant number of contributors, and working across a large span of the Eastern coast of Australia and New Zealand—often in different time zones—has been a fascinating process and an enriching challenge.

In the process of putting this book together, there are many people to thank.

Firstly, we thank all the contributors who so generously worked with us and each other to develop the chapters in this collection. Everyone was so professional, creative and agreeable in their approach to this volume— and especially diligent and generous in offering commentary and feedback on each other's chapters, as well as quick in responding to our editorial queries—that working with such a large group was never anything but a pleasure.

We must also thank our universities which continue to support this area of research. This is Central Queensland University (Brien and Ellison), the University of Technology Sydney (Batty) and the Australian Catholic University (Owens). Professor William Blayney is a Dean who understands both learning and the humanity that underpins it. Thank you, Bill, for your support of this project, and approving the School of Education and the Arts seed grant funding, which financed the initial workshop that provided the impetus for this book. Professor Bobby

Harreveld generously supported the lead editor in her development of that funding proposal and then approved its funding. Associate Professor Susan Davis then oversaw the delivery of this funding. Thank you all for this support.

We would also like to thank the Noosa campus of Central Queensland University for its generous support of campus-based research events. As universities become more and more fiscally driven, many of our colleagues cannot even hold such research events on campus without incurring large fees. We thank the campus management and staff for their assistance and support.

Very sincere and appreciative thanks go to Professor Gina Wisker for providing such a perceptive and engaged foreword to the volume.

A special thank you to copyeditor, Virginia Birt, for her close reading of this volume and insightful input in terms of her probing questions, always gently put, but often resulting in significant improvements to the text.

The publishing team at Palgrave have been a dream to work with. Thank you all!

Finally, we acknowledge and thank all our colleagues, doctoral and other students, friends and family members who have either offered comments about, or encouragement and love during the process of working on, this book.

Contents

Notes on Contributors

Craig Batty is Head of Creative Writing at the University of Technology Sydney. He is the author, co-author and editor of ten books, including *Writing for the Screen: Creative and Critical Approaches* (2nd ed.) (2019) and *Screen Production Research: Creative Practice as a Mode of Enquiry* (2018). He has also published over 50 book chapters and journals articles on the topics of screenwriting practice, screenwriting theory, creative practice research and doctoral supervision. In 2016, he received an Australian Award for University Teaching (AAUT) Citation for his contributions to PhD supervision in creative writing.

Virginia Birt is a former DFAT officer with wide-ranging policy experience including as executive officer for the Australia-New Zealand Foundation and South Pacific Cultures Fund. A freelance writer, editor and script consultant, Virginia's research interests include screenwriting, screen production, visual art, children's and young adult literature, and promoting literacy in the community.

Donna Lee Brien is Professor of Creative Industries at Central Queensland University, Australia. Author and editor of over 30 books and exhibition catalogues, and author of over 200 book chapters and journal articles, Donna has completed major nationally-funded research projects on doctoral degrees, has successfully supervised almost 50 research students to completion and has examined over 100 Masters and Doctoral research theses for Australian and international universities. In 2014, she received the Vice-Chancellor's Award for Excellence in Research Higher Degree Supervision.

Lisa Brummel is an Australian multi-award winning, and internationally exhibited, artist. Her work is held in numerous private collections worldwide, including in Australia, Singapore and Paris. Lisa is currently researching an alternative firing technique for the raku kiln at Central Queensland University, Australia.

Margaret Cook is an Australian historian, cultural heritage consultant, a Post-Thesis Fellow at the University of Queensland and an Honorary Research Fellow at La Trobe University. Her PhD, completed in 2018, explored the history of floods in the Brisbane River and her findings have been published in national and international journals and in a book, *A River with a City Problem*, with University of Queensland Press.

Susan Currie BA/LLB (UQ), MLaws/MArts (QUT), PhD (CQU), has worked as a lawyer, academic, teacher and librarian. The major component of her PhD thesis, *A Prescription for Action: The Life of Dr Janet Irwin* was published by Australian Scholarly Publishing. Susan has also written biographical profiles for *A Woman's Place: 100 Years of Queensland Women Lawyers* published by the Supreme Court of Queensland Library, and co-authored a textbook on legal studies for Queensland schools.

Leanne Dodd is an Australian author and lecturer in creative writing at Central Queensland University. She acts as a mentor for emerging writers at Queensland Writers Centre and facilitates writing for well-being community workshops. She has published and presented nationally and internationally on writing about trauma in fiction. Her practice-led PhD explored the therapeutic potential of creative writing and the novel produced was longlisted for the 2018 Richell Prize for Emerging Writers (Hachette Publishers).

Elizabeth Ellison is a Senior Lecturer of Creative Industries at Central Queensland University in Noosa, Australia. Her research focuses on Australian writing, film and television, with a special interest in the Australian beach. She has ten years of teaching experience across all tertiary levels, and specialises in teaching and supervising in postgraduate creative industries programs. She coordinates the Creative Arts Research Training Academy, and has been involved in two national learning and teaching grants.

Carmen Gray is a visual art teacher at Central Queensland University. She has spent more than a decade creating course content for both online and face-to-face delivery. During this time, she has also pursued her own creative interests including printmaking and drawing. Along with her visual art practice, Carmen writes and illustrates books for middle-school readers. She is currently continuing her postgraduate studies at Central Queensland University.

Peter McKenzie is a lecturer of jazz and contemporary music within the Bachelor of Music degree at Central Queensland University, Australia. Peter is an accomplished woodwind specialist and has focused on being an in-demand saxophonist performing and teaching throughout Australia and the USA. Peter holds a Bachelor of Jazz Studies, a Grad Dip. Ed, and a Master of Learning Management degree. Peter is currently undertaking a Doctor of Philosophy specialising in developing regional jazz communities.

A. K. Milroy is an intra-disciplinary researcher who works in both art and science, publishing in journals as varied as *Australasian Journal of Popular Culture* and *Review of Palaeobotany and Palynology*. Milroy creates works of art/science and recently produced an exhibition for the Queensland Museum: 'Deep time', a sensory experience of life thirty million years ago using visualisations produced by synchrotron radiation and specimens from the museum's palaeobotanical collection. She is currently Associate Vice Chancellor, Central Highlands region, Central Queensland University.

Justine Newport is a studying towards a PhD investigating revision in contemporary poetry. A moderator for Jamyang Institute, London, in an on-line course in Buddhist studies for ten years, she has also run a counselling private practice. A professional exhibiting oil painter, Justine previously owned and ran Harmony Wood pottery, selling to galleries in Sydney, Melbourne and Canberra.

Charmaine O'Brien completed a PhD in Creative Writing at Central Queensland University. She also holds a Master of Science in coaching psychology. Her doctoral thesis focused on the writing of food, cookery and cooks in Australian history, and the psychology of creativity and coaching creativity. She has published widely on Australian food history including *The Colonial Kitchen: Australia 1788–1901*. Charmaine is also the author of several books on Indian food history and culture, including *The Penguin Food Guide to India*.

Susannah Oddi is a PhD candidate in creative writing with Central Queensland University, Australia. Her practice-led research examines the influence of an online community on digital writing, comparing contemporary digital serial frameworks with Victorian techniques. Susannah has a background in professional writing, corporate research and communications. Her research interests include digital serial narratives and Victorian and contemporary Gothic media.

Alison Owens lectures in the Graduate Certificate in Higher Education at the Australian Catholic University in Sydney, and is an adjunct Associate Professor of Education at Central Queensland University. She has taught university courses in English, education, communications and social research methods for over twenty years and has a special research interest in internationalization of education and curriculum as well as second language learning. Alison has a Doctorate of Education and a PhD in Creative Arts.

Gail Pittaway is a Senior Lecturer in Creative Writing, Drama and Storytelling, Myth and Ritual at the Waikato Institute of Technology, in the School of Media Arts. She is also a doctoral candidate at Central

Queensland University, undertaking a Creative Writing thesis in creative nonfiction—a food memoir. Gail has had both creative work and academic papers published, and has co-edited journal special issues, conference proceedings and a collection of academic essays.

Irene Rogers PhD (CQU), is an Adjunct Senior Lecturer at Central Queensland University Australia. Her research interests are in the history of nursing and medicine. She has jointly published articles on the use of drama in nursing education, oral history and Australian nursing in WW1. She has worked extensively in humanitarian nursing in areas of conflict as a clinician and educator.

Bernadette Ryan PhD (CQU), MHProfEd (JCU), BHealthSc (CQU), RN, is freelance musician, composer, teacher and writer. Her PhD study on Thai popular protest music, completed at Central Queensland University Australia, marked a culmination in her music interests by bringing together Southeast Asian and Western music forms involving classical, popular, and folk styles. Her approach to music—music as social practice—is inspired by art's connection to social critique. She is author of several published articles and has presented her research in Thailand, Singapore, USA, and Australia.

Colleen Ryan is a lecturer in nursing at Central Queensland University. Her research focusses on nursing education for clinicians and students. She has co-authored nine published manuscripts and has presented at international conferences in New Zealand and Australia, and a variety of national nursing and simulation conferences. Currently she is completing doctoral studies around the professional development needs of nursing clinical teachers.

Alison Vincent has qualifications in science (BSc Hons UNSW) and history (BA MLitt UNE), and experience of both the quantitative and the qualitative research journey. She has just completed a PhD at Central Queensland University researching the role of restaurant reviews in the shaping of tastes for dining out. She has published widely both online and in print and regularly presents at conferences both in Australia and internationally.

1

Introduction

Donna Lee Brien, Craig Batty, Elizabeth Ellison, and Alison Owens

The doctorate represents the most advanced form of adult education and qualification. Although considerable effort, research and training has been expended on the process of completing a doctorate, there has been far less interest or focus on the lived experience of doing one—the human, and often relatively veiled dimension that underpins the highest level of formal learning achievable. With this is mind, this book offers a wide

D. L. Brien (✉) • E. Ellison
School of Education and the Arts, Central Queensland University,
Noosaville, QLD, Australia
e-mail: d.brien@cqu.edu.au; l.ellison@cqu.edu.au

C. Batty
School of Communication, University of Technology Sydney,
Sydney, NSW, Australia
e-mail: Craig.Batty@uts.edu.au

A. Owens
Learning and Teaching Centre, Australian Catholic University,
North Sydney, NSW, Australia
e-mail: Alison.Owens@acu.edu.au

© The Author(s) 2019
D. L. Brien et al. (eds.), *The Doctoral Experience*,
https://doi.org/10.1007/978-3-030-18199-4_1

1

variety of personal insights from creative arts and humanities research students into the challenging yet rewarding journey of undertaking a doctorate. Recognising that the doctoral journey is simultaneously cognitive, emotional, spiritual, ethical and transformational, the book presents a range of chapters written by current or very recently completed doctoral students (as well as one intending candidate) that capture the essence of what it means to undertake a doctorate in the twenty first century. Unlike other books that focus on the degree milestones that completing doctoral level study entails, this book is uniquely organised around the themes and concerns that students themselves have identified as centrally important to successfully completing their research degrees—the invisible work of the doctorate. From assessing the self to working with others, from building resilience to developing networks, and considering how ethical conduct permeates a researcher's practice, this book takes its readers—both students and supervisors—on a journey towards successful doctoral learning. Each section is framed by ideas and concepts suggested by the editors, who are experienced doctoral supervisors, but the core content of the book is purposely student-driven and authored. This, we hope, will provide an authentic and user-friendly account of the doctoral experience.

On Doctoral Learning

In the students' accounts of their experiences and journeys, it is not surprising to see them demonstrating sophisticated levels of conceptual, procedural, declarative and metacognitive knowledge, as defined in Benjamin Bloom's Taxonomy (Anderson and Krathwohl 2001). Constructivist accounts of adult learning emphasise the sequential and developmental process of assimilating new knowledge with existing knowledge, and then applying this newly assimilated knowledge to practice. In his model of the Experiential Learning Cycle, David Kolb (1981) emphasises the cyclical process of theorising abstract conceptualisations, testing these theories through application to concrete experiences, and then reflecting on outcomes to generate further and more refined theorisations. This cyclical process applies very clearly to doctoral study, which aims to develop new knowledge (and/or theories) supported by evidence drawn from real-world investigations through research, and implying further research through a process of reflective analysis, evaluation and further theorisation. As the students in this book discuss, the challenges and complexities of undertaking a doctorate have been embraced and overcome to produce resilient learners who are not only able to complete research projects, but who are also able to understand the journey they have undergone and fold it back into their ongoing practice—as researchers, practitioners, teachers, and so on.

Other constructivist models of learning organise the development of cognitive complexity as a hierarchical process, for example, Bloom's Taxonomy (Anderson and Krathwohl 2001), John Biggs' SOLO (Structure of Observed Learning Outcomes) (Biggs and Tang 2011), and Matthew Perry's 'nine positions'. Perry's model (1975) progresses from a dualistic—right or wrong—approach, to acquiring knowledge through a multiplistic understanding of knowledge as context-dependent and uncertain, to a sophisticated response to relative values and contingent knowledge through a process of commitment to a reasoned position. The doctoral journey represents an engagement with knowledge and reality that is necessarily performed at the higher end of the hierarchy of cognitive complexity. Doctoral students 'theorise the unknown', performing what Biggs (Biggs and Tang 2011) has defined as 'extended abstract' thinking in a sustained and structured process, engaging with the higher order cognitive processes of evaluative and creative thinking (Anderson and Krathwohl 2001). With many of the doctoral projects described in this book drawn from students of the creative arts, creative thinking is particularly evident. In this context, each chapter provides an evaluative account of an aspect of doctoral study that has challenged the student-author, whose reflective assessment and subsequent 'breakthrough' can help inform and support others undertaking their own research journeys.

This book thus celebrates the lived experience of undertaking a doctorate—the human dimension of high-level learning—and taps into some of the common personal challenges that students face and, ideally, learn how to overcome. Chapter authors are each at different stages of their doctoral journey (with some just completed), and their stories reflect on key aspects of the journey that had such an effect as to 'stop them in their tracks' and encourage them to think more widely than their specific research project. The book therefore does not follow what many other doctoral study guides would consider to be the 'standard' journey of candidature. Rather than taking readers through stages related to the project itself—for example, developing a literature review, selecting and enacting a methodology, conducting pilot work—this book centres on the often non-linear, iterative and sometimes messy cognitive journey, which we characterise as a transformation that comprises challenges, breakthroughs and reflections on the process. In editing this book, we found that it was sometimes more useful to place chapters by students further along the journey alongside those who were just beginning, because early insights were useful segues into the very issues that the latter students were then writing about. We hope the structure presented is rich and rewarding, and encourages an interactive relationship with the stories presented, rather than simply following them in a preconceived order.

On Doctoral Transformation

The doctoral learning experience is also strongly transformational in both the personal and the social sense (Mezirow and Taylor 2009), in that new knowledge created from an original research enquiry informs and progresses the understandings of a specialist community of practice (discipline), and also transforms the individual through "self-critique of deeply-held assumptions which leads to greater personal awareness in relationship to others" (Taylor in Mezirow and Taylor 2009, p. 5). This process is evident in Alison Vincent's chapter, which positions identity at the centre of doctoral learning and emphasises self-discovery in what is firmly framed as a process of life-centred learning. It also provides the focus of the chapters from Leanne Dodd, Justine Newport, Alison Owens and Charmaine O'Brien, which explore the personal and interpersonal implications, benefits and risks involved in telling your own and other people's stories.

A strong theme of self-care and self-awareness emerges also from the student stories. Further evidence of the life-oriented nature of adult learning, and the centrality of formal and informal relationships, is provided in chapters by Peter McKenzie, Susannah Oddi and Colleen

Ryan, for example. Empowering experience-based guidance is drawn from chapters by AK Milroy and Carmen Grey, which speak to tactics for achieving university approvals, recognising and realising the role of creativity in doctoral research, and developing personal resilience for unplanned outcomes. Gail Pittaway and Bernadette Ryan further demonstrate the personal, professional and intellectual transformations that are a direct flow-on from doctoral study. Transformation, therefore, permeates the entirety of the book's content, as well as its structure.

On the Creative Arts and Humanities Doctorate

Despite the various paradigms of doctoral degrees that exist internationally (with such features as coursework, numbers of milestone review points, the *viva voce* and the ways examiners are asked to report varying from location to location, and sometimes even within individual universities), the human experience of doctoral study—our research, and this book, suggests—is much more universal. As such, while the focus of this book is on PhD students from the creative arts and humanities, we suggest that all of the aspects written about by the students—personal and cognitive—are applicable across disciplines and doctorate types (for example, PhD, Doctor of Creative Arts, Professional Doctorate, Doctor of Education). The fact that this book concentrates on the creative arts and humanities is a testament of sorts to its focus on unearthing the personal and human facets of doctoral study, given that many creative arts and humanities research topics relate to people, cultures and personal processes.

The Development of This Book

The foundations for this book emerged via a two-day workshop with current or newly completed research students as facilitated by the editors. Throughout the two days, the students were invited to share their experiences of doctoral study in a collective setting. Specifically, they were asked to prepare responses in advance to three questions:

- What were the main challenges encountered in your doctoral study?
- What were the breakthroughs you experienced in your doctoral study?
- If you could start again, what questions would you ask yourself, your supervisor, and your university, before beginning?

Students shared their responses about their challenges and breakthroughs throughout the first day, and the editors used large whiteboards in the room to record and collate the key themes that emerged as the conversation progressed. At the conclusion of the first day, students were asked to map their research journey overnight, identifying cognitive (learning) and emotional (personal) obstacles or milestones. On the second day, students shared their responses to the third question, sharing insights about what information they wished they had received earlier in their candidatures. Specific findings from the workshop and the data generated have been reported separately in journal publications. The final part of the workshop was the collective planning of the book's structure, in which students and the editors worked together to identify thematic trends—in particular, the journey metaphor—and volunteered topics for chapters. Each student chapter is sole-authored but students worked collaboratively in small groups, and then pairs, in order to refine this work, and respond to comments from the book's editors. Although there have been some expected changes to this initial plan through this writing and editing process, many of these original ideas remain and speak to the co-created approach the editors and authors took for the development of this book. In devising this process, we were inspired by such research as that by Jazvac-Martek, Chen and McAlpine which suggests that "student agency emerges strongly in negotiating with others in order to achieve intentions" (2011, p. 18), and our own belief that doctoral students are the experts when it comes to the doctoral experience.

The workshop was developed as an action learning event in recognition of the fact that collaborative learning through cyclic processes of questioning and reflecting is appropriate to a group of cognitively advanced, adult learners with developing research experience and expertise. Action learning is one form of action research, which also includes critical action research, participatory action research and collaborative inquiry (Kemmis and McTaggart 2005; McTaggart et al. 2017). Action learning entails "real people resolving and taking action on real problems in real time, and learning through questioning and reflection while doing so" (Marquardt and Waddill 2010, p. 186). The workshop was envisaged as a tool to support students to develop both an individual, and a collaborative, capacity to identify, recognise and negotiate problems that are frequently encountered in the research journey; to empower these students through collaborative problem solving; and to generate research outcomes and reportage that could be used to assist research degree students and supervisors.

We acknowledge that there are some limitations to the collective authorship of this book. For example, the workshop participants were representative of a predominantly female, older demographic, with only one younger male participant and one male editor. This is reflective of the demographics in Australia in the broad Field of Education areas of Society and Culture, and Creative Arts (Department of Education and Training 2017). There was also limited cultural and linguistic diversity in this group: all students were enrolled as domestic students (that is, Australian or New Zealand citizens or permanent residents). Again, this is not dissimilar to the national demographic of this type of cohort which usually has less international enrolments. Participants were representative of a number of institutions, although a majority were from Central Queensland University, the host organisation for the workshop. Within the group, the students represent both on-campus and distance, and full-time and part-time study modes.

Using This Book for Doctoral Success

Considering the human dimension within doctoral research has largely been lacking, it is our hope that this book will inspire others to also focus on this important aspect. While presenting the journey, and voices of students undertaking their doctorates, was a key motivation for this book, it was also produced with doctoral supervisors in mind.

Although experienced doctoral supervisors and thesis examiners ourselves, we were still surprised, enthralled and moved by the stories that emerged, and what these revealed of the students' aspirations, struggles, resilience and achievements—and we have taken these learnings back into our own supervisory practices. As such, we hope that other supervisors reading this book will share the same sentiments and use the stories presented to assist them with their development as successful supervisors of their own doctoral students.

The book is structured with a framing commentary introducing each thematic part in order to situate and contextualise these parts in terms of the broader ecology of doctoral study and supervision, and to tease out some of the more general nuances that we, as editors and supervisors, can see in these individual narratives. As a result, this book can be read from beginning to end, or used for 'just-in-time' learning to meet the challenges and issues that arise during every candidature. Chapters and parts of chapters can be visited and revisited by students and supervisors as various needs arise, including the personal, italicised vignettes that bring the challenges and breakthroughs to life. This will assist in meeting problems, not only in a timely manner, but crucially, before they are compounded. The book has been purposely structured to include personal perspectives, case studies, scholarly signposts, and key take-away points that are relevant in all doctoral settings—regardless of geography—and to all students, at any stage of their own research journeys.

The centrality of experience to learning has long been acknowledged by influential theorists in education including John Dewey, Jean Piaget and Lev Vygotsky. In adult learning, defined by Malcolm Knowles (1984) as 'andragogy', experience plays an even more critical role in learning as adults have a greater breadth of experience than children and adolescents, and resource their learning by drawing on their past and present life experiences. The doctoral stories collected in this book are thus supplied to engage the reader with the lived experiences of these students, including study, work and home life, and are intended to implicitly recognise the convolution of learning experience and life experience. As such, it is our hope that this book provides both interesting and helpful information as well as personally engaging stories that can be of use to students and supervisors currently working on a doctorate, as well as interested potential students wanting to learn more about what a successful and enjoyable doctoral journey might look like.

References

Anderson, L. W., and D. Krathwohl, eds. 2001. *A Taxonomy for Learning, Teaching, and Assessing: A Revision of Bloom's Taxonomy of Educational Objectives*. New York: Longman.

Biggs, J. B., and C. Tang. 2011. *Teaching for Quality Learning*. 4th ed. Open University Press.

Department of Education and Training. 2017. *Higher Education Statistics Data Cube (uCube): Enrolment Count by Mode of Attendance by Type of Attendance by Gender by Course Level by Field of Education*. http://highereducationstatistics.education.gov.au.

Jazvac-Martek, M., S. Chen, and L. McAlpine. 2011. "Tracking the doctoral student experience over time: Cultivating agency in diverse spaces." In *Doctoral Education: Research-Based Strategies for Doctoral Students, Supervisors and Administrators*, edited by L. McAlpine and C. Amundsen, 17–36. Dordrecht: Springer.

Kemmis, S., and R. McTaggart. 2005. "Participatory action research: Communicative action and the public sphere." In *The SAGE Handbook of Qualitative Research*, edited by N. Denzin and Y. Lincoln, 3rd ed., 559–603. London: SAGE.

Knowles, M. 1984. *The Adult Learner: A Neglected Species*. 3rd ed. Houston: Gulf.

Kolb, D. A. 1981. "Learning styles and disciplinary differences." In *The Modern American College*, edited by A. W. Chickering and Associates, 232–255. San Francisco: Jossey Bass.

Marquardt, M., and D. Waddill. 2010. "The power of learning in action learning: A conceptual analysis of how the five schools of adult learning theories are incorporated within the practice of action learning." *Action Learning: Research and Practice* 1 (2): 185–202.

McTaggart, R., R. Nixon, and S. Kemmis. 2017. "Critical participatory action research." In *The Palgrave International Handbook of Action Research*, edited by L. Rowell, C. Bruce, J. Shosh, and M. Riel, 21–35. New York: Palgrave Macmillan.

Mezirow, J., and E. W. Taylor. 2009. *Transformative Learning in Practice: Insights from Community, Workplace, and Higher Education.* Jossey Bass.

Perry, W. G. 1975. "Intellectual and ethical development in the college years." In *How Students Learn*, edited by N. Entwistle, and D. Hounsell, 139–148. Lancaster: University of Lancaster.

Part I

Orienting Towards the Doctoral Journey: Introduction to Part

Donna Lee Brien, Craig Batty, Elizabeth Ellison, and Alison Owens

In this section, students outline the very personal nature of undertaking a doctorate. They discuss the importance of the research project itself to each candidature, and how this strongly intersects with the personal and professional development of the researcher (in-training). This is intended to encourage readers to take themselves on a journey along with the student-authors. The various chapters in this section also offer strategies

D. L. Brien (✉) • E. Ellison
Noosaville, QLD, Australia
e-mail: d.brien@cqu.edu.au; l.ellison@cqu.edu.au

C. Batty
Sydney, NSW, Australia
e-mail: Craig.Batty@uts.edu.au

A. Owens
North Sydney, NSW, Australia
e-mail: Alison.Owens@acu.edu.au

for effective self-reflection that will assist both existing and intending students on their journey as they read the various student stories in this volume. Citing Kandiko and Kinchin (2012), who argue that doctoral education "is a process of development and learning that is much broader than the production of a research outcome", Holbrook et al. (2013, p. 3) highlight the need "to develop a model for doctoral education and supervision that incorporates learning, intellectual practice, scholarly expertise, technique and contextual expertise as well as attitudinal and personal change". In their chapters, these students argue the same point.

AK Milroy explicitly discusses how the doctoral journey often requires a revision of previously held paradigms. As she identifies, students have ontological, epistemological, methodological and axiological paradigms that need to be addressed and rethought, because new thought creates new knowledge. What is so valuable about this discussion is Milroy's focus on how this active re-visioning functioned in her own PhD. Alison Vincent makes a case that, while undertaking this reorientation, students should also be doing everything they can to ensure they enjoy the experience of their doctoral studies—an aspect which is often lost in the focus on reaching the desired goal—explaining that the two are not mutually exclusive. Like Milroy, Vincent stresses the importance of planning as a key part of the process engaged with before commencing a doctorate. Both these chapters underscore the importance of completing some deep thinking on personal goals, strengths and weaknesses, and ways of working, before commencing a doctorate.

The next chapters develop this line of thought, but add how students also need to envision how they will operate in the larger academic system. Irene Rogers charts the evolution of the academy since Classical times to provide a context for her argument that, as well as their own processes, it is important for students to understand the nature of the transformations the academy has undergone in order to find their place in it. This knowledge is also essential so that students can align their personal expectations with the contemporary academy and what it does, and can, provide for—and to—them, both while studying and after the completing of their doctorates. Margaret Cook underscores this thinking, reflecting on her own just-completed doctorate. Cook explains that while many research students may think they know the skills they need to develop to complete a doctoral degree, these are often—following many of the guides available—focused on what she describes as the mechanics of the process. This includes honing the essential research and writing skills that are necessary to produce a thesis. Yet, in her experience, as Cook explains, many students are not aware of the less tangible skills and knowledge that a research student must acquire in order to be successful, in terms of an awareness of, and adherence to, the academic culture that Rogers outlines. By recasting the steps of the research process in these terms, Cook outlines the transformative steps and transferable skills that are required to achieve a doctorate. These are in line with some previous research (Kroll and Brien 2006), but—importantly in this context—expressed in terms of the reality of the student experience.

Each of these students are all well aware of what contemplating, beginning, working through and completing a doctorate entails, and the planning that is involved in successfully reconfiguring their persona to that of a doctoral student operating in the contemporary academy. This can be amplified when a student comes to this from a professional or creative practice background. From their study of fine arts doctoral students, Holbrook et al. (2013, p. 5) argue quite rightly that "A practice-based research paradigm requires candidates to engage in a dialogue between their art-making practices and their conceptual thinking about art as research, and yet candidates tend to be more familiar with the expectations of art-making and less with the academic expectations associated with doctoral study". Simmons and Holbrook (2013, p. 205) also discuss how "Strongly held creative identities, unrealistic expectations about candidature, and underestimation of the requirements of research, can all serve to destabilise the experience of research for the newcomer in fine art research". We suggest this mismatch can also operate in both professionally-experienced students and those from other disciplines. As well as potential frustrations, this can result in academic mismatch—an incongruity between what doctoral students want from a program, and what the program is preparing them to do, and be in the world, after they graduate (Hoskins and Goldberg 2005, cited by Holbrook et al. 2013, p. 4)—and if students and supervisors do not orient themselves accordingly early on in the process, it can lead to dissatisfaction and, worse, a tumultuous journey that might never be completed. We are, however, inspired by

Holbrook et al.'s study that found many fine arts doctoral students viewing the research degree "as an excellent opportunity to improve or change their practice, to explore new directions and inject new rigour into their art-making" (2013, p. 7). In other words, both the personal and academic aspects of the doctoral journey should be embraced for their potential to expand and enhance what the student already knows and does, in order to foster a criticality in their practice to move it forward, and a new sophistication in thinking—which helps new students to orient towards the doctorate accordingly and proceed in a way to ensure success.

References

Holbrook, A., B. Simmons, J. Scevak, and J. Budd. 2013. "Higher degree research candidates' initial expectations in fine art." *TEXT: Journal of Writing and Writing Courses*, special issue 22: 1–16. http://www.text-journal.com.au/speciss/issue22/Holbrook_et_al.pdf.

Kroll, J., and D. L. Brien. 2006. "Studying for the future: Training creative writing postgraduates for life after degrees." *Australian Online Journal of Arts Education* 2 (1): 1–13.

Simmons, B., and A. Holbrook. 2013. "From rupture to resonance: Uncertainty and scholarship in fine art research degrees." *Arts and Humanities in Higher Education* 12 (2–3): 204–221.

2

Making Time (and Space) for the Journey

A. K. Milroy

Introduction

Completing the doctoral journey takes a considerable amount of fortitude and self-discipline. It also requires that the student undertaking
doctoral studies re-examine, and perhaps abandon, previously held
hypotheses if their data shows anomalies or unexpected, contrary results.
Recognising the new is difficult, for if it is truly new knowledge, there
will not be any pre-existing way of expressing what has been discovered
or created. How to recognise and then textualise and/or visualise this
new knowledge in a thesis is the challenge. To allow such a poetic revealing (Heidegger 1996), the researcher has to create space: to suspend time,
schedules, books, writing and all of the usual 'procrastination by being
busy' that inevitably follows the doctoral student, and especially those
who are perpetually burdened by a cloud of guilt and thinking, 'I really
should be writing'.

A. K. Milroy (✉)
Central Queensland University, Emerald, QLD, Australia
e-mail: a.milroy@cqu.edu.au

© The Author(s) 2019
D. L. Brien et al. (eds.), *The Doctoral Experience*,
https://doi.org/10.1007/978-3-030-18199-4_2

The doctoral journey necessitates a revision of previously held paradigms—ontological, epistemological, methodological, axiological and rhetorical—as new knowledge is created by new thought. In my case, the PhD (which is, after all, a Doctor of Philosophy) required deep sustained cogitation (and lots of it) to contribute to knowledge. The importance of contributing to knowledge, across all disciplines, is inherent as a key criterion for excellence in a doctoral examination (Bourke and Holbrook 2013). Such deep thinking requires dedicated time; the ancient Greek philosophers knew this and valued it accordingly. Think Archimedes, and the epiphany he (allegedly) had while bathing, which resulted in a principle of how to determine the volume of an object with an irregular shape. Further, some of the most revolutionary theories of our time, such as Darwin's Theory of Evolution, were born not only from periods of sustained observation but also from periods of sustained thinking about that observation. Making time to think is a very individual process: for Darwin, taking regular walks around his property was how he made the time to think about, and to ruminate on, what he had observed and studied. In such relaxed synaptic meanderings, new thoughts had space to evolve. These breaks from concentrated observation, experimentation and recording allowed the 'new' knowledge to reveal itself to him (Stone 1980).

I found that *poïesis*, or the generation of new knowledge, was a process of 'revealing' (Milroy 2017). It required sustained quiet sitting in a peaceful place and allowing my mind to wander freely, to follow whatever synaptic meanderings it wanted, and free of needing to achieve 'something'. It also compelled me to avoid the distraction of people, books, writing, digital technologies and the constant 'doing' associated with my course of doctoral study. I was surprised at how effective and essential this practice became, although initially it was a struggle to justify not 'doing' something thesis specific. Scientific studies confirm this strategy of unconscious processing. Doidge (2007) highlights that even when thoughts are consciously—not actively—accessed in reality, the neuroplasticity of the human mind means it never actually stops or shuts down, but rather keeps changing with each new stimuli and the constant processing that takes place in the unconscious.

'Mind-wandering', or the study of spontaneous task-unrelated thoughts, is a recent research field in neuroscience and experimental science. According to Metzinger (2018), its results have radical implications for many fields. He uses the metaphor of 'porpoising' or a 'dolphin model of cognition' to describe how our conscious thoughts are like dolphins jumping briefly out of the 'ocean of our unconscious' for short periods before they submerge again. But as he points out, the control we have over our cognition is at best tenuous, thus how to harness these brief flashes is not yet understood. However, providing an environment with as few external stimulants as possible—that is, one that avoids competing with our subconscious thoughts—and allowing an activity such as mind-wandering, appears to be a way of encouraging these cognitive 'jumps' from unconscious to conscious thought to occur.

I often find these 'porpoising' events occur at unexpected times, however, I notice that many arise while driving (my epic car journeys provide a wonderful place to allow these to emerge, no telephone, no computers, no ability to write, just the open road, and my body on almost-automatic pilot that comes with a lifetime of driving long distances). Long walks in nature also provide a similar atmosphere, as does sitting outside on the couch in the morning sun, waking slowly with my morning tea or coffee. Occasionally these flashes occur in the middle of the night. And as my phone is often near, I can scribble or record a note, or even send an email to myself as a means of capturing these. In other circumstances (such as driving), I relate the thought to something else and write it into my journal/diary when I am physically able to do so.

Time

If the doctoral journey requires students to embrace mind-wandering and high levels of cogitation, it is imperative that we give ourselves time and space to do so. Elizabeth Grosz, in her book, *The Nick of Time: Politics, Evolution and the Untimely* (2004), challenges us to think of time as an ontological element. What exactly is time? Is it knowable or real? In her introduction to the book, she states: "Time is neither fully 'present', a thing in itself, nor is it a pure abstraction, a metaphysical assumption that can be ignored in everyday practice" (Grosz 2004, p. 5). She further refines this definition and states:

> Time is real, its characteristics are unique, and its effects cannot be explained in other terms. It distinguishes itself from space, from objects, from its multiplicitous representations in mathematical, formulaic or geometrical terms, or in the images and representations provided in the visual arts, through effects that are not spatial, objective, measurable or quantifiable, although it has no language of its own, no models on which to base itself except those provided by the impulse to spatialisation. (2004, p. 249)

Physicist Carlo Rovelli, on the other hand, has a very different ontological viewpoint. He writes:

> Fundamentally time does not exist. Time exists for us. Up and down exists for us but there's no up and down in the universe. The idea that time is not integral to the structure of reality is not something everybody agrees with, but many people are working on it. It might be true, and this would mean that the universe is something very different from what we think. (2016, p. 45)

These two opposing views on the nature and reality of time are a great example of how one's research paradigm, or worldview, may change during the doctoral journey. In my own experience, I examined both positivism and constructivism as the major paradigms for the production of new knowledge in science and art. However, neither fully encapsulated a useful methodology for my art-science hybrid research. As a result, I found myself drawn to quantum studies and Karen Barad's (2007) notion of an ethico-onto-epistemology. Barad furthers the work of Donna Haraway (1997), and both challenge binary-type thinking. As Barad notes, it is the measuring apparatus that determines the characteristics of what is being measured. Hence photons (of light) may have the characteristics of a particle under one measuring apparatus and a wave under another, despite these characteristics being considered mutually exclusive. I was excited by the possibility of quantum physics being able to define a research paradigm that could be applied to any discipline, and have been investigating its potential. I have tentatively described this research paradigm as Quantum | ivism (Milroy 2017). Under this paradigm, time can simultaneously exist and not exist, its state depending on how the individual chooses to measure it. For the doctoral journey, however, it is Grosz's definition that the thesis (as an apparatus) measures, and time is a 'real' entity.

As time in any of its measurements is inextricably linked with space, we also need to consider where we are and how this affects our doctoral journey.

A Room of One's Own

Virginia Woolf's *A Room of One's Own* ([1929] 1989) empowered many female writers to further careers with a private space in which to work. She advocated "a room of one's own" for maintaining a clear head—advice that arguably applies across disciplines and gender. Making a place for solitude and creative work (research) is a resonating comment throughout the ages:

> The mind is sharper and keener in seclusion and uninterrupted solitude. No big laboratory is needed in which to think. Originality thrives in seclusion free of outside influences beating upon us to cripple the creative mind. Be alone, that is the secret of invention; be alone, that is when ideas are born. (Tesla quoted in Dunlap 1934, p. 9)

Here, Tesla is promoting solitude as a way of stopping the relentless march of time by removing oneself from the things that are constantly reminding us of its advance. To complete a doctorate, students need to acknowledge that most of their daily life is entangled with the thought of time as a 'real' thing, in this case, a countdown towards a completed thesis. However, paradoxically, this sustained focus on getting things done according to a schedule competes with the mind's equally important need to 'un-plug', to allow the gestation and birth of new ideas, new thoughts, new knowledge. As Grosz proposes, "this space and time for invention, for the creation of the new, can come about only through a dislocation of and dissociation with the present" (2004, p. 261).

Making Space for Time

The typical doctoral journey is structured for the student to complete in some three to four years of full-time study, and this necessitates considerable planning to make space for time. The strategy I developed during my course of study was to analyse and break down the complicated doctoral journey into a manageable, achievable process with clear tasks and an imaginable destination. I have summarised these tasks into a checklist and present this as a Doctoral Journey Planner, which can be modified and used to incorporate other university requirements, timelines and planning tools.

The Doctoral Journey Planner (see Appendix 1) is also provided as a template for student and supervisors to develop an effective way of planning the research—with agreed destinations and milestones. Kearns and Gardiner observe that highly successful research students treat their doctoral journey as a job, complete with holidays and breaks (2012, pp. 30–31), and this may require the student to establish such factors as a dedicated space in which to work, and the appropriate equipment required, alongside an evaluation of other time demands and external expectations.

Towards the latter half of the doctoral journey, I devised a useful personal strategy when I purchased two whiteboards and divided them into days as a planning calendar. I chose to put the smaller one up in my kitchen and the larger one in my office. Not only did this motivate me and remind me of how many days were left to complete each task, but it also provided a visual cue for friends and family, so they had some idea of the amount of work involved, and were understanding when I had to excuse myself from social events. Learning "not to say yes" (Kearns and Gardiner 2013) became a key strategic response to ensure I gave doctoral priorities the attention they deserved.

The countdown calendar also provided a visual check of goals versus time available, and assisted with culling less important tasks to make room for more important tasks. The kitchen planner also serves (yes, I still use the system) as a discussion point at meal times, when I can confer with other members of the household and pencil in events that they need me to attend. In this way, I am able to respect their needs as well as my own.

I still struggle with scheduling down time, however, my aim is to have at least one day of proper rest every week. Scheduling downtime is crucial to re-energising and topping the tank up. Working a constant seven days soon becomes a false economy and any progress erodes as fatigue sets in.

There are digital time counters available online, and students may like to set one for their doctorate. A perpetual calendar can also be sourced online, and annotated with significant milestones, as per the Doctoral Journey Planner. Similarly, there are apps available that can be programmed for certain key events and milestones. These can be used on a smartphone as a daily reminder. A number of online support mechanisms exist to support students in their research journey. Twitter users can follow hashtag conversations such as #phdchat and #acwri (short for academic writing). Initiatives like 'Shut Up & Write', which encourages writers to meet (in person or virtually) and write for an hour or so in collegial silence (Mewburn et al. 2014), are also growing and are available in settings such as cafes and co-working spaces. Some further online material is generic and not specific to discipline; see, for instance, *The Thesis Whisperer* (Mewburn 2018) or 'iThinkWell' (Gardiner and Kearns 2018). Discipline-specific support is also available, such as the creative writing resources available through the journal *TEXT: Writing and Writing Courses* and, in particular, the exegesis structure suggested in Brien et al., "Exegetical essentials" (2017), in Batty and Brien's *TEXT* special issue, titled *The Exegesis Now* (2017).

Strategic Side-Trips

All doctoral programs allow the student to take leave, and it is important to schedule time off. In addition to honouring commitments for family and friends (an essential support team), time should also be used for rest and regeneration. This may differ from institution to institution. Typically, up to twelve months is available across candidature, however, it can be beneficial to schedule time off after every significant research milestone, or once every year. The doctoral journey can be intense; it requires endurance and it is important to build a supportive home base that involves the key people in the student's life. In the planning stage, it is paramount to ensure these people understand the work that lies ahead, and also that they too are being respected by being included in the planning process.

Some students also produce research outputs along their journey, such as journal articles, book chapters, papers in refereed conference proceedings, and 'non-traditional' research outputs such as creative writing, performances and exhibitions. While still clearly part of the research journey, sometimes a side-trip like this can freshen the mind and give a new perspective to the PhD being undertaken. It is useful to discuss the requirements of the doctoral program and career ambitions with the supervisory team, and schedule side-trips carefully and strategically. Attending conferences is often a great way of networking and finding out what is happening in a specific field of research. Presenting research at conferences allows students to gain valuable feedback from peers, and to clarify what is needed to answer their research question(s). It is, therefore, important to consider scheduling at least one international conference into the doctoral journey, to gain exposure to a broader pool of academics from the field, and access to their recent research. Taking on commentary and feedback from such conferences can help strengthen a student's work greatly.

An Apple a Day

Last, and by no means least, is planning for a healthy mind and body. Proper self-care through exercise and food is also paramount. Where and what to eat, and the type and duration of exercise on a daily basis, should be a key consideration in maintaining the physical health required to complete a doctoral course of study. As the writing stage can be quite sedentary, strategies like standing while typing, or setting a timer to ensure a ten-minute walk after every hour or so, or a series of yoga stretches during a particularly long session in front of the computer, can be productive. I also found that regular therapeutic/remedial massage helped me both physically and mentally. It is up to each student to find and manage the healthcare regime that suits them as an individual. It may be helpful to think of the doctoral journey as one's own personal Olympic Games, and the conferral of the award as the gold medal. Thus, like an

Olympic athlete, the student has to be focused, dedicated and take the utmost care of their award-winning assets—the mind and the body.

Conclusion

The doctoral journey takes time, in a structured and planned way, to ensure the student arrives at their destination. It also requires periods of unstructured mind-wandering and solitary explorations, as a means of discovering something truly new. It is a challenging, albeit rewarding, personal and public journey, as the student forges into unknown territories and adds discoveries to the map of human knowledge. It is important to consider the best strategies for mind-wandering and generating new knowledge, and also for the practicalities of achieving results within the appropriate deadlines. Plenty of resources and strategies exist, and I have presented the Doctoral Journey Planner as a template for use here. However, even the best tools cannot increase the number of hours in the day. Knowing the importance of time, how to make time, how to stop time, and identifying when to take strategic side-trips, are all key skills to learn and engage with during the doctoral journey.

In many ways, the doctoral journey is an apprenticeship into a career as a researcher. The notes suggested on planning for time and space are important and significant skills to develop during candidature, and will not only enhance the doctoral journey but will also continue to serve graduates as they progress to the next step in their careers as researchers. The final step in the Doctoral Journey Planner, "Post-doctoral opportunities", is highlighted to encourage students and their supervisory team to think about life *after* the doctoral journey, and to plant the seeds for employment opportunities along the way, ready to sprout upon graduation.

References

Barad, K. 2007. *Meeting the Universe Halfway: Quantum Physics and the Entanglement of Matter and Meaning.* Durham and London: Duke University Press.

Batty, C., and D. L. Brien. 2017. "The exegesis now: Where are we, and where are we going?" *TEXT: Journal of Writing and Writing Courses*, special issue 44: 1–9. http://www.textjournal.com.au/speciss/issue44/Batty&Brien.pdf.

Bourke, S., and A. P. Holbrook. 2013. "Examining PhD and research Masters theses." *Assessment & Evaluation in Higher Education* 38 (4): 407–416.

Brien, D. L., A. Owens, G. Pittaway, and I. Waters. 2017. "Exegetical essentials: A framing structure and template for a comprehensive exegesis in the creative arts." *TEXT: Journal of Writing and Writing Courses*, special issue 44: 1–18. http://www.textjournal.com.au/speciss/issue44/Brien_et_al.pdf.

Doidge, N. 2007. *The Brain that Changes Itself.* Melbourne: Scribe.

Dunlap, O., Jr. 1934. "Tesla sees evidence that radio and light are sound." *New York Times*, April 8.

Gardiner, M., and H. Kearns. 2018. Thinkwell [website]. https://www.ithink-well.com.au/about-us.

Grosz, E. 2004. *The Nick of Time—Politics, Evolution and the Untimely.* Durham and London: Duke University Press.

Haraway, D. J. 1997. *Second_Millennium.FemaleMan©_Meets_OncoMouseTM Feminism and Technoscience.* New York: Routledge.

Heidegger, M. 1996. *Being and Time.* Albany: State University of New York.

Kearns, H., and M. Gardiner. 2012. *The Seven Secrets of Highly Successful Research Students*, 3rd ed. Adelaide: ThinkWell.

Kearns, H., and M. Gardiner. 2013. *Time for Research: Time Management for Academics, Researchers and Research Students.* Adelaide: ThinkWell.

Metzinger, T. 2018. "Are you sleepwalking now? Given how little control we have of our wandering minds, how can we cultivate real mental autonomy?" *AEON*, 1–14.

Mewburn, I. 2018. *The Thesis Whisperer.* https://thesiswhisperer.com.

Mewburn, I., L. Osborne, and G. Caldwell. 2014. "Shut up & write! Some surprising uses of cafes and crowds in doctoral writing." In *Writing Groups for Doctoral Education and Beyond: Innovations in Practice and Theory*, edited by C. Aitchison and C. Guerin, 218–232. Routledge.

Milroy, A. K. 2017. *Epistêmê, Technê and Poïesis Visualisations of Evolution and Extinction in Queensland Flora.* https://cqu-primo.hosted.exlibrisgroup.com/primo-explore/fulldisplay?docid=TN_trove_thesis228725896&context=PC&vid=61CQU&search_scope=61CQU_Library&tab=61cqu_library&lang=en_US.

Rovelli, C. 2016. *Seven Brief Lessons on Physics.* London, UK: Penguin.

Stone, I. 1980. *The Origin.* New York: Doubleday.

Woolf, Virginia. [1929] 1989. *A Room of One's Own.* New York: Harcourt Brace & Co.

3

Who Am I, Where Am I Going on This Journey, and Why?

Alison Vincent

Introduction

A successful holiday journey may well involve aimless wandering and chance encounters without overdue concern for timeframe or final destination. Although no-one would describe undertaking a doctorate as a vacation, there is no reason why both research students and their supervisors should not enjoy the experience *and* reach the desired goal—the two are not mutually exclusive. The pathway to a completed thesis is intended to involve discoveries and surprises, and research breakthroughs often arise in response to hurdles that at first may seem insurmountable. It is important to recognise that undertaking a doctorate is about learning to be a researcher, which involves overcoming obstacles and crossing conceptual thresholds (Kiley 2009; Kiley and Wisker 2009). It is not possible to know in advance all the stumbling blocks and sidetracks that might be

A. Vincent (✉)
School of Education and the Arts, Central Queensland University, Sydney, NSW, Australia
e-mail: alison.vincent@cqumail.com

© The Author(s) 2019
D. L. Brien et al. (eds.), *The Doctoral Experience*,
https://doi.org/10.1007/978-3-030-18199-4_3

encountered. However, conscious and thorough preparation helps with anticipating some potential problems, and makes them easier to recognise and solve, if not avoiding them altogether.

This chapter proposes that there are two fundamental questions every research student should ask before they commit themselves to a research higher degree. These can be put very simply as: Who am I, and why am I doing this? How well prepared and equipped am I to undertake the journey involved? Answering these questions does not require a deep psychological analysis, but it does require some introspection and a degree of honest soul searching.

Asking Questions About Yourself

I started with making two lists, one of my personal strengths and the other of what I saw as my weaknesses. These were for my private use. No one else needs to see these and there are no right or wrong answers. My advice is to take time to reflect on your life, your history, your current circumstances and your relationship with the project you are planning. I tried to think of all the things that might in some way impinge on my doctoral journey, and that might help or hinder my progress.

In completing this list, it is a good idea to start asking yourself some general questions about what personal qualities you bring to your project. For example, what are you passionate about and what do you enjoy doing? What are you good at? What have you not been so successful at doing?

Following this, it is useful to consider the patterns of behaviour you tend to follow, and how they might be strengths or weaknesses. Lovitts (2008) suggests that students who successfully transfer from undergraduate studies to independent research generally demonstrate patience, a willingness to work hard, initiative, persistence and intellectual curiosity. It is, therefore, important to consider how you would rate yourself in these areas. What could you improve on? Think about how well you cope with frustration and failure for example, and how receptive you are to advice and criticism. Self-discipline is another consideration. How well do you deal with deadlines and pressure? Perhaps you are a procrastinator, or a perfectionist. You might identify other self-handicapping strategies such as overcommitting, not prioritising effectively and setting yourself unrealistic or impossible goals (Kearns et al. 2008).

The doctoral journey will put you in a variety of situations, some of which you may not have encountered before, some of which will be all too familiar. At a number of points along the way you will need to talk about your thesis with others, so it is essential to be honest about how you rate as a communicator. You might be good at written communication, but can you confidently express your ideas orally? There are technical skills to consider as well. This affects those entering academia from other fields, as well as students returning to study after a long break. How comfortable are you with computers and online tools—spreadsheets, editing programs, and so on—and do you need to update your knowledge in any of these areas?

Postgraduate-level research is often described as self-directed learning and so undertaking a doctorate requires you to take initiative in many areas. Ask yourself, how much experience have you had as an independent researcher or working autonomously? You may have unique skills or knowledge which will give you an advantage. For instance, you may have advanced skills in asking questions and formulating problem-solving strategies. On the other hand, perhaps you might need to think about what prejudices you would bring to a project, and how your background and prior experiences might hinder your study plans.

The specific questions commencing students need to ask themselves will depend very much on their circumstances and the sort of research they are planning to undertake. The examples above are intended to be prompts rather than an exhaustive list of all areas for consideration. The lists each student develops should be embraced as a tool to help their individual progress. Knowing what type of worker and thinker they are, for example, will help identify what skills are needed in a supervisor and how the student sees that relationship working. It may also help to define their research question and determine an appropriate research methodology.

Identifying weaknesses and any potential threats will help to pre-empt future problems and signal areas where assistance may need to be sought, either from supervisors or through other services available at the university. Having considered some of these issues will also be of significant benefit when it comes to working towards and meeting key candidature milestones, such as the Confirmation of Candidature or its equivalent. This list can also be used to develop an action plan—the steps needed to be implemented to overcome acknowledged weaknesses or avoid the threats—and a rough timeline for achieving those goals. At this early stage, however, it might be that all you need to do is prioritise the issues you see as potential hindrances to your progress. You will then be in a good position to identify the help you are looking for. I was very conscious that I needed to update my computer skills and had no idea how to go about editing or formatting my thesis, nor had I ever had to think about version control. As it happened, solutions to all these issues were offered by my university. Many new students may find a short computer course or even a communication skills or public speaking course useful.

Asking Questions About Managing the Project

Perhaps the most crucial question for a research student to ask is: how am I going to fit this project into my life? A doctorate will certainly take three or four years, or as many as eight—and even more if leave is taken. It is important, then, for students to consider how they will manage research, and thinking and writing time amongst all of their existing obligations and commitments to friends, family, work and hobbies. It is essential that, before you make any commitment to undertaking a doctorate, you carefully consider how it will impact physically and emotionally on you, your family and friends. According to Kearns et al. (2008), most full-time doctoral students overestimate the time they have available; but for a full-time student, who should treat the doctorate as a full-time job, weeks and months can go by in the blink of an eye. Good project management is crucial here.

Planning the management of the doctoral project involves a number of considerations. A good place to start is by looking at the big picture. For example, when and where will you conduct your research? This may be affected by factors such as being an on-campus student or working at a distance from supervisors. Will you access libraries or laboratories in the daytime, in the evening or at the weekend? Most libraries, museums, galleries and archives impose restrictions on parts of their collections, and gaining permission to access some documentation may be involved and time consuming. Some repositories have odd hours and they temporarily close altogether for one reason or another, and/or relocate their collections to somewhere that might be more remote and/or inconvenient. This is usually advised well in advance, so it pays to check that the research material needed will be readily available when you want to access it. You may need to be supervised in your field work, so find out what the requirements are. If you need to conduct interviews, it is important to consider when your interviewees will be available.

Before I submitted my final thesis proposal, I went and had a look through the archival material I wanted to use to gauge how much time I might need to find what I wanted. I also trawled through the catalogues of a number of libraries and joined those which would give me online access to resources I thought might be useful. I focused on trying to access as much reading material as I could from home to minimise the amount of time I had to spend travelling to and from, and sitting in, libraries. Of course, it was not possible to avoid actually going to the library altogether, so I visited the library where I would do most of my research to become familiar with the layout. I also learnt how the microfilm readers worked and how to negotiate the printers and photocopiers. All this gave me a head start and allowed me to efficiently use the time I spent there. I also made a point of understanding how to negotiate interlibrary loans and copying services. In this, my primary concern was maximising the amount of time I could devote to writing.

This is because, while you might be able to exercise some control over the time spent collecting material, it is also vital to consider the time you might need to devote to writing. If you are required to submit an 80,000 word thesis and you write 1000 words every day, for five days every week you could have your first draft written in around four months. Say, like me, you write painfully slowly. If, on average, you are lucky to manage 500 words a day and can only write for 3 days every week, your first draft will take a year. If you want to publish some of your findings as you go along, this will also add to your writing time. Then of course you need to do some editing, rewriting and revision. You will need to format all your chapters, check all your references and quotes, check tables and calculations, proof read again and again, perhaps allow time for professional proofreading, and so on. These figures are not meant to deter you altogether but to make it clear that you can never underestimate the time you will need to devote to your doctorate.

From my own experience, and as AK Milroy has spoken about in Chap. 2, I would also suggest that a research student can never overestimate the time needed to just sit and think. Writing takes time, but actually formulating what you are going to write and how your ideas are all going to fit together takes even longer. Where will you do your thinking and writing? Will you use the campus to do procedural work, and contain your thinking time to your home? Or are you able to think deeply in a shared setting? I was able to find a place at home where I could spread out and not be disturbed, but I know of other students who needed to find their quiet spot elsewhere. I used to get up early every morning and sit at my computer for a couple of hours before I did anything else. Others have to cut down on the hours worked or take leave from their employment to find dedicated study and writing time.

In terms of a support network, what sort of arrangements do you have? In other words, how are you going to juggle everything you do now and commit yourself to working even harder than you already do? Again, the point here is not be overwhelmed by potential problems but be aware that they may exist; not to pre-empt or have immediate solutions for everything that might come along, but to have some idea of what alternatives and solutions might be possible.

Maintaining a social life, away from your books, tools and computer, is important for your general well-being. Retaining contact with friends should be a priority if you want them to be there when you finish the journey, a sentiment echoed by Lisa Brummel in Chap. 11. Exercising, keeping healthy and eating well all play a role in staying on track. So, what could be given up if necessary? I still joined my friends for our book group meetings, but gave up on always finishing the set book every month. I was still able to make a contribution to the discussions but, above all, I enjoyed keeping up to date with life beyond the immediate concerns of my doctorate. I found, too, that I could still have my friends around for dinner, but rather than try to cook everything myself, I asked my guests to bring a dish. Considering the compromises that might have to be made and what you might need to sacrifice, albeit temporarily, brings us to another fundamental question: why am I doing this research?

Why Am I Doing This in the First Place?

Making a list of personal strengths and weaknesses relates to a research student's competence to undertake serious, independent research and the necessary high level skills training. Success as a researcher depends not just on your abilities but also on your motivation. Lovitts describes motivation as "a key factor that mediates between what a person *can* do and what a person *will* do" (2008, p. 313, emphasis in original). She further suggests that a high level of intrinsic motivation means research students will devote more time and energy to all aspects of their project, will be more amenable to taking risks and more likely to think creatively. It is, of course, fundamentally important that students are interested in and enthusiastic about their area of research and the question chosen to investigate, but even the most fascinating project will have its frustrations and setbacks.

The motivation for undertaking a doctorate can be personal, collective, or led by another, but it is oftentimes difficult to *clearly* define (see Guerin et al. 2015, emphasis in original). Motives usually overlap and involve some combination of professional development, professional advancement and self-enhancement (Brailsford 2010). You might be stimulated by lack of current job satisfaction, the aspiration to join academia, a desire to make a difference in the world, or to make a significant contribution to knowledge in your particular field. You may, like me, have simply always promised yourself that you would rise to the challenge. For some, just the idea of studying and writing is attractive.

Whatever the reason for embarking on the research project, a satisfactory outcome is more likely if enthusiasm and commitment to the area of research interest are married to a serious desire to achieve academic success in terms of the completed thesis (Brailsford 2010, p. 25). In other words, "if you don't love it and really want it, it won't get done" (Lovitts 2008, p. 315). I was driven by a long-standing interest in my area of study, the pleasure of undertaking original research and the challenge of completing a long-term project.

Kearns and Gardiner (2007) argue that having a clear sense of purpose makes planning, setting goals and prioritising easier. They emphasise the importance of reflection on what is being done, and where this fits into the researcher's life. The considerations here are: what is the researcher trying to achieve and what are their long-term goals? Asking these questions, Kearns and Gardiner (2007) suggest, leads to greater commitment and motivation which translates to greater effectiveness and well-being. Brailsford (2010, p. 16) also proposes that some of the problems which may arise in the course of the research journey might be avoided if students clearly understand their motives and aspirations. Managing time, calling in favours, having to make sacrifices and compromises, taking friends and family on the journey all become easier if the student is certain about where they are going.

My friends and family have indulged me. They have forgiven my physical absences and acknowledged that I am often thinking about my thesis and not quite on their wavelength, because they know how much completing my doctorate means to me. They have even managed to look interested when I tell them about my latest discoveries. I recognise that it may not always be easy for others outside the academy to share my enthusiasm for my area of research, but I have usually been able to convince them of my ultimate goal. In this way, being clear about the purpose of the doctorate allows students to define what they expect to achieve or gain from their experience, which also helps others to come along on the same journey.

To complement your list of strengths and weakness and to complete what is in essence a preparatory checklist for the doctoral journey, it is useful to prepare a short statement, no more than one or two sentences, or perhaps two or three dot points, which encapsulate what it is you want to achieve. Mine was neither complicated, nor particularly eloquent. I just wrote myself a little note that said: "This is what you always wanted to do. Now is the time to get on and do it!". The outcome of the doctoral process is a completed thesis, the result of the original research conducted, but the end of the journey always provides something more personal.

Conclusion

This chapter has argued that before a student makes any final commitment to their research proposal, and certainly before a research question is finalised, they take time to think clearly and unemotionally about the road ahead. The end result should be two documents. The first is a list of personal strengths and weakness, along with safeguards and possible threats to the successful completion of the thesis. The other is a brief statement of why the student wants to undertake this journey—a list of aspirations and expectations. Together they provide a picture of who the student is, how they work and think and where they stand in relation to their research project. They will assist you in making decisions about a number of the stages on your journey. Defining your research topic and selecting the appropriate methodology; identifying a supervisor who is right for you; selecting the right institution—one which will not only allow you to follow you chosen field of research but will also provide you with the support to help you achieve your goals; and not least of all, taking your support network, your friends and family on the journey with you: all these issues hinge on how well you understand your own personal strengths and weakness, and how clear you are about your reasons for undertaking the journey. It is useful to keep these two documents and refer back to them from time to time. Somewhere down the track, when progress is slow or when it seems the whole project has jumped the rails and nothing is going right, it is helpful to consult these checklists. This will enable you to examine how you have taken advantage of your strengths, how you have overcome your weaknesses, and the potential obstacles you anticipated and overcame. Reassessing the headway you have made, and reaffirming why you started the journey in the first place, may be just the motivation you need to keep going.

References

Brailsford, I. 2010. "Motives and aspirations for doctoral study: Career, personal, and inter-personal factors in the decision to embark on a history PhD." *International Journal of Doctoral Studies* 5: 15–27.

Guerin, C., A. Jayatilaka, and D. Ranasinghe. 2015. "Why start a higher degree by research? An exploratory factor analysis of motivations to undertake doctoral studies." *Higher Education Research & Development* 34 (1): 89–104. https://doi.org/10.28945/71010.1080/07294360.2014.934663.

Kearns, H., and M. Gardiner. 2007. "Is it time well spent? The relationship between time management behaviours, perceived effectiveness and work-related morale and distress in a university context." *Higher Education Research & Development* 26 (2): 235–247. https://doi.org/10.1080/07294360701310839.

Kearns, H., M. Gardiner, and K. Marshall. 2008. "Innovation in PhD completion: The hardy shall succeed (and be happy!)." *Higher Education Research & Development* 27 (1): 7–89. https://doi.org/10.1080/07294360701658781.

Kiley, M. 2009. "Identifying threshold concepts and proposing strategies to support doctoral candidates." *Innovations in Education and Teaching International* 46 (3): 293–304. https://doi.org/10.1080/14703290903069001.

Kiley, M., and G. Wisker. 2009. "Threshold concepts in research education and evidence of threshold crossing." *Higher Education Research and Development* 28 (4): 431–441. https://doi.org/10.1080/07294360903067930.

Lovitts, B. E. 2008. "The transition to independent research: Who makes it, who doesn't and why." *Journal of Higher Education* 79 (3): 296–325. https://doi.org/10.1080/00221546.2008.11772100.

4

Understanding the World of the Academy, and Aligning Expectations with Realities

Irene Rogers

Over coffee with friends one day, a discussion arose about the relevance of universities in a contemporary world and many compelling arguments were voiced about their irrelevance. I was busy preparing my thesis for submission and I was surprised by how swiftly strong feelings of defensiveness arose in me. Despite, or perhaps because, of this, I found myself voicing rather weak counter arguments that were not convincing even to me. Someone in the group challenged me to return the following week with my best shot at convincing them. In that week, I found myself pondering the question of whether universities were an historical anomaly or an enduring necessity and how they had changed. This led me back to the historical sources to try and understand how universities had survived to this point through many extreme and revolutionary changes in society. And how they had changed and were still changing. As the investigation continued, I was reminded yet again that the insights of history are a powerful way to see our own times and experiences in context. The arguments below are those I presented the following week.

I. Rogers (✉)
School of Nursing, Midwifery and Social Sciences, Central Queensland University, Noosaville, QLD, Australia
e-mail: irene.rogers@cqumail.com

© The Author(s) 2019
D. L. Brien et al. (eds.), *The Doctoral Experience*,
https://doi.org/10.1007/978-3-030-18199-4_4

Students enrol in doctoral degrees for many reasons. They come driven and dedicated, gifted and versatile, with long nurtured passions and a fascination for knowledge (Smith 2015, p. 1). They settle into an intellectual journey that is a mixture of pleasure and pain, and find "a shifting terrain of tradition and change and a cauldron of anxiety" about the future (Smith, p. 2). Many believe they are facing a unique set of circumstances that render them powerless to influence the future. This chapter recognises that university learning has a long history and ancient antecedents, and so doctoral students are joining a world with its own history, language and culture, although this may not always be articulated to, or obvious to, students or their supervisors. At the same time, change has also been a constant in the nature of the academy. Engaging in this "essential tension" (Kuhn 1977, p. 1) around higher education is an important part of moving forward successfully, and it is hard to anticipate what the new 'normal' may look like. Having this expanded view will help prepare doctoral students to cope with the academic world they are orienting towards in undertaking a doctoral degree. In short, this entails having a birds-eye view of the world being stepped into, and understanding of how the research project and the researcher themselves do not exist in isolation, but are always subject to the broader academic ecology. It suggests that students need to be nimble and ready for change, as well as realistic about both the world of university study and the future of both knowledge generation and dissemination.

A History of the Academy

History provides the opportunity to understand change; it illuminates the context for contemporary issues and enables a richer view of possibilities for the future. Universities have not been immune from the pressure of change since the first academy was founded by Plato in the fourth century BC. Historical evidence suggests that some women were allowed to participate in Plato's Academy, that survived for five centuries before it was destroyed. Unfortunately, it was another nineteen centuries before women were again included as part of the academy in the West. This first academy was free to attend, and academicians posed problems to be studied and solved using discussion and logic, with the aim of creating universal thinkers (Baltes 1993). In the fifth century AD, a similar type of academy was re-established but it lasted less than a century. It was closed by the Emperor Justinian when he instigated a general prohibition of non-Christian teaching. Academicians fled with their scrolls to the Persian Empire and the tradition survived into the ninth century in the Arab world, leading to the establishment of major centres of new knowledge and learning (Anderson 2004).

The word 'university' comes from the Latin *universitas*, and was first associated with medieval guilds and specialised knowledge. It was self-regulating, and academic freedom was demanded as early as the twelfth century at the University of Bologna. A travelling scholar was permitted unhindered passage in the interests of education, and this became an important tenet of the values adopted by universities to this day. The university became a formal institution in the West under the aegis of the Latin Church in the eleventh century, and universities grew rapidly. Europe developed a great thirst for knowledge, and leaders saw the benefit of patronising scholarly expertise. The rediscovery of the works of the ancient Greeks fuelled a spirit of enquiry into science and logic, and universities developed specialties and formalised the awarding of degrees and standards of teaching. Higher education, as a construct of society, was controlled during this period by contemporary political and religious dogma, a situation that has been a feature of university life since. However, history is resplendent with examples of scholars who have pushed boundaries and refused to be contained by their universities or their dogmas, despite the pressures to conform to the status quo (Anderson 2004).

Changes continued unabated over the centuries, and the seventeenth century was rife with events that affected universities, including wars, plagues and bitter debates about curriculum and academic authority. In 1793, the new government of the French Revolution decided to close the University of Paris and sell their property despite six very successful centuries of operation. This was cause for a great deal of anxiety within universities all over Europe who feared a similar fate. By 1917, in response to the rapid and radical changes in German universities, the sociologist Max Weber visited Munich University to give a series of lectures titled "Intellectual Work as Vocation" (Wellmon 2017). These debates centred around whether the university should be an intellectual community involved in moral education and the formation of students, or a place to further specialised knowledge born of the industrial age. Within decades, the Nazi enthusiasm for pseudoscience and anti-Semitism resulted in Einstein's theory of relativity being called a Jewish plot, and the establishment of what was termed and taught in universities as 'Aryan physics' (Cassidy 2017).

Knowledge Creation and Transmission

The idea of the university as an exclusive place where knowledge is created, cultivated and transmitted has frequently been under attack, in both history and the contemporary academy. Dewar (2000) argues that parallels between the invention of the printing press and the current so-called Information Age are sufficiently compelling to suggest that new and developing technologies are both causing change currently, and will continue to create dramatic change in the future. The printing press has been implicated in the Reformation, the Renaissance and the Scientific Revolution, and similarly profound contemporary technological changes, including the internet and social media, are already affecting future history. As with the printing press, there will be unintended consequences, speculated upon at present but uncertain and unclear, and it will be decades before the implications of these changes are understood, and the winners and losers who have resulted can be identified. Significant and permanent cultural change takes time and it is difficult to anticipate outcomes. In addition, the impact of individuals on such processes is often underestimated. Countries that embraced the invention of the printing press were advantaged by better access to, and distribution of, information across all aspects of society. Universities survived and thrived, despite fears the printing press would take away their control over knowledge and authority. Ultimately, the new technology became one of their greatest assets. An optimist sees the impact of rapid technological advances of the Information Age on universities as one more challenge (and even an exciting one) to embrace.

Thomas Kuhn ([1962] 1977) argued there is an "essential tension" between tradition and innovation, often leading to a crisis in belief and disruption in agreement about how problems can be understood. He created the term "paradigm shift" to identify this pattern. This disruption takes place in the form of intellectual battles, possibly leading to a fundamental shift in thinking, or at least the development of new tools or ideas to resolve or contain the anomalies. However, it appears to be much easier to identify a paradigm shift in hindsight than when it is occurring. This notion, from the history and philosophy of science, was soon taken up, and the term "paradigm shift" quickly gained broad application throughout society.

Higher degrees by research, and education in general, are currently under scrutiny through the lens of the paradigm shift. For example, in *The Paradigm Shift: Redefining Education*, Evans-Greenwood, O'Leary and Williams argue:

> The questions confronting the education sector are not just those of pedagogy or technology, but of purpose and role. There seems to be a fundamental shift occurring in how we use and think about knowledge and skills. Knowledge is becoming something that we now pull in as required, rather than being pushed out by an institution via instruction in anticipation of a future need. If this fundamental shift turns out to be real, then it will usher in a new paradigm and transform the education sector. (2015, p. 7)

It is understood by many educationists that there is a fundamental shift in how we use and think about knowledge and skills but, as Kuhn suggested, it is hard to see the future when you are in the centre of the grand upheaval of a paradigm shift. The anomalies are plain to see and new initiatives can be discovered in the attempt to find the new tools to handle these anomalies. What cannot be forecast with certainty is whether the crisis will cause a fundamental shift in beliefs about education and qualifications. For a doctoral student, it may feel like the ground is continually shifting beneath them.

The Creative Arts and Humanities Doctoral Degree Now

Higher degrees by research in the humanities and creative arts are currently particularly under scrutiny (ACOLA 2016), despite the arguments affirming the world of the twenty first century needs high quality humanities' and practice-based research and teaching more than ever (Smith 2015, p. 9). For Smith, the overarching theme of the current reports on, and initiatives in, doctoral level research training, is that an untraditional doctoral education is needed:

> To meet these goals, and to prepare a generation of humanists to be change agents for the humanities, the Academy needs flexible, imaginative, and rigorous doctoral programs, ones that encompass all kinds of experiences … opportunities to develop expanded repertoires of skills and competencies, that prepare future faculty for the new scholarly and teaching life … prepare the way for success in as-yet-unimagined professions inside and outside the academy. (2015, p. 9)

This involves looking broadly at career options post the completion of a doctorate. Supply generally outstrips demand, with academic jobs—even casual—typically being available to less than fifty percent of graduates (National Science Foundation 2015, p. 9). In the world outside of the university, there is also often a poor perception of the range of skills and experience higher degree research students gain during their studies, including a belief that doctorates remove a student from the world outside the university, and wisdom does not equate to experience (Prince 2018, p. 1). However, many universities, including Stanford and Toronto, have undertaken studies of student careers and have developed websites showing the successful career paths of their alumni after their higher research degree. Both universities' studies show the career landscape is far more varied than assumed, and extends far beyond traditional positions at universities. This has enabled potential graduates to make informed decisions prior to embarking on their higher research journey, and has also challenged universities to provide the best possible training and advice to prepare graduates for this variety of career paths (Cook 2017).

Figures for graduates worldwide are hard to find, but in a 2016 report commissioned by Forbes, it was estimated that at least 244,000 doctoral students graduated with a PhD worldwide in 2014—with numbers then increasing exponentially (McCarthy 2016). In Germany, the *Habilitation* post-doctoral degree is required for teaching and supervising doctoral students. This degree is more substantial than a PhD, takes longer to complete, and must be accomplished independently, without the direction or guidance of a faculty supervisor. It has arisen, in part, because of the large number of doctorates awarded (Zeppelin University Graduate School 2018).

We can also consider some other aspects of the 'academic industry' around the research produced in universities, including in doctoral programs. Online and open access journals have placed the print publishing system under pressure, and the idea of 'publish or perish' may be open to more radical changes in the future (Mrowinski et al. 2017). An optimist may suggest that in a world of unchecked circulation of information with a frequent lack of capacity to make sense of it, and where epistemic authority is near collapse, the core functions of the university may be critical as a place of trustworthy knowledge.

It is, therefore, useful for all students to take the time, before embarking on their doctoral journey, to become familiar with the nature of some of the transformations taking place. If they learn to embrace change and align their personal expectations to the possibility that they may not recognise the academic world they are a part of by the end of the research journey, a great deal of anxiety and worry could be avoided. The world needs doctoral graduates who can think in complex ways and solve problems, but who also have passion, imagination and the courage to embrace a future they cannot clearly see.

References

ACOLA. 2016. *Review of Australia's Research Training System.* https://acola.org/wp-content/uploads/2018/08/saf13-review-research-training-system-report.pdf.

Anderson, R. D. 2004. *European Universities from the Enlightenment to 1914.* Oxford: Oxford University Press.

Baltes, M. 1993. "Plato's school, the Academy." *Hermathena* 155: 5–26.

Cassidy, D. C. 2017. *Farm Hall and the German Atomic Project of WWII. A Dramatic History.* New York: Springer. E-book edition.

Cook, B. 2017. *The Stanford PhD Alumni Employment Project.* Dataset viewed 21 January 2018. http://web.stanford.edu/dept/pres-provost/irds/phdjobs.

Dewar, J. A. 2000. *The Information Age and the Printing Press. Looking Backward to see Ahead.* Rand Corporation. https://www.rand.org/pubs/papers/P8014/index2.html.

Evans-Greenwood, P., K. O'Leary, and P. Williams. 2015. *The Paradigm Shift: Redefining Education.* Centre for the Edge, Deloitte Australia. http://landing.deloitte.com.au/rs/761-IBL-328/images/deloitte-au-ps-education-rede-fined-040815.pdf.

Kuhn, T. S. [1962] 1977. *The Essential Tension: Selected Studies in Scientific Tradition and Change.* Chicago and London: University of Chicago Press.

McCarthy, N. 2016. "The countries with the most doctoral graduates." *Forbes.* https://www.forbes.com/sites/niallmccarthy/2016/12/19/the-countries-with-the-most-doctoral-graduates-infographic/#4b8f6a8a4fa9.

Mrowinski, M. J., P. Fronczak, A. Fronczak, M. Ausloos, and O. Nedic. 2017. "Artificial Intelligence in peer review: How can evolutionary computation support journal editors?" *PLoS ONE* 12 (9). https://doi.org/10.1371/journal.pone.0184711.

National Science Foundation. 2015. *Doctorate Recipients from U.S. Universities: 2014,* p. 9. https://www.nsf.gov/statistics/2016/nsf16300/digest/nsf16300.pdf.

Prince, G. 2018. "PhD students: Australia needs them to aspire to working in the private sector." *Financial Review,* 27 May. https://www.afr.com/news/policy/education/phd-students-australia-needs-them-to-aspire-to-working-in-the-private-sector-20180525-h10jip.

Smith, S. 2015. *Manifesto for the Humanities: Transforming Doctoral Education in Good Enough Times.* Digitalculturebooks. E-book. http://quod.lib.umich.edu/cgi/t/text/text-idx?cc=dcbooks;c=dcbooks;idno=13607059.0001.001;rgn=full%20text;view=toc;xc=1;g=dculture.

Wellmon, C. 2017. "The university is dead, long live the academy! Reflections on the future of knowledge." *ABC Religion and Ethics Report,* 6 November. http://www.abc.net.au/religion/articles/2017/11/06/4760850.htm.

Zeppelin University Graduate School. 2018. "Frequently asked questions: Habilitation." https://www.zu.de/info-wAssets/forschung/dokumente/en/Habilitation-Process_FAQs.pdf.

5

Building Confidence About the Academic Journey

Margaret Cook

Introduction

While many research students may think they know the skills they need to develop to complete a doctoral degree, these may be entirely focused on the mechanical part of the process. For example, the need to read, research, gather information, conduct experiments or complete field work and write a thesis to defend the findings or hypothesis are all necessary for the journey. Yet many students may not be aware of the less tangible skills and knowledge that a research student must acquire, in terms of an awareness of, and adherence to, an academic culture. This chapter considers the research journey as a master/apprentice model where both skills and culture are imparted to the student. Various tests must be passed along the way to prove the student has acquired the necessary academic proficiency to become a master or scholar, but they also must display the professional attributes, behaviours and codes of conduct

M. Cook (✉)
University of Queensland, Brisbane, QLD, Australia

La Trobe University, Bundoora, VIC, Australia

© The Author(s) 2019
D. L. Brien et al. (eds.), *The Doctoral Experience*,
https://doi.org/10.1007/978-3-030-18199-4_5

43

required to become a member of the academic world. By recasting and explaining the steps of the research process—with its mandatory milestones—in these terms, this chapter demystifies the process and explains the transformative steps and transferable skills that are required to achieve a doctorate.

The Academic Culture

At the beginning of candidature, the student is a novice. Whether they have an honours or master's degree, or even another doctorate, they begin as a first day doctoral student on the bottom rung of the ladder. For a student who has progressed straight from high school through honours and master's study without a break, it may be disappointing to effectively start again. A mature age student with years in the workplace may struggle even more as work experience, previous publications and awards may count for nothing. This can shock or frustrate a new student, but there is no escaping this reality. In her book *Being Bright is not Enough* (2010), Peggy Hawley suggests that the first rule of a PhD is that you accept the role of a neophyte or beginner, albeit a talented, educated one. Whether you appreciate it or not, you have much to learn. This learning process ahead is far more than the mechanics of the doctoral degree—the research and writing—it includes gaining an understanding of the academic culture within your school or department, your university, your academic field and beyond.

The current university system can be compared with the medieval guild system that flourished in Europe, a concept based on the progression from apprentice to master craftsman (Heathcote 2005). An apprentice would learn the skills of the trade until producing a masterpiece, thereby earning the status of master. The doctoral process is similar. The student begins with a question, then researches, interrogates, writes and defends the work along a path of enquiry, with supervisors to guide the way. The finished product is the thesis, designed to display mastery of both a particular subject and the academic discipline. For some, the completion of a PhD is a 'rite of passage' into the academic world of continued scholarship.

Throughout their candidatures, students have to complete set tasks, reach milestones and demonstrate the attainment of the necessary skills and intellectual maturity. They also have to complete numerous forms, possibly an ethics application, consider health and safety issues and more, all of which can, at times, seem endless, overly bureaucratic and pointless. Students will submit draft after draft of chapters and present the content of their thesis in various formats and lengths to different audiences, incrementally refining and improving their argument. It is easy to complain about the system, but students should be mindful that this has existed for centuries and is unlikely to change soon (Petre 2010, p. 10). Knowledge of the system and the rationale behind the stages required may help a student through the doctoral process. Acceptance, rather than frustration or resistance, could help build a student's resilience and their determination to continue as the inevitable challenges or stumbles come their way.

The Journey to Becoming a Scholar

Previous education and experience does not necessarily prepare a student for the advanced level degree that is a doctorate (Deconinck 2015, p. 361). Hawley (2010) notes a major difference between a PhD and previous study: whereas previously in their academic careers students have received knowledge, in a doctoral degree, there is a necessity that a student creates knowledge. A PhD is not just a larger master's thesis. Its duration, word count, and intensity will most likely be the most significant academic work the student has undertaken to date. There is an accepted structure, language and style, which is reasonably prescriptive and, in part, formulaic. Studies have found that the required thesis style can present even the brightest scholars with problems and result in delays in completion (Gearity and Mertz 2012). Perhaps most daunting of all, they start with a blank page on which to craft their academic masterpiece. The good news, however, is that underpinning the notion of master/apprentice is an understanding from the university that the student is not expected to know how to complete their doctorate at the beginning of enrolment. That is what the student is at university to learn and why the doctorate is known, and in some contexts funded, as a process of research training.

Students first locate and/or are assigned a team to help them with this task—their supervisors. With their guidance, a student will undertake preliminary research and refine the thesis question, arguments and structure. Supervisory meetings are designed to challenge these theories and findings, testing a student's writing and strength of argument. In worst cases, these meetings can be combative, counter-productive and can destroy a student's confidence, as discussed in other chapters below. Even positive meetings can raise doubts, anxieties and problems, or bruise the student's ego (Gearity and Mertz 2012, pp. 6–10). The challenge for the student is to respond positively to any comments or criticism, respecting the expertise and professionalism of the supervisors. Students should remember that most supervisors have been involved in guiding many more PhDs than theirs. As academics, they are usually also conducting and publishing their own research, and spend significant time peer reviewing that of others. Where necessary, however, students must also feel at ease, and confident enough, to stand their ground—and this is something supervisors must respect, and foster, as well. The doctorate in question is the student's project, and their research, and the student must not only test it, but also defend their thinking and approach when required. In this way, supervision should be a collaborative process, strengthened by debate and constructive criticism (Gearity and Mertz 2012, pp. 19–22).

Writing draft thesis material early on in the candidature is critical so that the work begins to take shape, and any holes are revealed. It is also essential to be brave and let others, including academic peers (that is, other students), read work in progress in order to offer insights and critique. Peer-to-peer groups, particularly at the discipline level, can provide a strong sense of community as well as invaluable input into drafts (Batty 2016). The review, rewriting and editing process is designed to produce the best scholarship possible, and it is also helpful to compose journal articles and submit these for publication to test the work in the external arena (Brien 2006). This strategy comes with a warning, as up to ninety per cent of articles are rejected outright, with the majority of the rest requiring revisions of varying degree in order to be published (Bartkowski et al. 2015, p. 110). Reviewers' and editorial criticism can be demoralising, but it can provide valuable insights into the field of work as well as guidance for necessary improvement—all of which will positively influence the thesis. It is also useful to present at conferences as the questions and feedback may help with refining ideas, and has the added bonus of making useful professional connections (Kroll and Brien 2006). As well as garnering engaged input, this constant review and public exposure of the thesis is designed to teach students the art of being an academic, particularly the need to defend their ideas and be able to withstand, and utilise, vigorous criticism.

Towards the end of their doctorate, students experience a mixture of emotions. Some are utterly sick of their thesis, dispirited and exhausted, frustrated and disheartened at the need to write yet another draft and feeling guilty about neglected family and friends. Others are exhilarated and excited as the finish line comes in sight. After all, the thesis is a marathon; an endurance test that only the determined will complete. The key word here is 'test': there needs to be challenges, obstacles, goals and milestones along the way, and it is meant to be hard. The PhD is regarded as the pinnacle of academic study, and only the strongest and most tenacious will finish (Brown 2013). Many have the intellectual capacity to complete a PhD, but not everyone has the fortitude, persistence or resilience to do so. Along the journey, a student's academic skills will regularly be tested and assessed, in order to enable them to meet the stringent requirements of the final examination process.

The Journey's Milestones

Regardless of the university, postgraduate studies now have in-built milestones. While the process and requirements may vary at different institutions, the underlying rationale is much the same—to check quality and quantity of work completed to ensure the student is on track. This can be a stressful process for the student, and perhaps for the supervisors as well. The process might involve presenting work to academics beyond the supervisory team in an oral setting, and will always include the provision of a written document that captures the research project to date. The requirements are likely to vary from university to university, but they usually reflect the expectations of the stage of study.

Students should not underestimate the work involved in preparing for, and attaining, a milestone. It is a formal process with mandatory conditions set by the university. Many former students will attest to the work required for each milestone, but equally they will remember the sheer joy and relief in attaining it, as well as the level of feedback provided. It is, moreover, vital to note the effectiveness of this process if conducted well. Each milestone is a timely intervention to check that the student work is progressing in the right direction or to provide guidance for its re-direction if necessary.

To meet my first-year milestone (Confirmation of Candidature), I had to prepare a 6,000-word research proposal complete with abstract, rationale, methodology, literature review and bibliography, along with a draft thesis chapter. The process was daunting and challenging, especially so early at nine months into my candidature. The documentation was read by two academics in advance. I had to present my work publicly at a twenty minute lecture and defend my work in an interview with the external reviewers and supervisors. "Why this torture?" I asked myself. I have since learned that abstracts are an essential part of having a conference paper or journal article accepted; rationales are mandatory for research grant applications; and articles without their scholarly context (the literature review), rationale or methodology will not be published. Recognising that I was undertaking an apprenticeship, I appreciated in hindsight that these difficult tasks were in fact crucial tools to learn to use as part of the scholar's trade.

At times, completing a milestone process can seem a time-consuming distraction from writing the thesis, a problem seemingly made worse if major changes are required which take considerable time. Progression is not automatic and is more than an administrative hurdle (Petre 2010). The milestone process is designed to help shape the thesis, raise issues of concern and offer guidance on how to proceed. Discussions about the milestone process also provide both students and supervisors the opportunity to raise issues about their relationship, timing or funding issues, and any potential problems the student or thesis may be experiencing. If the review goes well it can also be extremely re-affirming, indicating that the student is on the right track, thereby providing a rare confidence boost along the way. These milestones are also an important part of the apprentice/master journey. Each milestone affords the student opportunity to take stock, review previous work and see where the thesis is heading. Each milestone completion should also mark a substantial advancement from the one before and make the task ahead clearer.

Dealing with Challenges

The PhD is designed to be challenging and most students will encounter difficulties of some kind. These will vary depending on personal skills or the project at hand, but meeting (and defeating) these obstacles is part of the test, the process required to attain the qualification. The challenge for a student is not to be deflated by criticism or take it personally, but to view it as an intrinsic part of the learning process.

Throughout their course of study, students will undoubtedly face rejection, whether in terms of a funding application, journal article or book chapter submission or conference presentation proposal. Competition in the academic world is fierce, and this is fought between equally intelligent, hard-working, qualified students and academics. But the important thing to note is that everyone faces rejection at some time, even experienced and esteemed professors. The correct response is to see rejection as a part of the learning process and move on. Rather than take it personally, students should accept the criticism, learn from it and respond positively, knowing it is part of the academic process.

At a PhD student workshop, a retiring professor confided trade secrets, revealing that many of his papers submitted to journals had received initial rejections or requests to revise and resubmit. One of his esteemed colleagues had wallpapered his office with the numerous article rejection letters he had received during his long and successful career. This was a pivotal moment in my PhD journey—the realisation that this experience happened to everyone, not just PhD students or worse, happened only to me. I experienced an epiphany as I realised what a PhD candidature was all about. It was an apprenticeship for the life of an academic.

Another challenge may be lodging an ethics application. More than a just a step to go through, which can cause further time delays, gaining ethics approval for a study is designed to confirm the student's professional code of practice and personal ethics in all that they do. Similarly, acknowledging the work of others in their own writing in the form of correct referencing, not only proves the student's knowledge of published scholarship but also demonstrates their application of required academic etiquette.

Finding a mentor is a perfect way to help a student through the various academic processes and assist them in learning about the academic culture. Most likely this will not be one of their supervisors, but ideally another academic who can shepherd the student along their journey. Either an early career academic (fresh from their own candidature experience) or a generous senior scholar may suit the purpose admirably. A mentor can: assist with (or explain) various bureaucratic processes; help steer a student's professional development by suggesting available conferences, workshops and funding opportunities; and provide strategic advice or provide an independent assessment of work. If independent of the supervisory team, this mentor may be able to offer advice regarding those relationships as well, offering a sounding board or an academic's viewpoint. A mentor could be included in a student's community of practice (see also Chap. 7).

A Transformative Experience

Undertaking a PhD is a transformative journey. The student begins with an embryonic question, an idea or problem that demands attention. With reading, research, discussion and writing, the thesis will begin to take form, as will the student as a future scholar. The long journey is at times exhilarating and occasionally hazardous. The thesis arguments will be tested along with a student's resilience, emotional fortitude, health and relationships. The student's work will be criticised by supervisors and readers, tested at milestones and conferences, and critiqued by peer reviewers, but with each defence, public airing, re-writing and editing, the thesis will become more honed, and the argument more robust.

Thirty months into my PhD study, I met a friend (with a PhD) at a function. She kindly asked how things were going, then cut to the chase. "When we last met," she said, "you were full of ideas and information. Have you worked out what it all means yet? What is your argument?" Much to my sheer delight I could give her a one sentence answer. In one conversation, I could mark my own journey from enthusiastic newbie to an emerging scholar.

Even a cursory revisiting of the original proposal, milestone documentation or early drafts of chapters will reveal how much the thesis and student's skills have matured and developed. As a student's growing academic expertise is evident in new work, so too are other changes. Their ability to weigh evidence and critically assess materials will have changed the way they think about the world and shape their future. The relationship between the student and the supervisors will also have evolved. As the student and supervisors work together on the thesis topic for several years, the balance will shift as the student becomes more expert in a particular topic. With the student's growing skills and professionalism, the positions of teachers and student may subtly shift away from that of master and apprentice towards that of colleagues.

Conclusion

The completion of a PhD allows students entry into a community of scholars. It is a recognition that they have acquired the necessary skills—an independent research capability, and the ability to formulate, write and defend a thesis. Undertaking and completing a PhD is, however, much more than the gaining, refining and demonstrating of these skills. Possessing a PhD provides evidence of the student's resilience and persistence. While respecting and building on the work of others, they have demonstrated mastery of a subject and critical thinking, and offered research insights which have added to the body of knowledge within the discipline. The student has also proven they have the necessary intellectual rigour and competency required to graduate from a novice to a master. But equally important are the intangible lessons learned—the "tools of the trade", "the rules of the game" and the "standards of engagement" (Petre 2010, p. 37). The student needs to have demonstrated knowledge and acceptance of the academic culture and the ability to implement the behaviours and standards required to become a scholar. In short, the student has shown they have earned the right to use the title of Doctor.

References

Bartkowski, J., C. S. Deem, and C. G. Ellison. 2015. "Publishing in academic journals: Strategic advice for doctoral students and academic mentors." *The American Sociologist* 46 (1): 99–115. https://doi.org/10.1007/s12108-014-9248-3.

Batty, C. 2016. "Collaboration, critique and a community of peers: The benefits of peer learning groups for screen production research degrees." *Studies in Australasian Cinema* 10 (1): 65–78.

Brien, D. L. 2006. "Creative practice as research: A creative writing case study." *Media International Australia—Culture and Policy: Creativity and Practice-Led Research Issue* 118: 53–59.

Brown, P. 2013. "Loneliness at the bench: Is the PhD experience as emotionally taxing as it is mentally challenging?" *Science and Society, EMBO Reports* 14 (5): 405–409.

Deconinck, K. 2015. "Trust me I'm a doctor: A PhD survival guide." *The Journal of Economic Education* 46 (4): 360–375.

Gearity, B. T., and N. Mertz. 2012. "From 'bitch' to 'mentor': A doctoral student's story of self-change and mentoring." *The Qualitative Report* 17 (59): 1–27.

Hawley, P. 2010. *Being Bright is Not Enough: The Unwritten Rules of Doctoral Study.* 3rd ed. Springfield: Charles C. Thomas.

Heathcote, J. 2005. "Trained for nothing." *Academe* 91 (6): 14–17.

Kroll, J., and D. L. Brien. 2006 "Studying for the future: Training creative writing postgraduates for life after degrees." *Australian Online Journal of Arts Education* 2 (1): 1–13.

Petre, M. 2010. *The Unwritten Rules of PhD Research.* 2nd ed. Maidenhead, UK: Open University Press.

Part II

Setting Out on the Doctoral Degree: Introduction to Part

Donna Lee Brien, Craig Batty, Elizabeth Ellison, and Alison Owens

The four chapters in this section emphasise the critical importance of building and maintaining relationships during the period of doctoral study (Kroll and Brien 2006). These relationships extend across university departments, include other researchers as well as those being researched, and exist in the home and workplace as well as in the university. Relationships are conceived as powerful resources for doctoral students as they help

D. L. Brien (✉) • E. Ellison
Noosaville, QLD, Australia
e-mail: d.brien@cqu.edu.au; l.ellison@cqu.edu.au

C. Batty
Sydney, NSW, Australia
e-mail: Craig.Batty@uts.edu.au

A. Owens
North Sydney, NSW, Australia
e-mail: Alison.Owens@acu.edu.au

mitigate the sense of isolation that may occur during a four (or more)-year journey of focused investigation, analysis and writing.

Virginia Birt offers a series of preliminary strategies for ensuring that students achieve the best fit with their selected university and supervisory team, and also discover and exploit the various support staff provided in a range of university departments, including information literacy, counselling and collegial networks. Colleen Ryan's chapter picks up on the central importance of developing a 'support team', in this case envisaged as a community of practice, to allow for sharing difficulties and solutions and promoting resilience on the doctoral journey, which inevitably presents challenges as well as breakthroughs. The chapters by Justine Newport and Alison Owens explore the ethics of research, attending to challenges that emerge despite the comprehensive ethics approval process undertaken by many doctoral students prior to the actual research beginning. These authors stress the necessity for continual mindfulness and reflexivity in considering the boundaries of one's own morality as the research unfolds and unforeseen ethical hurdles emerge. Establishing authentic and sensitive methods for researching intimate friends and/or family about potentially distressing topics are examined.

Overall, then, this section highlights both the importance and the benefits of working closely, widely and respectfully with individuals and groups to generate mutually beneficial experiences and a high-quality, publishable thesis.

Reference

Kroll, J., and D. L. Brien. 2006. "Studying for the future: Training creative writing postgraduates for life after degrees." *Australian Online Journal of Arts Education* 2 (1): 1–13.

6

Managing Relationships with Your Institution, Its Staff and Your Peers

Virginia Birt

Introduction

The decision to undertake postgraduate research is a life-changing one, and all related decisions, including where the student elects to study, exactly what they will research and who are the most appropriate supervisors, will impact upon the quality of both the research produced and the student experience. While the relationship with supervisors is of vital importance, a student's relationship with their institution, including their understanding of its aims and objectives and how their research fits under its academic umbrella, is important to both consider and value. This chapter examines this and other aspects of the student's 'institutional relationship', including the areas and individuals who provide a wide range of support and guidance, from libraries to IT to student services. It will consider how to best manage and maintain respectful working relationships across these support areas in order to best facilitate the doctoral journey. Undertaking research within a faculty and

V. Birt (✉)
Cairns, QLD, Australia

© The Author(s) 2019
D. L. Brien et al. (eds.), *The Doctoral Experience*,
https://doi.org/10.1007/978-3-030-18199-4_6

along with other research students can be a bumpy ride, and so it is important to be alert to potential problems and have strategies that can be utilised to manage interpersonal difficulties that may arise. Using examples of real (but de-identified) student experiences, the chapter provides practical steps for minimising and managing problematic working relationships that may arise within an institutional setting and between peers. It also discusses ways of managing, and benefitting from, relationships with fellow students during the doctoral journey, and ways to work successfully within the sometimes competitive and alienating postgraduate research environment.

Assessing Your Wants and Needs

As Alison Vincent notes in Chap. 3, undertaking a PhD calls for some serious self-reflection and self-analysis before you begin the journey, to understand how your personality traits and attitudes may benefit or impede the experience. It is impossible to complete a PhD in isolation, and your ability to manage the varied relationships you establish and negotiate will be both challenged and expanded as you travel the research road. It is therefore important to consider from the start what interpersonal skills and strategies you may need to develop or strengthen.

It is important to spend time at the very start of a research journey establishing the kind of institution that would best suit the research you are interested in pursuing, and the support that institution can provide to you. Finding the 'right' institution, supervisor, topic and research process will inevitably depend upon how you employ your interpersonal skills to establish, and then negotiate, the institutional relationships that will impact your journey. These skills and traits include communication, flexibility and resilience. Time spent on strengthening these three skills and traits will pay valuable dividends as you interact with your institution, its staff and your peers, both as organisational and support structures and as groups of individuals.

Communication: Waru's Story

I was encouraged to do a PhD after successfully completing my Honours year majoring in postmodern American literature. My thesis supervisor was really interested in the topic I had examined in this degree, and suggested I begin a PhD as he felt I could take my research a lot further. Frankly, I was over it. I was quite interested in doing a PhD, but in my final year I had begun working on some short stories and felt I wanted to take this creative writing process further. I am not a very assertive person, and I felt uncomfortable talking to my supervisor about this, especially as he was so enthusiastic about my abilities and my thesis topic.

I was pretty stressed about what I should do, and felt my choices were quite limited—my university didn't offer much in the way of creative writing at undergraduate level, and so there probably wasn't anyone who could supervise me as a creative writing PhD student. I decided I would get a job for a while and write in my spare time.

I ran into my old supervisor at the supermarket a few months later and he asked me what I was up to. When I told him I was working on some short stories he suggested we have a coffee and talk about writing—turns out he was working on a novel. He pointed me in the direction of another university with a strong creative arts focus, and now I am writing and researching short stories as part of my PhD project at that institution. It was just luck that I ran into him—I should have asked for advice in the first place. I was too caught up with how I would start the conversation, and worried about how it might end.

It was a scary process to enrol in a PhD at an unfamiliar campus, but I pushed myself to find the right people to talk to before I enrolled, and my supervisor gave me some really helpful contacts. Seems all these literature academics know each other! It is going really well—my department is really supportive and I have met other research students who are doing similar creative writing doctorates. It is a really stimulating research environment.

If a student is embarking on a doctorate, they presumably already have proven communication skills; but they may be shy or lack confidence when dealing face-to-face with administrators or academic staff. They may feel that asking questions makes them look foolish. In fact asking questions, and making sure you get the answers you need, is the most empowering thing for a student to do at the start of, and during, their doctorate. It is, for instance, important to research and compare universities to be comfortable and confident about your choice. Most universities provide a significant amount of information to potential postgraduate students, including the research foci of the institution, doctoral student profiles and stories, internship possibilities, and peer and other support groups and services. At this stage is useful to think carefully about whether any information is missing that you feel you need.

If you are unwilling to ask for help, you will get lost. While you may rely on technology to help you out, it cannot provide answers and advice in the same way another person can—someone with specific skills, experience and empathy. Establishing strong and comfortable lines of communication with key people within your institution and department will smooth your journey and also give you confidence in asking for assistance when difficulties arise. The relationships you form with academic, administrative and service staff at a university—including those working in IT, library, and the various health and well-being support services, and with other students taking similar journeys—will help to smooth the inevitable bumps you encounter, assisting you to reach your goals quickly and effectively.

Here are a number of tips that will help to ensure you have the best knowledge base from which to choose a university:

- Write down your questions, and identify where you might find the answers you require.
- Use the internet to research topics and institutions that may suit your interests. Find the names or positions of people to follow up with online. Initially, ask questions via email, but be prepared to find someone to talk to if necessary.
- Research how your preferred institution supports postgraduate students. Consider the quality of information on the website. How easy is it to find what you want to know? How comprehensive is the information? How easy is it to find someone to speak to?

- Get a feel for how your research project aligns with the academic focus and culture of the university, as this is an indication that you may be well supported in your studies.
- See if you can find out whether the institution provides employment, external internships or mentoring programs for postgraduate students.
- What industry connections do they have?
- Is there financial assistance for students to undertake field-work or attend conferences?
- Contact current PhD students within your proposed department or discipline and, if possible, post-graduate students who have completed (and perhaps students who have withdrawn from) similar research projects and/or have studied in your proposed faculty, regarding program-specific information.
- Be respectful. University staff are there to assist you, but they often have to deal with difficult situations and individuals. Like you, they have complex lives both within and outside their work environments. If you find someone unhelpful, seek advice elsewhere. There are many paths to finding information.

Do not forget to note down the names and contact details of university and faculty staff when seeking advice and assistance. Keep this list of support people/areas handy, so you can refer to it quickly and request advisors by name, or at least refer to the advice provided by a particular individual. It is also not only polite, but also politic, to thank those who help you. The quality of your institutional relationships will be enhanced if you show that you value the advice and support of those who provide it to you.

Flexibility: Bianca's Story

It's a learning thing I guess. Starting my PhD, I was so organised. I had been thinking about going back to study for a long time—I am a primary school teacher and had become really interested in a specific area of educational policy. When my youngest child finished high school, I decided to switch to part-time work and devote my new spare time to hopefully doing a research PhD. It was something I had been considering for a while. I discussed it with my principal and she thought it sounded interesting, but I don't think she really understood what I wanted to do. But I did manage to negotiate shorter work hours. My local university has an Education department, and I did my research and was accepted into their doctoral program, with a supervisor who I thought I would get along well with. She was not immediately enthusiastic about my project, as she thought it may be difficult to get data from primary schools, and that there might be ethical implications, but I think I impressed her with my enthusiasm and confidence.

In the end it was a lot harder than I imagined—especially because my supervisor wanted me to change my topic when I came up against a lot of obstacles, such as when I needed to interview students and their parents. I don't think I'm stubborn, but once I get an idea in my head I can be pretty determined, and I don't give up easily.

I really thought I could just push through, and work around the issues as they came up. But it got complicated, because I didn't want to adjust my project, and the issues weren't resolved. I devoted over a year to the PhD but, in the end, decided not to complete it. I wasn't prepared to compromise, but in retrospect I think I made a poor decision. I was totally inflexible. I would do it differently next time—definitely be more open to advice. I'm actually already thinking about how I might take it in a different direction, and how a lot of the work I have put in could be useful.

Undertaking a research degree demands flexibility, particularly when managing relationships with those working in the institution. There may not be a perfect fit between your preferred university and your desired research topic, and this will necessitate negotiation and compromise. For example, you may need to adjust your project numerous times, filter advice from supervisors, which can sometimes be contradictory, or deal with changes in personal and professional circumstances. Compromise is about negotiating the path to your research goal. It may seem more convoluted that initially expected, but it is a crucial part of the learning process—and especially when working at the doctoral level, which involves being able to solve complex problems and think both critically and creatively.

Here are some tips that are helpful in having a flexible approach to the doctorate, which encompass both institutional policies and personal practices:

- Be prepared to communicate any concerns and state your case succinctly if your research runs into problems.
- Accept, though, that there are often very legitimate reasons for you having to adjust your topic, approach and/or research schedule, and that your supervisors are often experienced in advising students regarding such modifications.
- Find out how others have dealt with changes or difficult situations, and whether they were successful or not.
- Remember that your supervisors have external lives too, and sometimes you may have to adapt to their situation or working practices.
- Sometimes universities change their policies—for better or for worse—and while these changes would usually not detrimentally affect your studies, be aware these are often in response to external drivers such as government imperatives.
- Personal circumstances and responsibilities might seem to come secondary to a research degree but, in reality, sometimes life will intervene and you have to give yourself permission to attend to whatever needs your attention.

These all point to how undertaking a lengthy and complex research project such as a doctorate is an evolving process, and students need to develop skills in flexibility and creative problem solving alongside their research training.

Resilience: Garry's Story

Starting my PhD while working full time was a challenge, but as my research project aligns closely with my work as a theatre company manager, I felt that I was in a good place—with financial security and a work environment that stimulated my research interests and provided excellent networking and data gathering opportunities. I was motivated and excited, and felt well supported by my university. My supervisor and I knew each other quite well via industry collaborations, and the Creative Industries faculty has a number of PhD students working on a really interesting and diverse range of projects. I knew there would be challenges, but I was very positive that I could manage them.

It didn't work out that way. While trying to cope and survive the stress of what felt like insurmountable difficulties, I realised that doing a PhD is incredibly challenging, and necessitates a high degree of resilience. Some may have this when they start, but others have to learn it as they go along—especially if they want finish.

Firstly, the theatre company I managed lost its funding and was forced to close. Not only did my salary disappear, I felt a sense of responsibility to the theatre, and had to deal with a lot of complex and stressful administrative issues as the business wound up. My faculty was very supportive, as were my peers—there was a lot of sharing of work stories of woe. The university assisted me in accessing scholarship funding, and my supervisor pointed me to campus services that helped me to deal with the stress. Talking to other students was also really helpful.

Further down the track, my senior supervisor was diagnosed with a serious illness, and left the university. I was devastated, as we worked very well together and I could not imagine working with someone else. I really felt like giving up at that point—too many obstacles—and I felt like my work and my mental and physical health were being compromised. Fortunately, the excellent staff and peer support continued, and I think I became a lot stronger having to cope with so many challenges and changes. Developing resilience is so important, and the excellent services provided by the university, and the mutually supportive relationships I had established with academic staff and other students in my faculty, definitely helped me to push through to completion.

Resilience is a quality developed from confronting difficulties and dealing with them, both successfully and unsuccessfully. Undertaking a doctorate will inevitably throw up difficulties to be surmounted, and as highlighted above, communication skills and flexibility are very important when negotiating issues that arise. To seek, assess, and accept or discard advice can be made easier when relationships within an institution are based on trust and mutual support. While you might not necessarily get along with everyone you work with, it is very important to build a set of professional relationships that you can rely on. There will always be individuals, and institutional circumstances, that create obstacles. Most obstacles are temporary, and with support from your 'team' you will continue on to complete your journey with renewed enthusiasm and strength. In this way, completing a PhD will inevitably build and strengthen a wide range of a student's skills, not all of which are academic. Undertaking a doctorate is also about committing to personal growth.

Here are some tips that are helpful in relation to becoming more resilient:

- Take responsibility for your personal learning journey, and be open to the possibility that all may not go to plan.
- Share concerns and experiences with your peers.
- Recognise the value of strong, mutually respectful and supportive working relationships.
- Avoid competition with your peers, and understand that everyone has different working processes, goals and ambitions.
- Recognise that you are not alone, and that it is okay to ask for help.
- Remember that most situations are salvageable, no matter how dire they may seem. Solutions may not be immediately obvious, but can often be found with perseverance.

Conclusion

Undertaking a research degree is a complex and complicated journey, during which interpersonal skills are important to develop alongside advanced research skills. Good relationships are built on strong communication, flexibility and the ability to be resilient. Recognising the importance of a student's relationship with their academic community—their institution, department, staff and fellow postgraduate peers—underpins the research training experience. Being willing to bring the personal into the research process, especially in relation to how professional obstacles can be negotiated with measured judgement and insight, in itself assists in further developing the useful life-long qualities of communication, flexibility and resilience.

7

Developing Communities of Practice

Colleen Ryan

Introduction

As highlighted by Margaret Cook in Chap. 5, the journey for the doctoral student may begin with returning to the uncomfortable position of novice. In the transformation from novice to doctor, the research student will travel many pathways. The journey can be long and exhausting, requiring learning to navigate the sometimes-challenging intellectual terrain, including gaining advanced skills in data collection and analysis, and critical thinking and theorising. Exhilaration when you succeed at one point may be bittersweet, because the journey is a long one and having a toolkit of quality resources is essential. This chapter discusses one such resource for doctoral success—being a member of a Community of Practice (CoP). Along with their definition and history, and the ways

C. Ryan (✉)
School of Nursing, Midwifery and Social Sciences, Central Queensland University, Noosaville, QLD, Australia
e-mail: c.l.ryan@cqu.edu.au

© The Author(s) 2019
D. L. Brien et al. (eds.), *The Doctoral Experience*,
https://doi.org/10.1007/978-3-030-18199-4_7

they can function to support a doctoral candidature, experiences from members of a variety of communities of practice are presented in this chapter.

Communities of Practice

The term 'community of practice' was first defined by Jean Lave and Etienne Wenger in 1991. This was then expanded upon, and refined, by Wenger (1998) and, then, Etienne Wenger-Trayner and Beverly Wenger-Trayner (2015) as the concept began to have traction. Communities of practice are "characterized by socialisation, knowledge sharing, knowledge creation and identity building" (McAllister and Brien 2017, p. 145). As Wenger-Trayner and Wenger-Trayner (2015) explain, communities of practice are pervasive and common in our lives, with members often operating in ad-hoc and unintentional ways, and without set processes or agendas. Communities of practice may begin informally, as when a group of like-minded people come together and, through sharing their stories, support each other to develop knowledge around their particular situations. One outcome of this coming together, albeit unintentional in many cases, may be to develop or improve practice. Here we might consider the staffroom in any busy workplace: workmates sit around the table having a meal, simultaneously sharing stories about various situations, problems or encounters they have experienced, or are encountering, at work. Invariably, members of the group will add their own stories, and offer commentary, advice, insights, support and guidance. This is a community of practice.

Communities of practice are not a new phenomenon. This form of practice development has its origins in pragmatism. Pragmatism is an American philosophical movement from the 1870s, attributed to the little-known Charles Sanders Pearce (1839–1914) and the more often acknowledged educational philosopher, John Dewey (1859–1952). Pragmatists believe thought is instrumental in problem solving and by enacting their thoughts hope they will assist in developing knowledge that can promote change (Hookway 2016). Wenger-Trayner and Wenger-Trayner (2015) explain that communities of practice may also be formed intentionally and formally, resulting in a group of members who are guided by an articulated purpose and are bound by three specific requirements: the domain, the community and the practice.

The *domain* speaks to the identity of the community that has formed. Each member is committed to this domain or identity, and will strive to develop a competence in this identity that sets them apart from other members of the community in which they live. The *community* refers to all the members working collectively and collaboratively to share knowledge and learn from each other, because of their interest in the common domain. Finally, the *practice* speaks to the fact that members of the community of practice are practitioners, each wanting to work together to develop a set of resources, particular knowledge and/or solutions to problems. In short, communities of practice that are guided by these three components are different to the informal and ad-hoc communities of practice taking place in the staffroom example above. The reasons why communities of practice might be beneficial for doctoral students are now explored.

Benefits to Adding a Community of Practice to the Toolkit

In 1991, when studying learning through apprenticeships, Lave and Wenger published findings around the concept of communities of practice as a learning strategy. What Lave and Wenger (1991) published was their observations of apprentices achieving various degrees of mastery from working alongside their peers. Learning *always* and *only* from the master (or in our case, the supervisors as doctors) was not deemed to be essential. Here is another example, taken from Jean Lave (Lave and Wenger 1991, p. 79): an Alcoholics Anonymous meeting. A new member is joining. The new member is embarking on a journey and will strive to learn to live without alcohol. Other members are available within the group to assist. These members have experiences and resources that may assist their new peer. One or several of these group members are paired with the new apprentice to offer assistance and support. These peers are not masters, as they often themselves are still striving to learn the skill of abstinence; they are fellow journeymen. In this same way, the new doctoral student may seek support and guidance from a group comprising of journeymen and masters, and this group becomes a community of practice.

The Breakfast Club

I inwardly (and perhaps outwardly) groaned when I was invited to join a community of practice. This was very early in my studies, before my enrolment was completed. I just did not have the time! Full time work, family commitments, other professional development activities and, of course, the PhD: no time at all.

Two of my peers, slightly ahead of me in their studies, invited me to join what could be considered an informal, ad-hoc version of a community of practice. We have no agenda, keep no meeting notes or minutes and do not meet regularly, however, after two years, we are now committed to holding our meetings far into the future. We are a Breakfast Club CoP and I was hooked from our first meeting. Here's what I experienced:

> *I remember sharing, "So I'm really stuck on my methodology. How will I ever get my head around this? I have pestered my supervisor, I'm sure she's regretting taking me on as a student. I just don't get it!"*
>
> *The responses went something like this.*
>
> *"I've got a great easy to read book about that, I will leave it on your desk tomorrow".*
>
> *"Have you looked at that thesis I said I was reading? I'll send you a copy. It has a great methodology section".*
>
> *"Keep talking to your supervisor and try writing a couple of hundred words on your current thinking. Your confusion is normal, keep going".*
>
> *And, from a colleague enrolled two weeks after me: "I am so relieved you brought this up. I am feeling quite stupid just now that I don't get methodology either".*
>
> *The thesis and the book were helpful and not long after my first Breakfast Club, I submitted a few paragraphs about the thesis methodology to my supervisor and received a good review. I was hooked!*

What Kind of Community of Practice Is Best?

You might discover your university already has a variety of formal and informal communities of practice that you could join. If this is the case, researching current members to understand the domain, community and practice, and how these will suit your needs, is essential. You might like to consider creating your own. This could have small member numbers or be something larger, and can be highly regulated and scheduled, or more casual, meeting when members feel the need to. Either way, both members and conveners will do well to understand the essential stages of facilitating such a group. Wenger et al. (2002) offer seven principles for cultivating a community of practice, which I adapt below for the doctoral context.

Evolution of a Community of Practice

First the CoP must be established and then continually evolve. Some kind of advertising to attract members must take place. Initial meetings might be held regularly but, at this early point in time, meeting notes might not be required. Simple problem solving for example might be the focus of these initial meetings. The CoP might not need to progress from this style of meeting (see *The Breakfast Club CoP*, above). However, if the vision was for a larger group to continue for some time and to tackle many problems, the core membership of the CoP might also incorporate the next steps.

Inviting the Outside In

This stage begins when core members realise they may benefit from inviting new members who are equipped with relevant knowledge and skills and/or able to assist in brainstorming ideas about solving particular problems. The core members remain experts about their domain or identity. Outsiders may only participate for a short period of time, or they may choose to, or be invited to, become regular members. Examples of practitioners for the research student to consider inviting to a CoP might include: a peer experienced in a particular methodology; an expert to instruct on thesis editing and presentation; or a mentor to advise about writing for publication. The options are limitless, depending on members' requirements. The membership status of participants is important to consider, to maintain the integrity of the group and their focus.

Membership: Who Is Who and Who Does What?

Wenger et al. (2002) describe three core levels of member participation in the CoP. The first are most committed to the domain and are present and active at every meeting, often driving the direction of the CoP. The second level are also active members, however their input may not be as regular or as intensive. The third may attend irregularly depending on what they want to achieve from a meeting. Finally, there is a fourth (non-core) level of membership, comprising those who may not attend the CoP but who observe the group's effects or output from a distance. These fourth-level members often still benefit from the CoP. If a CoP is focused on academic writing and publications, for example, the department, research centre and/or university will benefit from any publications without having any direct involvement in the CoP. Members join the CoP for different reasons and Wenger et al. (2002) suggests one way of keeping members interested and continually participating is for core members to stagger activities and delegate various work to all members.

Convening Meetings and Events

Core CoP members are encouraged to consider a variety of options to conduct their meetings, such as holding small group meetings or larger networking events, and utilising telephone conversations, online meeting technology and group email chatter. As members develop mutual trust and honesty, the meetings will occur in ways and places that are best suited to the group's identity. This enriches the community and its activities. Some CoP secure funding for a variety of member projects. After a success, such as doctoral completion, members may decide to celebrate.

This might range from something informal such as cake and coffee in the student common room or similar space, to a barbeque at a member's home, or a more public display such as renting a function room and inviting members and their partners. The CoP must decide as a group what is best for its members and what will be true to their domain and community. It is also important to ensure members are delegated tasks and responsibilities in the various events. This develops a sense of involvement and can enhance commitment to the group.

The Value of the Community of Practice

Discussing the value that arises from the group is recommended. Its value may not be apparent until the community is well formed, and the value may differ for each member. The value may be tacit, for example emotional relief when a member discovers they are not the only student worrying about the same issue; or it may be more tangible, such as receiving feedback on a thesis chapter in progress. Members exploring and developing an understanding of the value of their CoP is critical in effective decision-making about the CoP.

Mixing Up the Activities

As members will each benefit in different ways from the CoP, it is important to offer a variety of activities. On the one hand, routine activities will promote stability and develop trust and relationships between the members. On the other hand, less frequent activities, such as attending conferences together, may stimulate new thinking, ideas and knowledge, which can be very exciting. Considering the timing and scheduling of meetings and activities to best suit members is essential.

When Will We Meet Again?

In terms of the rhythm of the community of practice meetings, regular timing of meetings is recommended initially to stimulate growth, membership commitment and useful sharing of ideas and knowledge. Then the CoP may evolve in a different manner. Some groups continue for long intervals, constantly evolving. Other groups may come to a natural end because the identity or shared interest, that is, the domain, no longer exists or stimulates the members.

What's on Offer?

In addition to the Breakfast Club, I now outline some of the CoP I have been involved in while undertaking my doctorate.

The Writing Club

I have been, and remain currently, involved in several versions of this CoP. Two I started myself, each with the intention of producing a joint authored manuscript for publication. Membership of these CoP was limited to the authors. We met fortnightly to achieve the output. In both cases, once the manuscript was published, the CoP dissolved.

In contrast to this, the first Writing Club CoP I was invited to join remains alive after several years. This CoP began as a six-member group of novices and mentors, with the shared purpose of developing the novices' research and writing skills. The key to keeping this CoP alive, as we decided at the first meeting, is that the volume of data from a project we had designed would produce multiple manuscripts. We envisaged the group would then aim for six publications with a rotating lead author. To this effect, authorship contracts were then signed by each member of the group.

Two publications have been published with two more manuscripts in varying degrees of completion. This COP relies on the lead author of the working manuscript to convene the meetings. As such, we do not maintain regular meeting times, rather we rely on the authorship agreement and our academic professionalism to keep the CoP alive. We meet face-to-face at times, but mostly online or by teleconference. Two members have moved to other institutions however remain members of the CoP.

Online CoP

Formed by a colleague of mine who shares the same role within our institution, working with stakeholders. We offer support and education to nurses who supervise students in clinical practice, who often work autonomously. We thought to offer these nurses a platform to problem solve and share ideas, knowledge and experiences in a supportive environment. This newly formed online CoP already has close to two hundred members from a wide variety of geographical locations. Our meetings are monthly. The format of the meeting is the same each month; welcome, sharing of current role experiences, sharing of recent professional development, research news. Each meeting is video recorded and shared with all members. The regular attendance is usually about twelve, and we are already identifying core members.

The Healthy CoP

This is for maintaining our work/life balance. The group has four members, two core and is open to new members. We meet weekly for approximately one hour. We swim for thirty minutes and then, after showering, share our study and work experiences whilst having our lunch, before then returning to our respective universities. Not all members are research students but all are academics.

Examples of other CoP to consider include:

- CoP for the purposes of data collection, most commonly utilised in participatory action research or community based action research (Israel et al. 1998).
- Supervisors who bring their students together to review and share their work, as a form of group supervision.
- Brown paper bag CoP where participants meet over lunch and participate in previously advertised activities such as workshopping their work, guest speakers and dedicated writing time.

- Group formed by a variety of members from geographically separate locations coming together face-to-face. Meeting destinations rotate, however, due to large distances between members, CoP are held a few times, or even just once, a year.

Conclusion

Reflecting now on the importance of these various CoP in my own doctoral journey, both as an academic and a PhD student, I realise that without convening and participating in the Writing Club, for example, I would not successfully have published a majority of my publications to date: six published and in press manuscripts. The Online CoP organised for nursing clinical supervisors has been a venue for many a robust, academic, pragmatic, ethical and moral discussion that has affected how I have approached my doctoral studies. Sharing in discussions with these clinicians and academics has helped me to deepen my thinking and develop my ideas about clinical supervision. I am also appreciative of the Healthy CoP. This CoP has enabled me to position exercise and friendship as a part of my doctoral life. This reminds me of the importance of work-life balance, especially when I am working hard and my regular exercise regime is forced to take a backseat. The conversations and activities experienced with this CoP have assisted me to keep focussed and to enjoy the luxury of quality thinking time as I complete my swim.

References

Hookway, C. 2016. "Pragmatism." In *The Stanford Encyclopedia of Philosophy*. Summer 2016, edited by E. N. Zalta. http://plato.stanford.edu/archives/sum2016/entries/pragmatism.

Israel, B., A. Schulz, E. Parker, and A. Becker. 1998. "Review of community based research: Assessing partnership approaches to improve public health." *Annual Review of Public Health* 19 (1): 173–202. https://doi.org/10.1146/annurev.publhealth.19.1.173.

Lave, J., and E. Wenger. 1991. *Situated Learning: Legitimate Peripheral Participation*. Cambridge: Cambridge University Press.

McAllister, M., and D. L. Brien. 2017. "'Pre-run, Re-run': An innovative research capacity building exercise." *Nurse Education in Practice* 27, 144–150. https://doi.org/10.1016/j.nepr.2017.09.002.

Wenger, E. 1998. *Communities of Practice: Learning Meaning and Identity.* Cambridge: Cambridge University Press

Wenger, E., R. McDermott, and W. Snyder. 2002. *It Takes a Community.* https:// global-factiva-com.ezproxy.cqu.edu.au.

Wenger-Trayner, E., and B. Wenger-Trayner. 2015. *Introduction to Communities of Practice.* http://wenger-trayner.com/introduction-to-communities-of-practice.

8

Approaching Research in a Prepared, Mindful and Ethical Manner

Justine Newport

Introduction

Little Red Riding Hood, carrying her basket of thesis ideas, is standing outside her grandmother's house. As she opens the door, her Grandma looks scarily different. We all know the story. In this case, however, Little Red Riding Hood is an avatar of a student researcher who has recently commenced their doctorate. Having worked through the ethics application, she has been overwhelmed by the number of questions she must think about. She feels she has, up to now, led quite a virtuous life. Surely that is enough, she asks, to equip her for designing a survey or interviewing a few people?

Reading the literature on ethical approaches to research, a student might imagine that ethics is principally about doing no harm (Guillemin and Gillam 2004, p. 4). Doctoral students soon realise, however, that ethical research practice is not only about setting out not to cause harm

J. Newport (✉)
School of Education and the Arts, Central Queensland University,
Noosaville, QLD, Australia
e-mail: justine.newport@cqumail.com

© The Author(s) 2019
D. L. Brien et al. (eds.), *The Doctoral Experience*,
https://doi.org/10.1007/978-3-030-18199-4_8

to participants—human or animal—but is also about developing ethical "know-how" (Varela 1999, p. 21) to underpin their research practice. This ensures that students operate in fair and transparent ways that are driven by ethical values throughout their degrees.

Ethical clearance application forms, which are often very detailed with many questions, are created to cover a wide range of possibilities and can result in students sometimes feeling overwhelmed regarding what they are being asked to disclose. This can result in students feeling like Little Red Riding Hood, with both their identity as researchers and basket of research project ideas they offer in danger of being savaged by those on the ethics committee, with their shiny procedural teeth and sharp academic claws. Understandably, students can find the idea of these gatekeepers, who wield the power to derail their often still-emergent research plans, an insurmountable difficulty. As a result, it is not uncommon for some to flee from the encounter, changing their methodologies, or even their projects, in order to avoid such scrutiny.

What if, however, the research student has already been successful in receiving their ethical clearance—but is then faced with a participant who reveals something sensitive (and off topic) in an interview? What if a participant cries during the interview, becomes angry, or worse? This discussion proposes that such unprepared-for situations are the real wolves to be avoided. If, from the outset, the researcher has considered all—or, at least, a wide range of—possibilities, they will be in a better position to deal with them. Guillemin and Gillam (2004) term this 'practical ethics': pre-planning for a series of possible, and sometimes unimaginable, hurdles, because when things happen unexpectedly, there will be little time to consider the most appropriate reaction. This chapter outlines how research students will benefit from learning how to approach their research in an ethical manner, including preparing themselves for the unknown when dealing with human participants.

Moira's Story

It is a bright spring morning and the student researcher, Moira, feels relaxed and confident as she is some way into the interviews for her project. Her next interviewee is Jane, a quietly spoken, single mother with a two-year-old son.

Jane is keen to answer Moira's questions about a relatively little known Irish author and so the interview goes well. Then, just as Moira is leaving the meeting, Jane says, "I deliberately broke my son's arm yesterday, he made me so mad I could not help myself". (Enter wolf, stage left.)

What should Moira do? Should she ignore the comment and do nothing because she thinks Jane made it up or is joking? If she does believe it, remembering her role as a doctoral researcher—who should not harm her interviewees, or even reveal their identities—what should she then do next? As Jane's admission sounds like child abuse, should Moira tell Jane that she is going to report what she said to her supervisor or the police? Would she be in danger herself if she did so? Indeed, the questions could be so many that Moira may well be paralysed by indecision. Moira is suddenly faced with a range of ethical dilemmas. These relate to: a child she has never seen; a mother who may, or may not, have done as she has claimed; the law that requires her to report potential child abuse; her own humanity; and the requirements of her research project's ethical clearance.

Although few doctoral researchers will undergo such a dramatic experience as Moira's above, there are other aspects of practical ethics which do come into play in many projects in the creative arts and humanities. Doctoral students should, for instance, interrogate their own motivation for pursuing the subject they have chosen and examine their approach before they start. Some ideas, such as the research being 'for the greater good', have seduced researchers into using distressing or intrusive experiments. An example of this is Milgram's Yale University research into the power of authority (Thomas 2009, p. 147). In this research the volunteer participants were lied to, so that their actions appeared to give other participants electric shocks. This was to test if fear of authority would permit people to obey without thinking. The findings of this experiment, which were at first refused publication, then went on to win a major research prize (Milgram 1963), but the ethics of the experiment have since been questioned and debated.

Researchers may also become tired, bored with a part of their research project, or uncomfortably short of time. These factors may lead them to forget to respect people's wishes sufficiently (Thomas 2009, pp. 146–152). Mindfulness, or reflexivity as it is termed in a research context, is essential to behave ethically throughout the considerable length of time it takes to complete a doctoral project. This is a process of looking inward to one's mind, investigating one's own thoughts and feelings, and evaluating them for the ability to take others into consideration (Mann, 2016). This is an ongoing process of interrogating and analysing, not only the data, but also the researcher's attitude, and any possible effects the researcher, and the research, may have upon their participants (Guillemin and Gillam 2004, pp. 273–274). Reflexivity involves observing one's own personal motivations and acknowledging how that person actually operates, as opposed to how they actually perceive their own behaviour, and how honest they are in their interactions with others. As reflexivity is an ongoing process, and not a one-off check of researcher's ethics, keeping a research ethics diary is a good way to record this self-reflection over time.

In the same way, although researchers apply forward thinking when filling in the ethics clearance form, this is just the beginning. Moira's story is based on a real incident, and emphasises that research in the field may not always be without moral dilemmas; or occur in a way that makes the student researcher feel comfortable. This is why the ethics clearance process and those detailed forms are so important. They give the doctoral student a chance to plan their research in sufficient detail to help them cope if, and when, real life intrudes.

Consent

The consent to use other's ideas in their work is taught to all university students via the rules and guidelines for citation and referencing. In research projects, the project participants' consent is the starting point for all research with individuals, but doctoral students need to consider consent of various kinds, and understand the differences between informed consent, active consent and implied consent.

Informed consent means that participants know exactly the kind of research in which they are participating. This means that participants should be advised clearly what topic the research addresses, as well as what benefits the researcher, the university and society may gain from it. Beyond this, the student researcher also needs to inform participants about any possible harm they may incur as a result of participating in—or contributing to—the research. Students also need to explain about confidentiality, anonymity, and both how long the data will be kept, and when it will be destroyed. This should be explained in clear, and preferably not too dull, language, with no unexplained or jargonistic terms (Thomas 2009, p. 150). This is not an easy task and sufficient time needs to be dedicated to its fulfilment.

Active consent concerns those people who are asked to join the study and need to be briefed on how they will indicate if they agree to take part (Thomas 2009). For example, the student researcher may take it as 'opting in' if the participant sends a survey back, takes part in a meeting, or otherwise makes contacts with the researcher. However, there is also implied consent, which can be summed up as 'unless I hear from you I will assume you will take part'. Implied consent is not applicable, or acceptable, in any situation where there are unequal power relationships between researcher and participant (Thomas 2009, p. 159).

Ethnographic Research

Ethnographic research carries special difficulties for any researcher who is embedded in an unfamiliar culture or a marginalised, or even illegal, group. The effect of this on the student needs careful monitoring and close supervision to ensure they have the personal resilience to make this research a positive experience. In Sanjari et al., the co-authors warn that such a project may need thinking about in terms of why the student researcher has picked that specific subject to explore (2014, p. 6).

Petra's Story

Petra is a research student interested in social justice. Her doctoral research project is to explore the relationships between prostitutes and their friends. Her university had some reservations about this topic but, as Petra was a qualified counsellor, they agreed. She had coped well as an embedded street worker. Then, she encountered Janet, a pre-operative transsexual man who she knew immediately she would get on with, until the point that Janet said to her: "I would like to tell my mother what I do, I love it. Mother is great, but she found my change hard. My father, he still doesn't know. I dress male the way I always did around him as I act as a male prostitute for gay men, so it is easy really".

Petra, who naïvely thought that she had seen it all, found her mind bending at the edges. Her own mother had no idea about Petra's sister, Amy, a working girl, who had been her entry point into the research she was doing. Importantly, Petra had never encountered a male prostitute before. Nor had she realised how conventional and narrow her views actually were.

She did not feel she could go to her university-appointed counsellor to discuss her discomfort because she knew he had deeply held views about the proper roles of men and women. In a previous counselling session, she had found this comforting because they echoed her own fathers' beliefs. But she knew that they would be wholly inappropriate for this situation, and she felt at a loss to know who to go to for help. She certainly could not admit anything to Amy in case her sister realised how like her father she really was underneath. Petra felt ashamed, a fraud and lost.

Such self-monitoring is important in both this kind of research, as well as other research projects, whether the people the research student is surveying, interviewing or observing are members of their family, other people they feel empathy for, or even those that they may have an aversion to (Guillemin and Gillam 2004). The student researcher also needs to develop rules about their own disengagement, and how—and when—this might be enacted. Some relationships need, moreover, to be clearly defined before the researcher begins to work (p. 270).

Autoethnography, which uses a researcher's selected experiences from their own past to reflect on a particular culture or part of society, can be another ethical trap-in-waiting (Ellis et al. 2011, p. 11). This type of research often cannot proceed without referring to the researcher's knowledge of their own family and/or friends, and seeking their permission becomes central. This is common, for instance, when a student is writing a memoir or another form of autobiographically-based creative work as part of their doctoral project. However, the ethics of permission are complex and reveal how even research into a doctoral students' own life can harbour wolves.

My Own Story

I sat many times with a close friend, Sam, drinking tea in the kitchen and listening to him talk about his research project, enquiring into the accidental drug death of his daughter Mary, whom I knew before she died. She was exceptionally bright; however, she was wedded to her heroin addiction. Father and daughter had a somewhat intense relationship which was a mixture of admiration and pain. When it came time for Sam to submit his work to the university, Mary's two brothers refused to read their father's work, or to talk about it. So right up until it was submitted, he was waiting for some refusal that would not allow his insights about the family to be published. It never came, but his sons have still not read the work years later. However, they watch their own two daughters for signs of addictive personalities, more than is usual in the parents of tiny children. (This story is based on a true one, but many details are altered to protect my friend who isn't very skilled around wolves, and too hurt to admit it.)

This case illustrates how anyone the student researcher writes about can withdraw their permission at any time; even if they have agreed to the inclusion of their story or an incident in which they appear in a doctoral student's research project. If they do withdraw their permission, their vital, poignant story can no longer be used in either the research analysis or the report of its findings.

Permissions can also be difficult to negotiate. Likewise, determining the language and parameters needed for the informed consent section of the ethics form is also complex before the project has been commenced. It can, at times, seem almost impossible as the research student will not yet know what will occur when they explore their families' views of the same events, and where this will lead. It is worth considering how, in such cases, the research could be a healing journey, but it may be very far from that. Before student researchers begin this form of research, it is important to look at the difficulties they may encounter and, even, the costs they may pay (Guillemin and Gillam 2004). It is important to realise that, whatever research is undertaken that involves their family, friends or colleagues, there will be some alteration in those group dynamics as a result (Guillemin and Gillam 2004, p. 264).

Certainly, however, researchers have achieved good and useful results from sharing stories, so it is clearly not impossible. Such sharing can, indeed, make a difference in ordinary people's experiences of their own lives. Two examples of this are the world's youngest Nobel Prize winner and survivor of political violence, Malala Yousafzai (2013), and Rosie Batty (2017), whose son was murdered in front of her by her ex-husband. Both women went on to campaign for violence-affected families, and have become an inspiration to others through their revelation of their life stories.

An Ethics of Researcher Self-preservation

There are another series of ethical issues that concern the doctoral researcher and how they can ensure their own wellness and safety during their research project. A project participant may, for instance, ask the student researcher personal questions about themselves during the research process and, therefore, the student needs to have considered how much of their own history they are comfortable revealing. The research project often already reveals a great deal about the student researcher. It is—after all—designed by them, on an aspect of life that they are curious about. This point may appear a minor concern; but opening up about personal information soon becomes a two-way street and the doctoral researcher could soon end up with more off-thesis topic information than they need, or want, to know.

Another wolf in the doctoral experience comes in the form of discovering someone else's unethical research behaviour. This is compounded if the person behaving unethically is someone of consequence. To whom is such conduct reported? A research student may need to work alongside them—or even for them—in the future, so the question of reporting such unethical attitudes becomes even more difficult and complex. This is where the various formal ethics personnel at the university can help.

If a doctoral student needs help or support as a result of their research, it is important that they have already researched to whom they might talk because, once they realise this is needed, the student may not have the mental clarity to select the best counsellor or therapist. The university may have someone available but the student should check their credentials as a trained professional is always best. A student should also remember that if, upon meeting a counsellor or therapist, they do not take to them, it is essential to find someone else. According to a study from the American Psychological Association (Novotney 2013, p. 2), it truly matters if clients like their therapists, as therapy works better in such circumstances.

Conclusion

The ethics of conducting research is an ongoing concern and process that requires much attention. Students should guard against wolves turning up at unexpected moments by preparing themselves and their research for a range of challenging eventualities in terms of ethical issues and dilemmas. If, however, the researcher keeps checking in with their ethical self and their supervisors, who will undoubtedly have seen similar wolves come and go, the researcher will ensure that both they, and their research participants, are protected from ethical, and other, research malpractice.

References

Batty, R. 2017. *Never Alone*. https://lukebattyfoundation.org.au.

Ellis, C., T. Adams, and A. P. Bochner. 2011. "Auto ethnography: An overview." *Forum Qualitative Social Research* 12 (1). http://www.qualitative-research.net/index.php/fqs/article/view/1589.

Guillemin, M., and L. Gillam. 2004. "Reflexivity, and ethically important moments in research." *Qualitative Inquiry* 10 (2): 261–280.

Mann, S. 2016. *The Research Interview: Reflective Practice and Reflexivity in Research Process*. Hampshire and New York: Palgrave Macmillan.

Milgram, S. 1963. "Behavioral study of obedience." *The Journal of Abnormal and Social Psychology* 67 (4): 371–378.

Novotney, A. 2013. "The therapist effect." *American Psychological Association* 44 (2): 48.

Sanjari, M., F. Bahramnezhad, F. K. Fomani, M. Shoghi, and M. A. Cheraghi. 2014. "Ethical challenges of researchers in qualitative studies: The necessity to develop a specific guideline." *Journal of Medical Ethics and the History of Medicine* 7 (14). https://www.ncbi.nlm.nih.gov/pmc/articles/PMC4263394.

Thomas, G. 2009. *How to Do Your Research Project.* London: SAGE.

Varela, F. 1999. *Ethical Know-How: Action, Wisdom, and Cognition.* Stanford, CA: Stanford University Press.

Yousafzai, M. 2013. *I Am Malala: The Girl Who Stood Up for Education and Was Shot by the Taliban.* New York: Little, Brown & Company.

9

Understanding Issues of 'Truth' and Integrity in Doctoral Research

Alison Owens

Introduction

It may be assumed that writing fiction is to be liberated from the tyranny of the factual past and the historian's necessary precision in identifying, verifying and justifying sources in order to establish the historical veracity of any account. However, a writer of a historical fiction work developed to fulfil the requirements of a PhD must articulate the relationship between their research, the data that they collect, and the creative process that results in the end product. In this way, they contribute new knowledge about what de Groot has termed "the spaces scholars have no idea about … the gaps between known factual history and what is lived to a variety of purposes" (2010, p. 217). As increasing numbers of creative artists and practitioners are undertaking PhDs (Boyd 2009; Webb and Brien 2011), the relationship between factual input (data) and creative output (art/practice) is further explicated, and the research processes that

A. Owens (✉)
Learning and Teaching Centre, Australian Catholic University,
North Sydney, NSW, Australia
e-mail: Alison.Owens@acu.edu.au

© The Author(s) 2019
D. L. Brien et al. (eds.), *The Doctoral Experience*,
https://doi.org/10.1007/978-3-030-18199-4_9

bind them are more closely examined. One important aspect of this type of research is the ethical experience of both the researcher and the researched.

This chapter discusses ethical issues encountered in a recently completed creative practice PhD that drew on family history as well as public records as contributing data informing the development of an historical novel. The novel sought to depict the experience of growing up in an urban, working class family in Woolloomooloo (an inner city, harbourside suburb of Sydney, Australia) between World War One and World War Two. The research method was structured as a creative practice narrative inquiry, and the accompanying exegesis explained the research undertaken and the relationship that occurred between creative and expository texts. As such, this chapter explores how other creative arts doctoral students might take advantage of the ethical stances encountered during their research, in order to produce a thesis that takes on a 'meta' narrative of what it means to conduct research into real events and people.

Establishing a Narrative Inquiry Research Method

For near to a century, research methodologists in the social sciences have embraced a constantly diversifying set of qualitative methods by which they might study complex social phenomena, to produce richly detailed accounts of lived reality for specific communities, often received from informants and represented to readers in the form of a narrative (Clandinin and Connelly 2000; Crotty 1998; Denzin 1989). Narrative inquiry is primarily employed for the purpose of understanding human experience(s) rather than solving specific social problems or informing decisions, as much applied research seeks to do. In narrative inquiry, "the stories that people tell are the vehicles through which experiences are studied" (Lal and Suto 2012, p. 6). This form of inquiry is based largely on the assumption that stories are a form of social action, and that the telling of stories is one way humans experience and make sense of their lives (Bruner 1991; Caine and Steves 2009; Chase 2005; Clandinin 2006; Lal and Suto 2012; Riessman 2008).

The personal narratives or stories of individuals who have experience of the historical phenomena under study are invaluable to the narrative inquirer; invaluable, that is, if the researcher can establish (or in this case, preserve) authentic and open accounts of experience. While one of the principal informants in my PhD, my mother-in-law, seemed ever-ready to discuss her deceased husband and relate incidents or stories about him whenever family were around and the mood took her, it was quite another thing to get her to talk like this on prompt. Indeed, a recent attempt to have her answer direct questions either on paper or in conversation delivered the following sparse exchange:

1. When you think of your husband, what do you see? Is there a scene? Multiple scenes?
   Just before dying, laughing with us all as I tried to support him.
2. What do you hear? Smell, feel/touch when you think of him? (These sensory images may seem silly but are important in fiction.)
   Can't do as last 10 years were overpowering.
3. Describe him in a few sentences. How do you think he would describe himself?
   Prior to above, conceited, macho, arrogant, caring, kind, almost a contradiction.
4. What did he look like? (Physique? Hair? Clothes?)
   Broad shoulders, very tall, brown hair, very well dressed always.
5. Describe his voice.
   Beautiful voice, very deep, a great singer.
6. What were his favourite sayings?
   Christ, very well read, articulate.
7. What were his favourite possessions?
   His records and camera, later music, easel and paints.
8. What did he enjoy?
   Enjoyed entertaining.
9. What did he not like?
   Me swearing.
10. What do you know about his childhood?
    Childhood would have been loving, caring. "The little prince".

11. What were his political and religious views?
    Ha ha, very Centre Right, did not trust Labour due to antics of local polies. No religious leanings.
12. Describe his family.
    Family, loving, caring, supportive.
13. Describe his relationships with family members.
    Generous, caring, loving, kind, very close to sister, responsible for Mum.
14. What annoyed you about him?
    Always right.
15. What was most endearing about him?
    Most endearing, willing to help where needed. Extremely well thought of by relatives.

This was not the same conversation as the rollicking, often interrupted or contested accounts of how he had told off a headmaster, or had sent his son to an oil rig because his son had thought he was a man and had got in a fight, or how he had danced and sang on the table in the back kitchen of the Woolloomooloo home, or flown into Mombasa from the Kenyan oilfields in the middle of the night to try to catch the birth of his second son, or lied about his age and enlisted in the RAAF to partake in the brutal battle for Tarakan, Borneo. Clearly, the former style of research was not going to get a story written.

It thus became apparent that this story had to be collected and inspired by participating in, and attending to, spontaneous conversations in much the same manner as I usually did, albeit with a new 'sociological' point of view. The much-admired interviewer, Studs Terkel, is remembered by one of his interviewees:

> Did Studs talk much during the interview?
> Oh yes. Something you say will remind him of a story or something somebody else said. Part of how he creates the atmosphere is it's not a one-way conversation. It really is a conversation. He contributes and you contribute, and out of that comes a real dialogue. It's not like he has a list of questions and he runs through them and you answer. It went places neither of us thought it would go, and that's very exciting. (Townley interviewed in Kovach 2002, n.p.)

In a narrative inquiry, relational issues are at the heart of the research process. These include the selection and initiation processes for establishing participation and consent, through to the representation of findings (Clandinin and Connelly 2000). As Dewey (1934, 1938) argued over seventy years ago, and Clandinin and Connelly (2000) and Clandinin (2007) have further expounded, continuity and interaction are crucial to understanding and accounting for experience. In narrative inquiry, the relationship between researcher and researched is consistently relevant and forms an important part of the story. From my own doctoral experience, I would argue that when researching those well known to you, this continuity also means maintaining the intimacy already established in the relationship that prohibits moving suddenly and artificially into the role of research scientist, leaving the participant abandoned in what suddenly becomes an awkward experiment rather than an extension or deepening of the existing relationship. This, I suggest, can be described as *relational continuity*.

For such reasons, narrative inquiry research has been practiced extensively in the fields of education and health, particularly nursing, where the relationship between teacher and student, or nurse and patient, is as important as the professional knowledge and skills of the practitioner, and may often pre-date and continue beyond any research period. In the case of researching family, narrative inquiry co-exists with peeling the potatoes and stacking the dishwasher, as if nothing has changed. For everyone but the researcher, nothing has, in fact, changed. As Fraser and Puwar (2008, p. 2) describe:

> The intimacies afforded by research materials and activities, those materials and activities that inform the making of knowledge, that shape power relations and that enable or constrain the practical negotiation of ethical problems, are not often foregrounded in debates on methods and methodology. The rhythm, smell, sense, tension and pleasure that go into producing what will become research and data remain largely outside of such discussions, even though these are the very ways in which we carry research into the library, the studio and the lecture hall.

Rather than interviews, then, the narrative inquirer engages in conversations that emerge from, and are in, naturalistic contexts. Encouraging people, creating time and space for them to spontaneously talk about the topic of interest rather than directly asking prepared questions, delivers a richer and more authentic account from participants as they nominate what is of interest through the detail of their own memories. The advantage of researching family is that these conversations take place as a matter of course over ordinary interactions, and detail builds over time. The problem is that the researcher is often unprepared, without a recorder or even pen and paper. Even if they have these items, asking speakers to repeat things or slow their account can lead to more self-conscious accounts that do not carry the conviction of their story as, and when, it occurred to them to tell it. Researching intimate others is not served by adopting conventional and formal research processes, such as the recorded interview.

Indeed, it is entirely foreign to relational norms and can befuddle and distract the participant to the extent that they become rabbits in the headlights of science rather than storytellers. Instead, the researcher may instigate events or get-togethers that are natural activities for participants, such as a visit to a museum, or a picnic at a specific location, or even a meal at a restaurant where the researcher can look for opportunities or leads into conversations on the topic of research. In short, narrative inquiry emphasises that "human beings ... draw on stories as a way to share and to understand, who we are, who we have been, and who we are becoming", and that storytelling carries obligations and responsibilities that come with "telling and retelling of experiences" (Huber et al. 2013, p. 213).

In these contexts, the participant is comfortable engaging in a stable and predictable relationship, even though the researcher is now attending to the conversation as 'data' and the intimate other as 'participant'. In other words, given that the participant is fully informed about the research objectives and processes, changes in the consciousness of the researcher should not impact on the norms of the participant. While the participant is fully informed, they are not required to do anything other than what is natural in the relationship. The researcher may guide these conversations to topics of interest, such as in my case, conversations about the Great Depression, politics and other family members, or they may trigger topical conversations by selecting to attend events or exhibitions with a connection to the era, or setting, of study.

The following is an example of such engagement from my PhD project:

As we wandered through the library exhibits of diaries and surviving personal objects of World War One soldiers, we came across embroidered postcards from France. "I had forgotten these," exclaimed G. "Isn't it funny how you forget about things entirely and then when you see them, all the memories come flooding back. I remember when my mother ..." It was just like the time we sat together over the old airline suitcase full of family photographs which had not been viewed for years. Many photographs triggered strong memories and elicited stories associated with the various characters and events portrayed. Some photos drew a blank and were dismissed as "someone or other ... who knows?". Part of family history that was not her part. So, central and marginal characters and events emerged from her story triggered by images and objects long forgotten. (Owens 2018, excerpt from unpublished PhD)

In this manner, a historical novelist as narrative inquirer travels "through time in our memories shifting our imaginings backwards, expanding out our life stories, enabling multiple possible resonances that may connect our storied worlds to others" (Hankins 1998, quoted in Caine and Steves 2009, p. 6), and thereby generating rich data for fictional inspiration.

Ethical Issues of a Creative Practice Narrative Inquiry

Ethical issues and concerns for research conducted in Australia are defined and governed according to the Australian Government's National Statement (National Health and Medical Research Council 2007), and overseen in the university context by Human Research Ethics Committees. The National Statement outlines the following values and principles for the ethical conduct of research: respect for human beings, research merit and integrity, justice, and beneficence. Respect for research participants involves the conduct of research that empowers people, and either ensures their autonomy or protects those with diminished capacity. Merit and integrity are achieved where research contributes to beneficial outcomes for participants and the general community without compromising well-being, and is conducted with honesty and full disclosure. Research is just when access to the benefits flowing from new understandings is fair and participation is open and non-exploitative. Beneficial research requires that any risk of harm or discomfort for participants is minimised, justified and clearly understood.

It should be acknowledged that the National Statement is authored by, and primarily designed for, the medical profession, where participation in research can have life-changing and even life-saving or life-threatening outcomes, such as trialling new therapies or medications. Craig and Huber (in Clandinin 2007, p. 269) propose a relational ethics for narrative inquiry that privileges relationships and relational knowing, thereby engaging, for example, in such processes as continual negotiation of free and open participant consent. The authors acknowledge that such an approach remains nascent, and suggest that narrative inquirers remain caught up in a formalistic and legalistic approach that demands compliance to criteria that may not always be relevant to narrative inquiry.

Narrative inquiry conducted as a background to historical fiction may seem, on the surface, to be ethically unproblematic. However, the historical novelist and academic, Ron Hanson, has suggested that even though "Courts have ruled that you cannot defame the dead", historical fiction should be "ethical, courteous, and jury-friendly" (2007, n.p.). There are many volumes of published material engaging with the ethics of qualitative research (see, for example, Crotty 1998; Denzin and Lincoln 2005; Denzin 1989; Punch 1994; Miller et al. 2012), as well as the ethics of qualitative research conducted as narrative inquiry (see, for example, Josselson 2007; Adams 2008; Clandinin and Huber (in press)). Further literature considers the ethics of writing creatively about real events, with many theorists focusing on the ethical issues associated with creative non-fiction (Bloom 2003; Bradley 2007; Brien 2009; Gutkind 1997, 2008; Hecq 2013; Finlayson 2011).

A further body of writing about ethics exists in relation to biographical writing and memoir (Carey 2008; Keighran 2011; McDonald 2010; Van de Pol 2011), and a developing body of work explores the ethics of fiction writing, particularly in relation to the crime genre (see, for example, Brien 1999; Finlayson 2011; Rose 2011). While the ethical issues involved in researching close family for the purpose of historical fiction writing are, of course, incorporated in more general discussions of the ethics of research conducted for fiction, I suggest there are specific relational characteristics that warrant further exploration in terms of ethical practice in the familial context.

Cosgrove (2009) has pointed out that "courses in creative nonfiction tend to include more discussion on matters of ethics and representation than those in fiction. For example, the writing program at Columbia University offers non-fiction subjects such as 'Can Truth Be Told? Ethics in Non-fiction Story Telling' and 'Investigations: The Craft of Non-fiction Research', without equivalent subjects in prose fiction" (p. 135). It may be assumed that the fictional status of the product neutralises ethical concerns, but I would agree with Finlayson (2011) and Brien (2009) that this is not the case. Ethical issues are simply different from those associated with research conducted for non-fictional practice. The possible identifiability of participants is not as problematic when the published story is fictional, and how participants feel about the fictional work becomes more a matter of taste than argument. On the other hand, the possibility that participants may feel exploited is powerfully evident in such a project where the researcher may be seen to be taking a story and making it their own. From undertaking my own PhD in this area, I would argue that the research conducted to write such a story needs to enrich the tellers of the story, even if theirs is a different story to the final published version. Sharing the journey of exploration and drafting, or fully engaging in 'relational continuity', can achieve this.

Even though some of the formal criteria constituting a human research ethics application may seem irrelevant, or even inappropriate, to narrative inquiry, particularly such a study conducted for fictional material, the basic values and principles of ethical research articulated in the National Statement remain important to research conduct and are appropriately addressed in an exegesis. The risk of discomfort, for example, is endemic to conversations with immediate family about deceased loved ones, especially to conversations with a widowed partner no longer accompanied in their life journey. The loss of a life partner is precisely the loss of a shared story: "To become a couple is to agree implicitly to live in terms of another person's story" (Bridges quoted in Baddeley and Singer 2007, p. 187).

Although it is also true that "personal stories are inevitably relinquished at death and become legacies merged with other similar stories, which belong to surviving generations and a larger historical record" (Baddeley and Singer 2007, p. 178), an invitation to re-tell a couple's shared story to a genuinely interested, empathetic and intimate listener can, in fact, be a joyous and welcome opportunity. Yet this also implies a grave responsibility on the part of the researcher to pace these events and guide the conversations so that the sadness that accompanies reminiscence is never overwhelming, and is always acknowledged and respected.

Academic literature about researching deceased people is generally clustered around the medical discipline, and frequently involves studies of grieving and the provision of care for those left behind. For example, Penman et al. discovered that:

> Supporting existing research, participants expected a finite period of grief with specific comments indicating an acute period of distress and impairment followed by resolution and "moving on" within the first six months (2014, p. 21).

This scientific study may seem to suggest that after a period of approximately six months, it is all right to discuss dead people with their surviving loved ones. However, I would argue that reactions to such tragic events as the loss of a loved one are individualised, and may involve an ebb and flow of emotion in response to the environment and circumstances of the subject. It is useful to assume that while the passage of time may diminish the degree of grief experienced by survivors in sharing their recollections of deceased and much loved family members, it is both ethical and productive to engage incrementally with these recollections. As the storyteller gains confidence in the listener's knowledge and understanding of the story, and as they become more accustomed to the regular discussion of their memories, the risk of discomfort diminishes.

A further aid to minimising discomfort is to involve more than one immediate family member in the telling of stories. In this way, the memories bounce off each other, triggering more memories and/or debates about the accuracy of recollections, or how complete they were. The event then becomes a family event, which relieves the individual of the entire burden of loss. Conversations and questions may not be about death *per se*, for example, but the fact remains that the person is gone, and this absence resonates in any discussion of their life and should be acknowledged: "Recalling a traumatic event by telling, writing or answering questions might raise the level of short-term distress but is unlikely to cause re-traumatization or long-term harm. The temporary distress must, however, be acknowledged (Jorm et al. 2007; Legerski and Bunnell 2010; Omerov et al. 2014, p. 3410). Planned trigger events for research conversations should also be more than research opportunities, and should contribute to growing relational intimacy. Sometimes the storytelling will be repetitive, sometimes slow and off topic, and at other times unexpected and explosively revealing.

> *He never forgave the Japanese. He felt they were a heartless culture.* (Owens 2018, excerpt from unpublished exegesis)

Regardless, these planned trigger events contribute to growth in relational intimacy that supports further revelation over time. Indeed, continuing the conversation, returning to events part told or poorly told, and re-starting conversations around different triggers is what families do naturally and is highly conducive to rich narrative inquiry.

> *When dad was fighting in Papua New Guinea …*
> *What? What do you mean Papua New Guinea? I thought he was posted to Borneo?.*
> *Yeah, but that was after New Guinea.*
> *But you haven't told me anything about New Guinea.*
> *You didn't ask about New Guinea. Anyway, when dad was fighting in New Guinea.* (Owens 2018, excerpt from unpublished exegesis)

"The sense of adventure, drama, mystery, fear—and sometimes, let's face it, the boredom—which produces research is not easily articulated in part because it risks revealing, perhaps even 'exposing', the so-called unscholarly, anecdotal, irrational and unscientific dimensions of the research process" (Fraser and Puwar 2008, p. 4). For narrative inquirers, these are not 'unscientific' dimensions. For narrative inquirers researching for fiction, these dimensions link the storied life to the tellings of the storied life, which provides the sociological and 'scientific' dimension for the creative work. Gregor McLennan acknowledged Runciman's point that novels "*are* sociology to the extent that their authors make them so" (McLennan quoted in Fraser and Puwar 2008, p. 3), but adds the proviso that "novels are never *just* sociology, and if they do contain good sociology, this will not be a matter solely of their imaginative accomplishment" (McLennan quoted in Fraser and Puwar 2008, p. 3). A 'good' historical novel contributes to a community's knowledge and understanding of itself, and if the research for the novel is conducted and iterated through ethical narrative inquiry, it can achieve this without compromising the well-being of informants and existing relationships between individuals, living or deceased.

Conclusion

The growing interest of artists in all creative spheres to reflect on, track and explain aesthetic decisions through the framework of a research higher degree promises to clarify the hitherto invisible processes of creative practice. Such work contributes to our understanding of how the complex, and sometimes chaotic, nature of lived experience is organised through a process of researching and imagining into meaningful works defined as art. This chapter has identified potential ethical issues and concerns for narrative inquiry research of close family conducted to inform an historical novel, and proposes possible solutions to these ethical dilemmas. Preserving 'relational continuity' is explained as an ethical approach to conducting such research in order to benefit all participants, and to respect the memories they are willing to contribute as inspiration for fiction.

References

Adams, T. E. 2008. "A review of narrative ethics." *Qualitative Inquiry* 14 (2): 175–194.

Baddeley, J., and J. A. Singer. 2007. "Charting the life story's path: Narrative identity across the life span." In *Handbook of Narrative Inquiry: Mapping a Methodology*, edited by D. Clandinin, 177–202. Thousand Oaks: SAGE.

Bloom, L. Z. 2003. "Living to tell the tale: The complicated ethics of creative nonfiction." *College English*, special issue 65 (3): 276–289.

Boyd, N. 2009. "Describing the creative writing thesis: A census of creative writing doctorates, 1993–2008." *TEXT: Journal of Writing and Writing Courses* 13 (1): n.p. http://www.textjournal.com.au/april09/boyd.htm.

Bradley, W. 2007. "The ethical exhibitionist's agenda: Honesty and fairness in creative nonfiction." *College English* 70 (2): 202–211.

Brien, D. L. 1999. "True crime fiction as criminal history." *Australian Feminist Law Journal* 13 (2): 133–144.

Brien, D. L. 2009. "'Based on a true story': The problem of perception of biographical truth in narratives based on real lives." *TEXT: Journal of Writing and Writing Courses* 13 (2): n.p. http://www.textjournal.com.au/oct09/brien.htm.

Bruner, J. 1991. "The narrative construction of reality." *Critical Inquiry* 18: 1–21.

Caine, V., and P. Steves. 2009. "Imagining and playfulness in narrative inquiry." *International Journal of Education & the Arts* 10 (25): 1–15.

Carey, J. 2008. "Whose story is it, anyway? Ethics and interpretive authority in biographical creative nonfiction." *TEXT* 12 (2): n.p. http://www.textjournal.com.au/oct08/carey.htm.

Chase, S. 2005. "Narrative inquiry: Multiple lenses, approaches, voices." In *The SAGE Handbook of Qualitative Research*, edited by N. Denzin and Y. Lincoln, 651–679. Thousand Oaks, CA: SAGE.

Clandinin, D. 2006. "Narrative inquiry: A methodology for studying lived experience." *Research Studies in Music Education* 27: 44–54.

Clandinin, D. 2007. *Handbook of Narrative Inquiry: Mapping a Methodology*. Thousand Oaks, CA: SAGE.

Clandinin, D., and M. Connelly. 2000. *Narrative Inquiry: Experience and Story in Narrative Research*. San Franciso: Jossey-Bass.

Clandinin, D. J., and J. Huber. (In press). "Narrative inquiry." In *International Encyclopedia of Education*. 3rd ed., edited by B. McGaw, E. Baker, and P. Peterson. New York: Elsevier. http://www.mofet.macam.ac.il/amitim/iun/CollaborativeResearch/Documents/NarrativeInquiry.pdf.

Cosgrove, S. 2009. "WRIT101: Ethics of representation for creative writers." *Pedagogy* 9 (1): 134–141.

Crotty, M. 1998. *The Foundations of Social Research: Meaning and Perspective in the Research Process*. Sydney: Allen and Unwin.

de Groot, J. 2010. *The Historical Novel*. New York: Routledge.

Denzin, N. 1989. *The Research Act: A Theoretical Introduction to Sociological Methods*. 3rd ed. Englewood Cliffs, NJ: Prentice Hall.

Denzin, N., and Y. Lincoln. 2005. *The SAGE Handbook of Qualitative Research*. 3rd ed. Thousand Oaks, CA: SAGE.

Dewey, J. 1934. *Art as Experience*. Toms River, NJ: Capricorn.

Dewey, J. 1938. *Experience and Education*. New York: Collier.

Finlayson, K. 2011. "Faking it: The ethics of transforming real life into fiction." In *Ethical Imaginings. Refereed Conference Proceedings of the 16th AAWP Conference, 2011*.

Fraser N., and M. Puwar. 2008. "Introduction: Intimacy in research." *History of the Human Sciences* 21 (4): 1–16.

Gutkind, L. 1997. *The Art of Creative Nonfiction: Writing and Selling the Literature of Reality*. New York: John Wiley & Sons.

Gutkind, L. 2008. *Keep it Real: Everything you Need to Know About Writing and Researching Creative Nonfiction*. New York: W. W. Norton & Company.

Hanson, R. 2007. *The Ethics of Fiction Writing*. http://www.scu.edu/ethics/publications/submitted/fiction.html.

Hecq, D. 2013. "Creative writing and theory: Theory without credentials." In *Research Methods in Creative Writing*, edited by J. Kroll and G. Harper, 175–200. New York, NY: Palgrave Macmillan.

Huber, J., V. Caine, M. Huber, and P. Steeves. 2013. "Narrative inquiry as pedagogy in education: The extraordinary potential of living, telling, retelling, and reliving stories of experience." *Review of Research in Education* 37: 212–242. http://journals.sagepub.com.ezproxy1.acu.edu.au/doi/pdf/10.3102/0091732X12458885.

Jorm, A. F., C. M. Kelly, and A. J. Morgan. 2007. "Participant distress in psychiatric research: A systematic review." *Psychological Medicine* 37: 917–926.

Josselson, R. 2007. "The ethical attitude in narrative research." In *Handbook of Narrative Inquiry: Mapping a Methodology*, edited by D. Clandinin, 537–566. Thousand Oaks: SAGE.

Keighran, J. 2011. "Into the badlands: Countering false shame in memoir." In *Refereed Proceedings of the 16th Conference of the Australasian Association of Writing Programs*. http://www.aawp.org.au/publications/the-ethical-imaginations-writing-worlds-papers.

Kovach, R. 2002. "Studs Terkel on the art of interviewing." *The Writer* 115 (5): 26.

Lal, S., and M. Suto. 2012. "Examining the potential of combining the methods of grounded theory and narrative inquiry: A comparative analysis." *The Qualitative Report* 17 (41): 1–10.

Legerski, J.-P., and S. L. Bunnell. 2010. "The risks, benefits, and ethics of trauma-focused research participation." *Ethics and Behavior* 20: 429–442.

McDonald, W. 2010. "Letter to my daughter: Ethical dilemmas in the writing of a memoir." *TEXT: Journal of Writing and Writing Courses* 14 (2): n.p. http://www.textjournal.com.au/oct10/mcdonald.htm.

Miller, T., M. Birch, M. Mauthner, and J. Jessop. 2012. *Ethics in Qualitative Research*, 2nd ed. Thousand Oaks, CA: SAGE.

National Health and Medical Research Council. 2007. "Section one: Values and principles." *National Statement on Ethical Conduct in Human Research.* https://www.nhmrc.gov.au/book/section-1-values-and-principles-ethical-conduct.

Omerov, P., G. Steineck, K. Dyregrov, B. Runeson, and U. Nyberg. 2014. "The ethics of doing nothing. Suicide-bereavement and research: Ethical and methodological considerations." *Psychological Medicine* 44 (16): 3409–3420.

Owens, A. 2018. "Researching and writing an historical fiction of the early-mid twentieth century Woolloomooloo community: A creative practice-led narrative inquiry." Unpublished PhD thesis. Rockhampton: Central Queensland University.

Penman, E. L., L. J. Breen, L. Y. Hewitt, and H. G. Prigerson. 2014. "Pathologising grief: An exploration of public expectations and grieving norms." *Grief Matters: The Australian Journal of Grief and Bereavement* 17 (1): 21.

Punch, M. 1994. "Politics and ethics in qualitative research." In *Handbook of Qualitative Research*, edited by N. Denzin and Y. Lincoln, 83–98. Thousand Oaks, CA: SAGE.

Riessman, C. 2008. *Narrative Methods for the Human Sciences*. Boston: Boston College.

Rose, J. 2011. "Theft is theft: The ethics of telling other people's stories." In *Ethical Imaginations: Refereed Conference Papers of the 16th Annual AAWP Conference, 2011.*

Van de Pol, C. 2011. "Fictionalising real people." In *Ethical Imaginations: Refereed Conference Papers of the 16th Annual AAWP Conference, 2011.*

Webb, J., and D. L. Brien. 2011. "Addressing the ancient quarrel: Creative writing as research." In *The Routledge Companion to Research in the Arts*, edited by M. Biggs and H. Karlsson, 186–203. New York: Routledge.

Part III

Taking Ownership of the Doctoral Experience: Introduction to Part

Donna Lee Brien, Craig Batty, Elizabeth Ellison, and Alison Owens

Undertaking a PhD is a life-changing decision, one that is usually made in consultation with the teaching and administrative staff of at least one institution, and discussion with—and advice from—other students working in both similar and quite different areas from the chosen research field. The decision-making process also necessarily involves, as raised in other chapters of this book, considerable self-examination and a focus on the relationship that each doctoral student has with their self, and how

D. L. Brien (✉) • E. Ellison
Noosaville, QLD, Australia
e-mail: d.brien@cqu.edu.au; l.ellison@cqu.edu.au

C. Batty
Sydney, NSW, Australia
e-mail: Craig.Batty@uts.edu.au

A. Owens
North Sydney, NSW, Australia
e-mail: Alison.Owens@acu.edu.au

this self may be changing during the process of undertaking a doctorate. In other words, during the journey and taking into consideration all the research learning that has taken place, doctoral students begin to question who they are. Learning to conduct research, and as a core part of that, learning to see and understand the world differently, will inevitably lead to questioning, self-doubt, fear of the unknown and, for some who reflect on their pre-doctoral lives, a sense that the work that have already done is 'wrong' or incorrect. For Finlayson, writing about creative writing students in particular, "they will try on various identities and will most likely experience a prolonged period of uncertainty of self as they explore what it might mean for them to shape an identity as an academic" (2012 p. 2). For Le Rossignol, also writing about creative writing students, there is an irony in that "the message of lost identity capital is ... linked to the very skills and experience which may have earned them a place as a doctoral candidate" (2015 pp. 4–5). Finlayson describes how McAlpine defines this

> in terms of an 'identity-trajectory', which is the idea of a path based on past identities, situated in the wider life context of the student and the perceived opportunities available to the present identity, which progresses towards potential future identities through the intentional actions of the postgraduate. (quoted in Finlayson 2012, pp. 4–5)

This sense of dissonance can be traumatic for some students.

Leanne Dodd outlines how the protracted nature of undertaking a doctorate can lead to students experiencing burnout, anxiety or depression, due to the uncertain direction that events may take. Dodd, therefore, posits that it is imperative that students take an active interest in mitigating the risks to their emotional well being while studying. Dodd uses her own doctoral work as a case study and provides practical self-care intervention strategies to build resilience and address well being over the long term. These range from developing positive habits to journaling to encourage personal exploration and increased self-awareness, through to knowing when to seek professional help. Lisa Brummel extends the notion of Occupational Health and Safety to a personal focus, urging students to maintain committed relationships with family and friends and utilise the benefits that exercise has for physical and mental health. Brummel suggests completing a personal plan to facilitate a smooth doctoral journey. In Chap. 12, Susannah Oddi extends this discussion to examine how researching within online social communities may provide for a connected and creative research journey for sole researchers. Oddi outlines, however, that while this can be an effective and efficient approach to research, like all other parts of the research journey, such online research requires careful navigation.

As other parts of this book reveal, maintaining strong relationships to provide support during this time is vitally important. As Finlayson describes: "A doctoral student does not undertake this identity formation process in isolation, and their supervisor and other faculty members can play a vital role in helping the doctoral candidate navigate the uncertainties of the complex process of identity formation" (2012, p. 6). That said, it is important for students to embrace this uncertainty and weave it into their becoming, rather than assuming others will solve these problems for them. As reported by Holbrook et al., "One common reaction to this dilemma among candidates was to avoid the unfamiliar and seek to place the responsibility for it with the supervisor, setting up a high degree of dependence on the supervisor" (2013, p. 5). These chapters suggest that, instead, students can take ownership of this process of identity formation and, by extension, the doctoral experience, leading to successful and productive outcomes.

References

Finlayson, K. 2012. "Encounters with future selves: Crafting an identity as a creative-writing academic." In *The Encounters: Place, Situation, Context Papers—The Refereed Proceedings of the 17th Conference of the Australasian Association of Writing Programs, 2012*, edited by A. Pont, P. West, K. Johanson, C. Atherton, R. Dredge, and R. Todd. AAWP. http://www.aawp.dreamhosters.com/wp-content/uploads/2015/03/Finlayson_1.pdf.

Holbrook, A., B. Simmons, J. Scevak, and J. Budd, 2013. "Higher degree research candidates' initial expectations in fine art." *TEXT: Journal of*

Writing and Writing Courses, special issue 22: 1–16. http://www.text-journal.com.au/speciss/issue22/Holbrook_et_al.pdf.

Le Rossignol, R. 2015, "Maintaining writerly identity during the creative PhD." In *Minding the Gap: Writing Across Thresholds and Fault Lines Papers—The Refereed Proceedings of the 19th Conference of the Australasian Association of Writing Programs*, edited by G. Pittaway, A. Lodge, and L. Smithies. Wellington, NZ: AAWP. http://www.aawp.dreamhosters.com/wp-content/uploads/2015/05/Le_Rossignol__R.writerly_identity.pdf.

McAlpine, L. 2012. "Identity-trajectories: Doctoral journeys from past to present to future." *Australian Universities Review* 55 (1): 38–46.

10

Instituting Self-care Strategies for Doctoral Students

Leanne Dodd

Introduction

Many research students embark enthusiastically on their doctoral journey based on their interests and passions. Subsequently, their expectations at the outset may be that the path to completion will be nothing but enjoyable and rewarding. However, being engaged in the same project for at least three to four years has its challenges. Added to the stresses of everyday life, therefore, the risks of such a protracted undertaking should not be underestimated. Despite the most detailed planning and the best intentions, personal and professional circumstances and interruptions that may occur over this lengthy period cannot be fully determined in advance. Research students have the potential to be impeded by the uncertain direction events may take, including personal burnout, anxiety or depression. Forethought and planning can help to mitigate against

L. Dodd (✉)
School of Education and the Arts, Central Queensland University,
Brisbane, QLD, Australia
e-mail: leanne.dodd@cqumail.com

© The Author(s) 2019
D. L. Brien et al. (eds.), *The Doctoral Experience*,
https://doi.org/10.1007/978-3-030-18199-4_10

107

some of the negative effects of undertaking a research degree, and a research plan might include strategies to overcome these hurdles to maintain emotional well-being and prevent possible impairment of a student's researching capabilities.

This chapter outlines the significance of recognising the causes and symptoms of adverse emotional responses that could arise from protracted research study and, for some, from dealing with sensitive material. It also considers the value of impairment prevention. The first section looks at causes specific to doctoral research, including, imposter syndrome, poor time management, stage fright, and dealing with traumatic or sensitive material. It suggests strategies that might be implemented to avoid impairment, including a case study from my own doctoral experience, which focussed on some of the consequences of dealing with stories of a personal, traumatic nature. The second section then offers a series of more generalised and practical self-care intervention strategies to build resilience and address well-being over the doctoral journey.

Facing Adversity: Specific Causes and Strategies for Overcoming Them

It is not uncommon for research students to suffer from imposter syndrome. This phenomenon was first identified in 1978 by psychologists Clance and Imes, and it is something students begin to experience when they have "intense feelings that their achievements are undeserved and worry that they are likely to be exposed as a fraud" (Jaruwan Sakulku and Alexander 2011, p. 73). It is said to be widely experienced in many occupations, even by famous people, so if a student begins to feel this condition at any time during their candidature, it is important that they recognise that they are not alone. However, this fear of failure has been shown to lead to clinical levels of anxiety, depression and dissatisfaction with life. The student might find that it triggers behaviours such as perfectionism leading to over-preparation and over-working, procrastination leading to last-minute panic, and self-doubt leading to discounting positive feedback (Jaruwan Sakulku and Alexander 2011, pp. 74–76). All of these behaviours could interfere with a student's priorities and their ability to complete the research workload, so it is important to address imposter syndrome as soon as it surfaces.

Awareness is the first step in gaining control. Students should learn to recognise the voice of the inner critic, then try and remind themselves that the story it is telling them is not reality. Clance and Imes (1978) suggest that making a list of the positive feedback received to date, and role-playing *being* successful, could help people self-affirm their view of their abilities in a more realistic way. This should help with them being constrained by their fear. Another strategy is to learn to take criticism constructively, rather than personally. Being told you are wrong does not make you a phony; rather, it gives you opportunities to improve your knowledge. Students should remember that they are not expected to know everything at once—their research project is a learning and skill-building process. Nor should they compare themselves with others; peers will be at different stages in their journey, so this needs to be factored in.

There is no shame in asking for help from supervisors and peers either. Even the adage 'fake it until you make it' has merit in the research training sphere. Most of us learn by doing, and there is evidence that 'pretending', or at least having a sense of self-fulfilment, may create new neural pathways in our brains. This is referred to as neuroplasticity: "an induced change in some property of the nervous system that results in a corresponding change in function and/or behaviour" (Shaw and McEachern 2001, p. 4). This strategy, combined with positive affirmations, could help the research student to manage imposter syndrome, so that it does not hamper their ability to undertake and complete research tasks.

Research students may also often find themselves overwhelmed by the sheer volume of work required of a doctoral degree, which may range from reading and synthesising academic material, conducting and recording interviews or experiments, presenting at conferences, writing for publication, and writing up their research in a recognised thesis format. This work may also compete with other life and employment commitments, as noted by both AK Milroy and Alison Vincent in Chaps. 2 and 3. It is therefore easy to see how a student might feel overburdened and suffer from poor time management. It is important to set up effective time management techniques from the outset to avoid burnout. Burnout is a result of chronic, or ongoing, stress. It can have dire consequences.

According to Bourg Carter (2013), this could lead to exhaustion, both physical and emotional; a tendency toward cynicism and detachment; and feelings of ineffectiveness and lack of accomplishment. Research students are advised to keep an eye out for the following signs that they may be suffering from burnout: chronic fatigue, insomnia, weight fluctuations, impaired concentration and/or performance, anxiety, depression including loss of enjoyment, apathy or hopelessness, anger and/or irritability, and a desire for isolation (Bourg Carter 2013). There are steps that students can take at the outset, however, to avoid reaching this chronic stage.

Do not put unnecessary pressure on yourself by trying to do everything at once. Completing a doctorate is a journey over a lengthy period. Begin by creating a plan to plot the steps and milestones in your journey, as Milroy describes. Set realistic timeframes for when you will complete each step. A Gantt chart or other such tool can, moreover, act as a constantly updated working schedule that is modified as circumstances change. Make sure that you build the potential for delays due to unforeseen interruptions into your plan. Also factor in recreational leave to give yourself a break. All doctoral programs have provisions built into them to cover the possibility of unforeseen events that may require a longer absence. This might include illness of oneself or a loved one, the need to grieve a loss or relationship breakdown, or the need to earn additional income, all of which could transpire over the course of a student's research journey. It might be essential to apply for a leave of absence to extend the maximum completion time in these circumstances, rather than risk your emotional well-being.

There are likely to be times when competing deadlines lead to a feeling of being overwhelmed. Allowing deadlines to float around, unconstrained in your mind, only serves to exacerbate this feeling. A useful strategy here is to write them down in the form of a to-do list, with dates for completion. Ticking them off as each task is completed can create a strong and very useful sense of relief and achievement, which can boost motivation and self-confidence. An alternative is to create a calendar for deadlines and plot them visually across the weeks or months. Make time for each task and cross them off as they are achieved. If the tasks themselves seem overwhelming, it can be useful to break them down into manageable steps and list these steps individually on the list or a calendar, again marking them off as they are completed. By concentrating on one step at a time, it is likely that you will feel less overwhelmed and more motivated as each task is achieved.

At some stage in the research journey, it is likely students will be required to speak about their research in public. This may be to present at a conference or seminar, or defend the research project or findings. Performance anxiety, or 'stage fright', is accompanied by sweaty palms, a racing heart, dizziness, and shortness of breath. Some students even experience this to some degree while interviewing participants and/or performing in front of a camera. The first thing to be aware of is that almost everyone feels some anxiety when they are about to speak in public. Yet it is well known that a little stress usually leads to a heightened performance. The trick is not to let anxiety take over and affect your performance in a negative way. Understanding that this is a physiological reaction that can be controlled assists with this anxiety. The good news is that 'practice makes perfect', and eventually your body will recognise there is no threat if you repeat an activity numerous times. Until then, there are some strategies you can implement to help you through it.

I remember the first time I had to present a paper about my research in public, which was at a student research conference. I was quite tense. This was surprising as, as a published novelist, I had spoken at writers' festivals and events and was an experienced facilitator of workshops. I recalled being advised to practice controlled breathing, and did this while I was waiting to go up to the lectern. I took a deep breath right down into my diaphragm for four counts, held it for two counts, then breathed out slowly for seven counts. I repeated this several times, and felt my heart rate and breathing slow, as it triggered a relaxation response in the brain. Deep breathing is a practice that comes naturally to me now if ever I feel nervous, which is far less frequent these days after all my conference presentations. The process can be remembered by thinking: "4-2-7".

Another common technique that military personnel are taught when going into combat, to gain control over negative physiological reactions to stress, is to practice task-related and memory exercises to engage the frontal lobe of the brain. This turns off the parts of the brain that activate anxiety because their functions are incompatible (Driskell and Johnston 1998). This can be achieved, for example, by rehearsing a speech in your head immediately prior to the presentation, which will not only enhance your delivery but also lessen your levels of anxiety. Being well-prepared by making notes, if needed, and rehearsing the performance until comfortable with it, might also help. Similarly, pre-empting the answers to any questions that might be asked, and formulating answers in advance, can reduce the fear of the unknown. While performing, focus outwardly on your material and your audience rather than inwardly on yourself. Taking advantage of opportunities to perform in public is also useful, because the more presenting experience doctoral students have, the less they will need to rely on these techniques. You may even discover that you come to enjoy the experience of performing, once the anxiety dissipates.

With my PhD, which dealt with trauma in crime fiction, I was aware that there could be potential consequences that I could not foresee or plan for, as my research could not avoid involving material of a personal and sensitive nature. It is imperative that the risks to emotional well-being in these circumstances are addressed in advance, so that the student does not lose sight of their sense of self, or suffer illness or impairment to their researching capabilities.

Kumar and Cavallaro have defined four types of research that present additional emotional demands on researchers. These are: research on sensitive issues (for example, violence, abuse, mental health, chronic or terminal illness, death); research similar to personal trauma previously experienced by the researcher; the researcher's experience of traumatic life events while conducting a study; and unexpected events that arise during research in what was previously *not* identified as a sensitive issue (2017, p. 1). If this sounds like it describes your research, then you need to be particularly vigilant for signs of adverse emotional impact. Kumar and Cavallaro further claim this type of research "demands a tremendous amount of mental, emotional, or physical energy and potentially affects or depletes the researcher's health or well-being" (2017, p. 1). While they agree these types of research can be beneficial in gaining deeper understandings of phenomena, they contend that insufficient attention is given to preparing novice researchers for these demands. Doctoral students also need to be aware of the potential consequences when dealing with stories of a sensitive or traumatic nature as these conditions could have an impact on their research outcomes as well.

As was the case with my own PhD, a student may be researching traumatic events for their project that bear no resemblance to their own life experience. There are still risks of vicarious traumatisation, however, or compassion fatigue that could arise when researching other participants' stories (Bradley et al. 2013). Vicarious trauma results from secondary exposure to traumatic events and material. Compassion fatigue occurs when preoccupied with the suffering of others, leading to secondary traumatic stress. These conditions could result from interviewing traumatised participants or accessing and/or working with other written material or images that are traumatic. Even as an experienced creative writer, I found that I spent so much time in my characters' heads that I risked taking on their emotions and trauma.

There is also a risk that a student immersing themselves in research similar to, or about, personal trauma they have previously experienced may lead to re-traumatisation (Kumar and Cavallaro 2017). In writing accounts of trauma based on one's own past, it is inevitable that memories will surface; yet, it is often imperative for the completion of the thesis that the merits of their use be analysed and incorporated into the process. This creates a dichotomy that needs to be resolved to maintain the authenticity of works produced, and to adequately support the student's health and well-being as their thesis nears completion.

Re-traumatisation, vicarious traumatisation and compassion fatigue have the potential to lead to symptoms similar to post-traumatic stress disorder and depression (Kumar and Cavallaro 2017). Some of the signs that a student may be suffering the effects of trauma are fear/terror, nightmares, flashbacks, panic attacks, hyper-alertness, a heightened startle response, sadness, emotional numbness/dissociation, avoidant behaviours, appetite or sleep disturbances, angry outbursts or substance abuse (Australian Psychological Society 2018). While not suggesting this *will* happen—and if it does, it might occur at a manageable level—this is something that all students should take precautionary measures against when dealing with traumatic or sensitive material.

There are pre-emptive strategies for self-care that could prove effective in limiting the potential for re-traumatisation or traumatic stress. It is important to learn to be in the moment when dealing with this type of material. Feelings should not be avoided, but should not be dwelt on either. Practicing mindfulness may help to stay present, and techniques that help to decrease the intensity of emotions by externalising feelings include both deep breathing and the act of writing. Engaging in activities that enhance the daily schedule and give life meaning outside of the thesis and the research for it can also be helpful over the longer term.

Working with a psychologist or therapist is another way to mitigate these risks. In my PhD, my research encroached upon issues of personal traumatic experience and fractured identity, as I endeavoured to change my self-narrative by exploring fictional traumatic experiences in creative writing. The following describes how, by approaching this topic in my actual research methodology, I was able to alleviate some of my own feelings of traumatic stress.

Bringing my memories back out into the light felt like the first step toward working through them and moving forward. I wrote scenes for my novel based on incidents I dredged up from the past, working toward my goal to change my cognitive perception. But 40,000 words later, I realised the story, my story, had not changed. I was still holding onto the past and feeling detached and numb. My creative writing hit a wall. I became paralysed and blamed it on writer's block but, in reality, I was resisting the need to explore these memories further as I had become re-traumatised. My university requested I engage a therapist to work with me on the project because of its traumatic content. I was resistant to this initially, feeling this would be burdensome rather than supportive. I remained locked in this paralysed state for months, focussing on my research as a distraction. I began to research narrative therapy and discovered the patient had full agency in this type of therapeutic relationship. I located a narrative therapist with complementary qualifications in creative writing that I felt secure in working with on my project. The narrative therapist became my mentor in my post-traumatic growth journey by engaging with my creative writing. As a result, I began to sense positive changes in my emotions and behaviours, and my writing began to flow again.

Writing forms a significant role in the doctoral journey, whether drafting material for the thesis or simply thinking through ideas by writing them out. In creative and professional doctorates, reflective writing is also a strong feature of the research journey. There are also various ways that reflective and other writing and narrative and storytelling approaches can be utilised to help the writer gain a stronger sense of perspective and control over their past and present. This may assist in avoiding the accumulation of excess baggage along the way.

Writing a journal provides a way to externalise thoughts and memories. It may, therefore, be useful to work through issues caused by stress and trauma by creating distance to observe the problem more objectively (Bradley et al. 2013). According to Bolton (1999b), journaling can be used for painful release, joyful discovery, sense-making and the reaffirmation of self. She likens the journal to a grown-up security blanket. The journal can also provide a place to explore overwhelming sensations in a safe environment, and this can be useful when completing a research degree as, unlike the thesis, the journal does not need to be shared publicly. Using stream of consciousness writing where whatever comes to mind is written down, abandoning any concern about structure, grammar or punctuation, may be a useful method for journaling to bring relief (Bolton 1999b).

Tara DaPra (2013) has suggested that writing a memoir can be a rewarding and potentially cathartic experience. In telling or writing the story of their life, a memoirist is both creating and re-creating their self. A memoirist is also creating a connection between the past and the future, a process that can assist in framing adversity as a challenge. The memoirist is then able to learn from the experience, grow and move on. DaPra adds that beyond the initial cathartic effect of writing, "the organizing, editing and structuring" (p.6) of the writing process may have lasting benefits for individuals to see their experiences in a new light. Delving into and seeking to write about other significant life experiences, such as rites of passage and adventures, might also provide a means to explore the self and its growth and development.

Creative writing provides another place to stand to revisit a difficult history. Writers may find opportunities to redevelop their life stories by writing about them through the perspective of fictional characters to explore emotional constancy, strength by example and possibilities for change (Detrixhe 2010). The creative process may itself be naturally cathartic in alleviating emotional stress when the concept of 'flow' is experienced. Introduced by psychologist Mihaly Csikszentmihalyi (1990,

p. 4), flow is that state of consciousness where someone becomes so absorbed in the process that any external concerns fade from their awareness.

Poetry, metaphor and song-writing are all ways to share feelings and experiences, and also have proven health benefits (Bolton 1999a). Experiences may, however, sometimes be too painful or deeply buried to be easily accessed. This might necessitate using more metaphoric and poetic writing strategies. Using metaphor, where one thing is likened to something else with similar properties, may help to convey complex memories, feelings and hidden meanings and could give voice to experiences that otherwise elude verbal expression.

Self-care

Many of the symptoms described in this chapter may be avoided or mitigated by implementing sound self-care strategies to build resilience and develop support systems from the outset of the doctoral journey. Self-care can refer to any practices that sustain well-being, ranging from simple daily activities, to creative interventions such as journaling, which encourage personal exploration and increased self-awareness (Bradley et al. 2013, p. 459).

The list below represents a range of strategies that might be included in a research plan. This list is not exhaustive.

- maintain a balanced diet and healthy sleep habits
- exercise regularly
- avoid overuse of caffeine, sugar, nicotine, alcohol or other drugs
- engage in relaxation activities—baths, meditation/prayer, listening to music
- keep a sense of humour
- practise gratitude
- maintain social networks and be socially active
- reach out and connect with your peers
- find a trusted mentor with relevant experience
- spend time with your loved ones and pets

- immerse yourself in nature and/or take photographs of nature
- engage in music or art-making and/or appreciation
- keep a diary or journal, and/or practise stream of consciousness writing

Conclusion

The doctoral journey should be an enjoyable undertaking, yet it is a protracted activity that can carry some risks to the researcher's health and well-being. Recognising some of the causes and symptoms of negative sequelae from drawn-out research study may be the first step to ensuring that students do not suffer impairment to either their research capabilities or their lives more generally. Following the suggested approaches in this chapter encourages doctoral students to incorporate self-care strategies into their research plans to mitigate such risks.

If any of the signs or symptoms listed in this chapter last more than two weeks, students should seek professional help. This is particularly important if you feel that you are unable to deal with the intensity of your feelings, you have limited social support or find yourself withdrawing from relationships, you increase your reliance on alcohol or drugs, or you experience suicidal ideation (Australian Psychological Society 2018). Most universities have support services available for students to speak to a counsellor without cost. These services are confidential and exist specifically to help students with such issues and questions, so there is no reason to suffer alone or to fear reaching out.

References

Australian Psychological Society. 2018. "Understanding and managing psychological trauma." http://www.psychology.org.au/publications/tip_sheets/trauma.

Bolton, G. 1999a. "'Every poem breaks a silence that had to be overcome': The therapeutic power of poetry writing." *Feminist Review* 62: 118–133.

Bolton, G. 1999b. *The Therapeutic Potential of Creative Writing: Writing Myself*. London, UK: Jessica Kingsley Publishers.

Bourg Carter, S. 2013. "The tell-tale signs of burnout … do you have them?" *Psychology Today Web Blog*, November 26, 2013. https://www.psychologyto-day.com/blog/high-octane-women/201311/the-tell-tale-signs-burnout-do-you-have-them.

Bradley, N., J. Whisenhunt, N. Adamson, and V. E. Kress. 2013. "Creative approaches for promoting counselor self-care." *Journal of Creativity in Mental Health* 8: 456–469.

Clance, P. R., and S. Imes. 1978. "The imposter phenomenon in high achieving women: Dynamics and therapeutic intervention." *Psychotherapy Theory, Research and Practice* 15 (3): 1–8.

Csikszentmihalyi, M. 1990. *Flow: The Psychology of Optimal Experience.* New York, NY: Harper and Rowe.

DaPra, T. 2013. "Writing memoir and writing for therapy." *Creative Nonfiction* 48. http://www.creativenonfiction.org/therapy-memoir.

Detrixhe, J. J. 2010. "Souls in jeopardy: Questions and innovations for biblio-therapy with fiction." *Journal of Humanistic Counseling, Education and Development* 49: 58–72.

Driskell, J. E., and J. H. Johnston. 1998. "Stress exposure training". In *Making Decisions Under Stress: Implications for Individual and Team Training*, edited by J. A. Cannon-Bowers and E. Salas, 191–217. Washington, DC: American Psychological Association.

Jaruwan Sakulku, J., and J. Alexander. 2011. "The impostor phenomenon." *International Journal of Behavioral Science* 6 (1): 73–92.

Kumar, S., and L. Cavallaro. 2017. "Researcher self-care in emotionally demand-ing research: A proposed conceptual framework." *Qualitative Health Research* 28 (4): 648–658.

Shaw, C. A., and J. C. McEachern, eds. 2001. *Toward a Theory of Neuroplasticity.* Philadelphia, PA: Taylor & Francis.

11

Handling Occupational Health and Safety and Its Impacts on the Doctoral Journey

Lisa Brummel

Introduction

Occupational Health and Safety (OHS) is about ensuring safe and healthy workplaces. Workplace hazards are many and varied, including environmental, chemical, physical, psychological and even ergonomic, and thus it is important that safeguards are put in place to protect everyone concerned. Universities must abide by government regulations by providing a safe environment for students and staff; they, in turn, expect the same level of commitment from research students. An OHS audit may form a mandatory part of a doctoral student's coursework, which might need to be woven into their confirmation of candidature paperwork. In this audit, the university expects a clear and fair evaluation of the potential risks associated with a student's project, how the student will ensure these risks are mitigated against, and if required, how they can be resolved.

L. Brummel (✉)
School of Education and the Arts, Central Queensland University,
Noosaville, QLD, Australia
e-mail: lisa.brummel@cqumail.com

© The Author(s) 2019
D. L. Brien et al. (eds.), *The Doctoral Experience*,
https://doi.org/10.1007/978-3-030-18199-4_11

There are, however, other aspects of OHS that are not usually covered in discussions, workshops and online training modules, and these relate to a student's relationships and their own self-care as they complete their research degree. I suggest this might be called 'Personal Occupational Health and Safety'. As Leanne Dodd has addressed in her chapter, looking after the doctoral self can make or break a research project—and this, I argue, extends to looking after your friends and family, and ensuring they look after you. Failing to address these areas at the beginning of candidature may, for some students, create problems that derail the research journey and worse, break their relationships to the point of being irreparable.

Drawing on my own experience of confronting OHS issues at the beginning of my candidature, this chapter firstly provides insights into the more compliance-related aspects of OHS risk management, and then discusses the need for managing relationships along with self-care risks while completing a doctorate. For many students, the research journey is a shared one, so being aware of what might go wrong for those fellow travellers is an essential consideration.

Occupational Health and Safety Compliance

I am a ceramicist who has been practicing for some twenty years, producing, exhibiting and selling work. My research project involves the marrying of two different disciplines: silversmithing which I studied in my BA, and the ceramic field I am now working in which I studied at Graduate Certificate level. To achieve this hybrid of disciplines, I melt glaze (a key element of the craft of ceramics) within a crucible (taken from the metal industry) and pour this onto a ceramic base at varying temperatures. This is to investigate rates and success of glaze adhesion achieved outside of the kiln environment and, in doing so, attempt to create an alternative method of finishing a ceramic work.

In my professional life, I had considered such issues as how studio safety is handled in a practical and iterative manner. Each new kiln or other ceramics tool is approached according to its specifications and capability to ensure safe practice, and my tacit knowledge is accepted and well known. Any issues are discussed and solved in situ. Instead of taking this approach, as part of my research proposal I had to explain in words on paper what I wanted to do, and deconstruct how I was going to it.

In this, I had to adopt a measured and neutral tone. I never considered, for instance, that the word 'explosion', which I initially used to describe what could happen to my pots, would raise so many red flags. Perceptions of this word may include massive fireballs and total destruction of property as seen in the action movies or, worse still, the aftermath of a terrorist attack. When used within the ceramics industry, this may refer to a small and well-contained activity, but I needed to imagine the alarming scenarios this word could conjure up in the minds of the readers of my documentation. This was important as it could possibly lead them to find problems with my processes where there were none. Instead, I learned to use different words that played down the likelihood of anything dangerous occurring. Using a neutral word such as 'popping' was useful here, as in, "When heat is added to the experimental clay body, it may cause some popping", instead of, "it may cause it to explode". 'Molten' for 'hot liquid' is another example that informs the reader but plays down the factor of heat and hopefully averts too many alarm bells. For those who are well acquainted with filling out OHS forms this may be obvious, but for those who are not, this aspect of careful language use cannot be overstated.

Every research project is unique and specialised, and university processes necessitate students to complete standardised processes and forms. It was important for me to learn that the terminology and language used within my industry (ceramics, specifically, and the arts, more broadly) would be understood differently outside of it. I also had to remember to write simply and clearly. Using large words in the attempt to sound impressive or more dramatic would have, in my case, had the opposite effect. What I needed was simple language that carefully explained my project. I found it useful to ask friends and family members who are unfamiliar with the language used in my field of practice (and study) to read through my work and make suggestions. Remember that the readers who are the decision makers, including the relevant Research Higher Degree administrative team, may have no knowledge of your area. They also cannot ask questions whilst they are reading, and may have a different way of thinking from you that puts them completely off track. If you know someone who is knowledgeable in OHS regulations, you could also ask them for advice and to make recommendations. Doing this in the early stages will avoid lengthy delays, rewrites, or in the worst-case scenario, the rejection of your project.

Similarly, if completing experimental work, it is important to be specific about the processes involved, and how safety procedures are going to be implemented. At my university, all students are asked to make a list of safety equipment, clothing requirements and the tools that will be used, including how they will be handled. It is important to be specific with quantities, weights, dimensions, and so on; as well as how any materials will be measured, mixed and formulated. In my case, the possibilities of cross contamination, the glaze application method, temperatures required and other such factors had to be meticulously planned and stated. This was, I saw in hindsight, of considerable benefit as this detailed project scoping allowed the experimentation phase to be completed relatively quickly and certainly more smoothly than it would have without this planning.

Environmental factors that may impact the gathering of data, such as heat, rain, sun, driving times involved per day, potential vehicle breakdown and how spent/excess materials will be disposed of, also need to be considered, and solutions provided. Never assume other people will know what all of this means or how it usually occurs, as they will rarely have the specialist knowledge or expertise that each student possesses of their own area of practice. In this, I learnt to seek guidance from the university's OHS personnel. Some universities my even offer workshops, but remember to use simple, non-threatening language and full explanations in all your interactions, even if these seem unnecessary.

If a student lives or is studying in a regional or rural area—like I am—this may present further issues with regard to gaining access to the necessary facilities. A third-party premises, such as a laboratory or artist's studio, which has all necessary safety requirements and protocols in place demanded by the university, may need to be located and engaged with in order for the project to proceed.

As my campus had no facilities in which to undertake my experimentation, I had to find a ceramics studio to do this work. This became a time consuming and difficult task as not all the studios in my area were OHS compliant, and others had long waiting lists (of over a year) to gain access to their facilities. Once I found suitable premises, I had to seek approval from the university. At this point I had to complete two OHS assessments in order to use this studio space. One was for the university using their template, followed by a meeting with the OHS officer to discuss the studio set up, experimental process and technician's qualifications. The second was the completion of the studio's OHS template, which then had to be discussed and signed off on by their OHS officer and ceramic studio technician. I had to hold meetings with the president of the management committee, the committee's ceramic studio manager, as well as the gallery director to which the studio was attached. Further approval was then required from the main council-run regional gallery. All of these people had to be briefed, and then they needed to provide statements that could be attached to the official university paperwork.

The university also required me to employ a technical assistant to help in the conduct of this experimental work. This assistant, therefore, also needed to be fully briefed on the OHS procedures of my work, and had to comply with all standards and procedures of the facility we were using. I was also advised that in some cases, the university may also require the student to use a third-party supplier to conduct the experimental work for them. If this scenario suits, then a lot of time can be saved, although this 'solution' would not be acceptable to most students in the creative arts.

Personal Occupational Health and Safety: Relationships

Many students do not have the luxury of a scholarship to undertake their studies or pay the bills while they are working on their research degree. That means that a large number of students are working at least part-time or casually while studying. This can make the work/life balance tenuous and place pressure on relationships in the workplace, at home and with friends. Just like workplace OHS, steps taken at the beginning of the doctoral journey to identify potential issues that could arise, and then putting plans in place to counteract these, could save untold hours of extra work, as well as considerable stress and angst in terms of maintaining these relationships safely and sustainably.

Respondents to Relationships Australia's *Relationships Indicator Survey* (2011) listed financial stress (26%), along with communication difficulties (25%), as among the top factors in a relationship breakdown. Duke University also found that another major contributor of relationship failure while studying can simply be the fact of undertaking a PhD itself (2018). Being honest about how these factors may impact personal relationships at the outset may hopefully keep everyone on the same page while the research is undertaken and completed.

It is important to also consider the financial implications of studying and how these will impact the household budget. Changing from full to part-time work, or taking a break from work to study, will certainly have an impact. Will your savings be sufficient, or do you have a partner or family willing to carry the financial burden for the duration of your degree? Although there are limited scholarships and bursaries available through each university, some companies and charities that have a vested interest in your research topic can be approached. As Virginia Birt has discussed in Chap. 6, universities provide considerable support through counsellors and other professional staff, and financial advice is often available. It is important not to be afraid or embarrassed to seek out their help.

The needs of those closest to you should not be overlooked or diminished as you focus on your work, either. Taking the time to communicate regularly with others allows them to join you on the journey, and sometimes they can provide the type of support and feedback that you need at a given time.

I have tried my hardest to keep to family routines throughout my candidature. These have had to be modified along the way, but stopped me feeling guilty. I followed Farkas's (2013) advice to schedule some fifteen to twenty minutes per day to connect and solve challenges with family, ensuring everyone around me stayed up to date and enabling them to provide me with extra support when I needed it. I also found Duke University's article "Committed relationships and grad school" (2018) useful, as it is a practical resource that provides strategies to put in place.

As a parent, I have joined a 'PhD Parents' Facebook page to link up with a wider community of people juggling similar issues and have received useful advice and support from this group. At times, compromises have had to be made such as getting up two hours earlier, sometimes more, to complete work in order to ensure I could attend my child's events. Time may be limited but that sporting event, concert or birthday cannot be replayed and children grow so fast, I did not want to miss anything and so made sure I always put my child's needs first. This was difficult at times but, when I was with my family, I made sure that I was there one hundred percent and totally in the moment, instead of thinking about my research all the time.

Telling my family and friends in advance that I had a paper or other work due in the coming weeks, enabled them to be more empathetic towards my needs during this time and aware of the possibility of mood changes, for when I am highly stressed (as I am in the days before a paper is due), I tend to become a little short and snappy. When finished, everyone is rewarded for getting through this period, for at times it is just as challenging for my family. This includes dinner on the night I finish, and then time doing whatever they want.

If you are single, be sure to take time to do something nice for yourself, such as booking in for a massage or going out with your friends. Rewarding yourself when you get through your milestones can also boost confidence and feelings of self-worth. All research students grow and evolve over the life of their projects. Good communication allows those closest to such students to be involved and grow with them.

Personal Occupational Health and Safety: Self-care

The World Health Organization (WHO) advises that "adults aged 18–64 should do at least 150 minutes of moderate-intensity aerobic physical activity throughout the week, or at least 75 minutes of vigorous-intensity aerobic physical activity throughout the week, or an equivalent combination of moderate and vigorous-intensity activity" (2011). This is the minimum activity required to "improve cardiorespiratory and muscular fitness, bone health and reduce the risk of depression" (WHO 2011). Godman (2014) expounds the benefits of combining exercise and study. These benefits include boosting brain health, which leads to a better retention of facts and better thinking skills. Further to this, exercising affects the chemicals in the brain, which in turn promotes new blood vessels to grow and new brain cells to survive. Some universities offer free or minimal cost exercise or yoga classes, and free workout guides abound online for exercise that can be completed in the privacy of your own home. Others in your research area can be approached to take a break and exercise with you. Many local councils also provide inexpensive classes or free access to gym equipment in local parks. There are walking, running and cycling clubs, many of which can also be joined for free. These types of activities relieve stress and stop social isolation, which can result in better work outcomes with the added benefit of providing a burst of endorphins, which boost mood and general feelings of well-being. Aware of this, some universities are beginning to offer programs that could be described as research well-being classes. Packages such as these equip students with strategies and resources that can transform the doctoral experience in an extremely positive manner as they focus on aspects of self-care such as time management, stress reduction and research productivity.

Personal OHS also incorporates being prepared for criticism of your work. This can come at many stages in your journey, and requires students to learn how to read and filter commentary that at times might feel harsh, but is actually aimed at getting the best out of the student, leading to an improved thesis. Gail Pittaway's chapter (Chap. 16) deals with feedback received from peer reviewers, and how to respond to this.

Very early in my candidature, I received a review that was confidence destroying and I wondered if continuing was in my best interest. Reading each comment caused vexation, angry words and prompted a walk around the block that was undertaken with great vigour. The importance of exercise for me at these moments for relieving stress cannot be overstated. This applies to me every day as it allows my brain to switch off completely. If I am in an exercise class or walking, I tend to sort slowly through the ideas in my head, discarding the vast majority before arriving home to jot down the keepers. It was also extremely important to keep clear communication lines open with my supervisor and, by discussing the feedback received on this paper, I learned a valuable lesson: the realisation my paper was not a failure, the feedback was overall of a constructive nature (though I could not see it at the time), and that the reviewer sought to improve my work rather than to knock it down. This was a difficult lesson to learn and presses home how essential it is to begin to develop a thick skin regarding feedback. I found what works for me is to read such comments and then walk away and come back the next day, or even the next week if necessary. It is tempting to make editing or other decisions in the heat of the moment, but given time and a calm thought process, the reviewer's comments can be digested and learnt from. I know now, too, that even the most senior academics regularly have their papers returned with less than completely positive comments. It is important to remember that standards are higher at this level and so not to think all is lost if work is rejected or attracts negative comment. Perseverance is the key.

Conclusion

As with many other aspects of life, maintaining balance while conducting research is essential. It is worth remembering that the university wants all its research students to succeed. Research students are their lifeblood, and universities are judged on the cutting-edge research produced and disseminated by their doctoral students. In many ways, a doctoral student is like a little boat on a large ocean. At times, all is smooth sailing but sometimes the vessel is tossed and buffeted by howling winds and huge waves, and can lose its bearings. At these times, it is prudent to put out a call for assistance, to be guided into a safe port where one can rest and recuperate, and undertake maintenance before setting forth again. Lone sailors can circumnavigate the globe, but it is their support crew that gets them safely home. Accomplishing this considerable journey is achievable by taking the time before setting forth to prepare a well worked-through health and safety plan. By thinking long-term—just like a sailor would study long-range weather forecasts—alternative plans can be devised and emergency action plans put in place to meet all kinds of weather. A clear OHS plan, both formal for the research project's experimentation and research, and personal for maintaining healthy relationships and the student's own well-being during their research journey, will ensure the voyage is completed safely and on schedule.

References

Duke University Counseling and Psychological Services. 2018. "Committed relationships & grad school." https://studentaffairs.duke.edu.

Farkas, D. 2013. *Why Relationships Matter in Grad School: 5 Ways to Maintain.* http://thegradstudentway.com.

Godman H. 2014. "Regular exercise changes the brain to improve memory, thinking skills." *Harvard Health Blog.* https://www.health.harvard.edu.

Relationships Australia and Credit Union Australia. 2011. *Issues and Concerns for Australian Relationships Today: Relationships Indicator Survey.* https://www.relationships.org.au.

World Health Organization (WHO). 2011. *Global Recommendations on Physical Activity for Health: 18–64 Years Old.* http://www.who.int.

12

Researching Within Online Communities

Susannah Oddi

Introduction

Digital social networks present a wide range of opportunities to design and implement innovative collaborative digital projects, dynamic participatory experiences and the sharing of experimental ideas across research teams, as well as for the construction of innovative creative works. While digital conversations may not replace experiences with real people, online communities allow the extension of practice beyond a physical location and may provide for a greater appreciation of global trends and developments through the creation of a global community of practice (Budge 2013, p. 19).

This chapter examines how a flexible approach to researching within online social communities may provide for a connected and creative research journey. Social media platforms are low cost and accessible tools that afford global networking potential, and can engage wider audiences

S. Oddi (✉)
School of Education and the Arts, Central Queensland University,
Melbourne, VIC, Australia
e-mail: susannah.oddi@cqumail.com

© The Author(s) 2019
D. L. Brien et al. (eds.), *The Doctoral Experience*,
https://doi.org/10.1007/978-3-030-18199-4_12

for research findings. Digital platforms annul temporal and geographical boundaries and allow for productive conversations with readers. Social media and collaborative online platforms can be a useful digital research tool for researchers; however, they require careful navigation. Designing effective methodologies for digital community research requires an inter-disciplinary approach that recognises ethical and practical considerations ranging from consent, privacy and moderation, to potential incivility. This chapter will map, using a reflective case study, practical strategies for minimising risk and managing digital research methodologies. Also discussed will be how ongoing reflection on activity and online relationships can shape both the research process and final work, and how evolving digital communities can expand traditional academic forums. Open-access publishing and emerging technological trends are also discussed.

This discussion examines how immersive research within social media offers far-reaching opportunities to tap into diverse audiences as research participants, and the ethical, practical and creative considerations of researching within digital communities as a doctoral research methodology. It highlights the advantages of social media research including the accessibility and reach of global platforms, and how this is countered by the risks of interacting with the public on a third-party platform, raising concerns over privacy, potential incivility and data security. Designing a research methodology requires interdisciplinary strategies that merge creative, scientific, technological, social, cultural, media and communication skills. While formal processes assess the suitability, feasibility and practicality of platforms and audience reach, a researcher requires an adaptable mindset to engage within a dynamic digital space, in which "ideas, practices, reflections—become entangled, and where disciplines spill into each other to form original constellations that inform the creative work that is at the centre of creative practice research" (Batty and Berry 2016, p. 249). Researching within social media is a process of trial and error, requiring continually evolving communication, creative and technical strategies. This discussion includes a case study of my own doctoral project—in creative writing—undertaken within a global social media community.

The Value of Researching Within Online Communities

My master's research examined the role of participatory readers in construct-ing Gothic fiction. The research was theoretical, as at that time there were few examples of creative writing research projects that had successfully engaged with a quantity of readers beyond classroom peers during its construction. My current doctoral project considers the potential of social media communities to foster creativity in a writer. The research focuses on my constructing a Gothic narrative within a digital community, and examines how taking on board feedback from the readers of this work online influences my creative writing skills and the narratives I create.

Due to the size/scale of social media platforms and their significance in contemporary culture, researching within social media provides a signifi-cant opportunity for researchers to engage with audiences. Posting work-in-progress or research ideas online reaches out to readers who may provide direction and depth to projects by providing individual com-mentary and, in some cases, an overall group sentiment. Comments, data and analytics provide a direct form of feedback that may shape the ongo-ing research process and its findings. Social media research is low cost and accessible, and provides significant advantages when accessing and liais-ing with participants over the traditional methods of research participant recruitment (National Health and Medical Research Council (NHMRC) 2007; Eysenbach and Till 2001). A social media platform is beneficial in attracting large numbers of subjects across the globe, provides the opportunity to develop relationships over time, and its interactive nature ensures the ongoing researcher-participant relationship is dynamic. Although social media research may reduce the ability to specifically tar-get individual participants, if specialist applications or interest groups within larger platforms are identified, it has the opportunity to approach and potentially engage a high number of people with a common interest.

I examined potential platforms and researched the ethical and practical considerations of undertaking research within them. I selected Wattpad.com, a global storytelling community of over sixty-five million monthly users, of which ninety per cent are readers (Wattpad 2016, 2018). While many niche writing platforms facilitate interaction with fellow writers, few offer significant access to a high number of readers across genres. As there was limited academic literature on Wattpad at the time, my decision centred on the analytics generated by the platform, its rising influence on creative production, the viability of the platform due to it being the pivotal business of the organisation, and its success in attracting significant investment.

Social media provides an opportunity to observe naturalistic users who interact with the platform as part of their daily lives (Moreno et al. 2013), and the anonymity of digital personas may provide a safe place in which participants can express ideas openly. Social media applications have technological capabilities to provide beneficial quantitative and qualitative user and engagement data, including user demographics, shares, likes and activity levels. Qualitative commentary may contribute to the development of new knowledge by enabling a better understanding of the social processes between researchers and their audiences, and by eliciting contextual data to improve the validity of statistical data (NHMRC 2007). Researching within digital spaces widens the audience for research beyond academic spheres, and when undertaken with integrity, forges quality online relationships that benefit the research undertaken.

Recent advances in mobile reading technologies have led to a resurgence of serial fiction, and online serials are now being cited as Dickensian storytelling for the digital age (Alter 2015). Wattpad affords writer-reader and creative connectivity through the addictive pull of social media. Writing my narrative in instalments online, and receiving reader feedback to consider, ignore or use as inspiration, creates a "practice-led loop" that both propels my research process and shapes my narrative (Kroll and Harper 2013, p. 2). My multidisciplinary research methodology applies Victorian serial writing techniques of Charles Dickens to digital culture, and encompasses creative practice scholarship and media theory.

Designing Digital Methodology

Well-defined research objectives guide social media research projects and their planning, practice and review. Aims propel the identification and the assessment of online platforms and their communities, their suitability to purpose, capabilities for communication and networking, provision of statistics and ease of data retrieval. Observational projects may require a formal schedule and technical methodology for content collection. Interactive surveys require timelines for content construction, dissemination, participant consent, collection of responses and analysis. Immersive projects, where the researcher becomes an active participant within a social community, require ample timelines to develop human research ethics frameworks and gain consent from fellow users. Timelines should not underestimate the level of interaction required in developing a new social profile and tapping into an interactive and valuable community. Social networks never turn off, and while many digital communities are suited to asynchronous communications, setting time limits for participation may provide less distraction and fewer opportunities for diversion. Allowing for regular reviews of processes enables project strategies to be adjusted as required throughout the research process.

At its heart, my methodology provides for spontaneity, as it is difficult to predict the outcomes of experimenting in digital spaces. I commenced my serial and fell into a paradoxical vortex. I had few readers and did not wish to continue my narrative without feedback, yet without posting regularly, I was unable to attract readers. Wattpad does not allow for self-promotion with the aim of soliciting readers. In order to be discovered, I worked to become a visible part of the social community, by reading and commenting on the works of others and participating in writing challenges. Rather than having a singular continuing narrative, my creative work-in-progress has developed as a collection of related episodes.

Considered and respectful digital communications appreciate the diverse cultural, technological and literary backgrounds of global social media users, and ensure the reputation of researchers and their institutions are not compromised on visible digital platforms. Researchers require a high level of expertise with the creation and use of digital data and platform technologies, an understanding of the conditions under which the data has been created, the skills to collaborate and network with others, and knowledge of risks associated with internet-based research (Clark et al. 2015, p. 19). Researchers engaging online with participatory communities seek to recognise cultural considerations and commonalities, aim to be minimally intrusive and to reduce bias. If a project is to be undertaken by a research team, it is important to consider how the technological and communication features of the platforms involved may influence collaborative dynamics. Social researcher and project designer Ioana Literat (2017) analyses how conducting a research project across three online sites resulted in diverse creative and leadership structures across platforms:

> When it comes to creative participatory projects, on the one hand there is an aesthetic and ethical aspiration to create an environment that is utmost collaborative, participatory and inclusive. But on the other hand, there is a practical need to retain some sort of control or coordination regarding the collaboration process (p. 86).

Digital social applications provide dynamic digital spaces for fellow researchers to drive projects and create knowledge. Researchers are participants simultaneously. This requires an interdisciplinary approach to technology, design, communication and leadership.

The digital footprints of researchers and the users they interact with are highly searchable. The exponential growth of social media, combined with the technological ability to draw vast amounts of user data from this media, have created methodological and ethical challenges for researchers (Williams et al. 2017, p. 1150). Many ethical guidelines provide principles relating to traditional forms of sourcing data, where consent may not be required if conducted in a public place where one may be expected to be observed by strangers. While digital social communities may feel very public, users may post information intended for their own networks within specific communities and may not intend for their words or content to spread across the wider Internet public and beyond into research publications, thus resulting in anonymity and privacy being compromised (Williams et al. 2017, p. 1160). To ensure the confidentiality of participants, no personal, identifiable, searchable quotations or user data should be copied from third-party applications for research analysis or publications without consent. Designing an ethical research methodology in this case requires reviewing and applying human research guidelines, as well as information privacy, social media policy, and codes of conduct of the institution and wider research bodies.

While my research commenced in a structured mode and adheres to ethical standards to ensure reader privacy, it has branched into a dynamic and diverse creative enterprise, demonstrative of how creative practice research within an online community suits an artistic methodology which embraces "serious play" (Cherry and Higgs 2011, p. 13). As a member of bespoke genre profiles on the site, I collaborate with fellow users across the globe to create engaging non-fiction content ranging from writing and graphic contests, to blog posts exploring pop culture and media tropes. By undertaking regular reviews of the research process, I avoid being swept away in a digital current—most of the time. On occasions, my research drifts into seemingly irrelevant online chats and I censure myself for such diversions. Such engagements, however, provide an increase of activity on my profile, leading to the generation of new creative ideas and an eddy of motivation.

Challenges of Digital Community Research

It is useful for students to consider that large social media applications, such as global blogging and social networking sites, have the potential to afford considerable exposure to a wide range of potential research participants and readers. Specialist niche communities, in addition, offer those with a close focus. Investigating the credibility and suitability of social media sites is more than analysing the feasibility of attracting a relevant audience. Digital content is vulnerable to data loss or technical threats, and data may be compromised if the organisation owning the site decides to no longer support the application. Copies of work thus need to be retained offline and regularly analysed in case data is lost, while also considering the privacy and security of participant data. Alterations to the site's terms of service, functionality, or statistical data offerings may impact the success of projects. Terms of service may affect the content and activity permitted, and the project's ability to attract and engage audiences. There are also intellectual property concerns regarding publishing online, including the risk of theft or copyright breaches, and retaining ownership of creative work. Publishing on an open access platform may, in addition, affect the ability to later publish in other media or academic journals that require exclusivity.

Undertaking a digital research project engaging a mass-audience suggests working in the realm of genre writing. By not restricting my outreach to intellectual circles, I may be reducing my literary credibility (Krauth 2016, p. 199). While my digital explorations are influencing my writing process, developing my digital communication skills, and strengthening my skills in community engagement, I acknowledge that presenting works-in-progress in social media spaces does not allow for the curation, polishing, or academic recognition that publishing in a peer-reviewed journal affords. Creative writing practitioners are, however, recognising the potential reach digital formats provide in terms of creating new artistic forms and building audiences (Fleming-May and Green 2016, p. 867).

A student's research methodology should consider the potential risks to participants, while appreciating that there is limited ability to identify age, demographics and other circumstances of individuals. Researchers have a duty of care to ensure their content or commentary, and participant activity associated with their work, does not cause offence. Commentary or feedback may affect a researcher's own motivation and mental health. Digital research is often viewed as low or negligible risk, as there often appear to be no foreseen physical, psychological, social, economic or legal risks associated with the research, though it is difficult to determine a direct connection between online data and how it may contribute to physical or psychological harm (Association of Internet Researchers 2012, p. 7). There is the potential to cause discomfort through digital communication due to the inability of predicting how posts, words and interactions may be interpreted. Challenges may arise and cause distress if commentary escalates into ongoing harassment or online incivility, as people may "say and do things under the distance and anonymity of the internet that they might never do in person" (Powell and Henry 2015). Many sites have functionality to mute or block user profiles and have dedicated community safety teams through which to report inappropriate activity. Researchers with a thorough understanding of the content guidelines and codes of conduct of the social sites they are researching within will be well positioned to ensure research practice mitigates potential risks.

While I adhere to overall project deadlines and objectives, the process requires flexibility and the altering of methodology due to shifting research trajectories. Regular reviews of my activity and reader commentary, or even the lack thereof, provide the opportunity to refocus. Researching within an online community creates an online portfolio of work and an enduring digital footprint of interactions. While it will be a challenge to construct my fragmented narratives into a cohesive whole, qualitative comments from readers have provided me insight as to the direction of my narrative—such as which of my characters are engaging and which are lacklustre. The quantitative data, including reader demographics, number of reads, votes and comments per chapter and by date, have revealed that my active narrative styles are most appealing.

In addition to ethical, technical and communication skills required to utilise social media platforms effectively, identifying wider digital applications and developing multimedia skills may assist in engaging with wider audiences. With so many digital entities vying for audience attention, a site consisting of plain text may not be appropriate in attracting and growing a research community, and tagging posts make work more discoverable. Adding visuals and multimedia suited to target audiences may add depth and understanding to content, promote research and sharing across digital spaces, and work to cross literacy and cultural boundaries. Assessing capabilities of applications and creating digital inclusions such as images, banners, videos, audios or graphics require additional time and resources. Third party images may be subject to obtaining copyright permission or purchase. Many social media platforms allow for the integration of applications such as surveys and forms that may assist with the collection of qualitative and quantitative data.

Many researchers are comfortable with technological applications and use social media and graphic applications as part of their everyday lives. While time may not be required to learn the practicalities of applications, consideration is needed of how they may be integrated into research projects and how long it may take to feel comfortable using applications within an academic context. Students who are 'digital natives' (Prensky 2001) are comfortable applying digital and social tools to their craft, yet they may be apprehensive about experimenting and presenting work in social media spaces. A study by University of Arts London (Robertson and Lange 2017), exploring the anxieties of researching in a continually evolving digital culture, asked students undertaking a MA in Fashion about their concerns regarding conducting research within social online communities, and found that:

> The pressure of working digitally, as in using social media, suggests that students feel that they constantly have to promote themselves and their work. Ultimately, this has an impact on their abilities to take creative risks, as they do not want to show all experiments and failures publicly online (p. 3).

The multiplicity of formats and platforms increases pressure, time and the decision-making process, yet evolving digital narratives and construction also provide exciting opportunities to expand traditional compositional boundaries (Skains 2017, p. 115). Undertaking research within creative online communities presents many twists and turns, and expanding literature on digital trends may be infused into projects. Comments, feedback and statistics can provide valuable information as to what is working and what needs to be altered, yet creativity may also be driven by the blank spaces—by recognising when community participation is lacking and developing new strategies is required to increase engagement.

Conclusion

As digital interactions continue to bridge traditional printed research and the attraction of online content, researchers experimenting within social media communities may anticipate engagement with online participants who are not merely consumers of data, but also influential over research outcomes. To overcome the lack of feedback and visibility afforded through traditional forms of academic publication, creative arts, humanities and other research is continuing to expand in the field of open publishing and communities of practice, where scholars provide online unrestricted access to informal and peer reviewed work (Fleming-May and Green 2016, p. 870). While artistic and cultural research continues to evolve utilising interactions and content within large social media platforms such as Facebook and Twitter, LinkedIn, Youtube, Instagram and Pinterest, diverse explorations of digital forms and kinds of engagement are emerging in specialist creative communities. These range from researching the psychology of artworks in Deviant Art, to the popularity of independent music in Reverberation, to typography portfolios on Behance, to promoting young adult literacy by writing in Fanfiction.net.

While creative research may focus on the produsage (Bruns 2008) of artefacts within digital communities, it also merges into commercialisation of creativity enterprises. As digital culture and creative enterprises continue to meld, research regarding intellectual property and ethical issues will continue to be debated (Flew 2017, p. 515). At the same time, political, social, educational and cultural networked economies, including practitioner branding, crowdfunding, geo-humanities, media fandom, digital learning and customer engagement behaviour, will continue to be explored. Creative economies are not exempt from the big data and analytical research that has been trending in business circles for years. In a world of spiralling algorithms and metadata, entertainment and conversations on our screens are being tailored to user preferences based on activity in digital communities.

Digital research is producing innovative creative technologists realising new forms of digital interfaces and networked community interactions, such as Massachusetts Institute of Technology's Media Lab's creation of a program which generates short horror stories on Twitter, trained on user data from the social community Reddit (MIT 2017). Applications of machine learning and artificial intelligence seek to meld human creativity with intelligent systems, and are forecasted to have immense potential on creative production, consumer predictions, and our society (Vivid Ideas 2017). Artificial neural networks compose music, write screenplays and animate graphics. The future creative researcher will digitise dynamic digital portfolios, highlighting their multidisciplinary expertise, to ensure discovery by the artificially intelligent talent acquisition systems of their future employers and creative enterprises.

References

Alter, A. 2015. "Margaret Atwood, digital deep-diver, writes 'the heart goes last'." *The New York Times*, 27 September. https://www.nytimes.com/2015/09/28/books/margaret-atwood-digital-deep-diver-writes-the-heart-goes-last.html.

Association of Internet Researchers. 2012. *Ethical Decision-making and Internet Research: Recommendations from the AOIR Ethics Committee (Version 2.0).* https://aoir.org/ethics.

Batty, C., and M. Berry. 2016. "Constellations and connections: The playful space of the creative practice research degree." *Journal of Media Practice* 16 (3): 181–194.

Bruns, A. 2008. *Blogs, Wikipedia, Second Life, and Beyond: From Production to Produsage.* New York: Peter Lang.

Budge, K. 2013. "Virtual studio practices: Visual artists, social media and creativity." *Journal of Science and Technology of the Arts* 5 (1): 15–23.

Cherry, N., and J. Higgs. 2011. "Researching in wicked practice spaces." In *Creative Spaces for Qualitative Researching: Living Research*, edited by Joy Higgs, Angie Titchen, Debbie Horsefall and Donna Bridges. Boston: Sense Publishers.

Clark, K., M. Duckham, M. Guillemin, A. Hunter, J. McVernon, C. O'Keefe, C. Pitkin, S. Prawer, R. Sinnott, D. Warr, and J. Waycott. 2015. *Guidelines for the Ethical Use of Digital Data in Human Research.* Melbourne: The University of Melbourne.

Eysenbach, G., and J. E. Till. 2001. "Ethical issues in qualitative research on internet communities." *BMJ: British Medical Journal* 323 (7321): 1103–1105.

Fleming-May, R. A., and H. Green. 2016. "Digital innovations in poetry: Practices of creative writing faculty in online literary publishing." *Journal of the Association for Information Science and Technology* 67 (4): 859–873.

Flew, T. 2017. "Social media and the cultural and creative industries." In *The SAGE Handbook of Social Media*, edited by Jean Burgess, Alice E. Marwick, and Thomas Poell. London: SAGE.

Krauth, N. 2016. *Creative Writing and the Radical: Teaching and Learning the Fiction of the Future.* Bristol: Multilingual Matters.

Kroll, J., and G. Harper. 2013. *Research Methods in Creative Writing.* Basingstoke, UK: Palgrave Macmillan.

Literat, I. 2017. "Facilitating creative participation and collaboration in online spaces: The impact of social and technological factors in enabling sustainable engagement." *Digital Creativity* 28 (2): 73–88.

MIT Media Lab. 2017. *Shelley: Human-AI Collaborated Horror Stories.* https://www.media.mit.edu/projects/shelley/overview.

Moreno, M. A., N. Gonui, P. S. Moreno, and D. Diekema. 2013. "Ethics of social media research: Common concerns and practical considerations." *Cyberpsychology, Behavior and Social Networking* 16 (9): 708–13.

National Health and Medical Research Council. 2007. *National Statement on Ethical Conduct in Human Research 2007*, updated May 2015. Canberra, ACT: National Health and Medical Research Council (NHMRC).

Powell, A., and N. Henry. 2015. "How can we stem the tide of online harassment and abuse?" *The Conversation*, 5 October. https://theconversation.com/how-can-we-stem-the-tide-of-online-harassment-and-abuse-48387.

Prensky, M. 2001. "Digital natives, digital immigrants part 1." *On the Horizon* 9 (5): 1–6.

Robertson, C., and S. Lange. 2017. "Looking: Thinking: Making: How is digital culture influencing practice?" *Spark: UAL Creative Teaching and Learning Journal* 2 (2): 139–143.

Skains, L. 2017. "The adaptive process of multimodal composition: How developing tacit knowledge of digital tools affects creative writing." *Computers and Composition* 43: 106–117.

Vivid Ideas. 2017. "Elevating creativity through artificial intelligence with Ross Goodwin." *Human & Machine 2017 Conference: The Next Great Creative Partnership*. https://www.vividsydney.com/elevating-creativity-through-artificial-intelligence-ross-goodwin.

Wattpad. 2016. *Almost 90% of Wattpad's 250 Million Stories are Serialized*. https://company.wattpad.com/blog/2016/05/18/almost-90-of-wattpads-250-million-stories-are-serialized-find-out-why.

Wattpad. 2018. *Press*. https://company.wattpad.com/press.

Williams, M. L., P. Burnap, and L. Sloan. 2017. "Towards an ethical framework for publishing Twitter data in social research: Taking into account users' views, online context and algorithmic estimation." *Sociology* 51 (6): 1149–1168.

Part IV

Staying on the Doctoral Path: Introduction to Part

Donna Lee Brien, Craig Batty, Elizabeth Ellison, and Alison Owens

This part of the book focuses on the ways that research students can make the most of the opportunities, and the peers and others they meet, while on their doctoral journey. It is about taking stock of what individuals themselves have to offer, and then developing effective networks and plans for what will happen once their doctorates are finished. Here the student chapters include advice about, and examples of, developing disciplinary and inter-disciplinary peer groups and research teams, contributing

D. L. Brien (✉) • E. Ellison
Noosaville, QLD, Australia
e-mail: d.brien@cqu.edu.au; l.ellison@cqu.edu.au

C. Batty
Sydney, NSW, Australia
e-mail: Craig.Batty@uts.edu.au

A. Owens
North Sydney, NSW, Australia
e-mail: Alison.Owens@acu.edu.au

to, and leading, events and publications that help to shape the field, and developing robust publication and research dissemination plans. These chapters also emphasise the importance of generosity in research education; becoming, and being, a peer in order to take others on the doctoral journey. Central to this is the importance of the varied relationships a doctoral student will develop with—and within—their chosen study institution. The chapters in this part provide tools to assist with managing these relationships in a professionally positive and personally beneficial way, and describe some common problems that can arise—with advice about how to effectively resolve them.

Peter McKenzie describes how, in his case, factors as prosaic as what he wore affected his ability to collect data in his doctoral project, due to how such elements influenced the relationships built with these individuals. This chapter highlights the benefits of establishing, building and maintaining ongoing relationships with study participants, benefits that will continue well beyond the PhD itself. Susan Currie tackles what can be, for some students, the most productive—or problematic—relationships during the doctoral journey; the relationships students have with their supervisors. Currie emphasises that the choice of supervisors should not be left to chance, and that it is an aspect of doctoral studies students should investigate closely before beginning their doctorates. Currie's chapter also provides invaluable information on styles of supervision to avoid and courses of action for students to take if the supervisory relationship breaks down. Both these chapters emphasise the importance of interpersonal relationships in both supervision and research, and the relationship between supervisors and students, and the relationships between the student and their research participants, are discussed in detail.

A relationship is often considered a one-to-one situation, and in the case of supervisors and individual research participants, this is usually the case. The potential for difficulties can be increased in these one-to-one relationships, where problems can be both unexpected and escalate quickly. They can be difficult to resolve because of the fine line between the professional and the personal and, in the case of the working relationship between a supervisor and student, because of the intensity and likely length of the relationship. The quality of the relationships between the student and their research participants determines the quality, quantity and accuracy of data, and ultimately contributes as much to the student's overall satisfaction with the research project as does the supervisor and university experience.

Carmen Gray's chapter picks up the point of enhancing student resilience—detailing how a student can recover from a catastrophic event that has derailed their studies: in her case, discovering that someone else had already conducted the proposed study. Taleb's useful concept of antifragility (2012) is considered in this context.

Reference

Taleb, N. N. 2012. *Antifragile: Things That Gain from Disorder*. New York: Random House.

13

Maintaining Good Relationships with Research Participants

Peter McKenzie

Introduction

Along the doctoral journey, research students will develop a range of critical skills that will inform their study and future research endeavours. One of the most important skills to develop concerns the development of relationships with the research participants. Undertaking the data collection phase of a qualitative research project can be met with excitement and trepidation. Despite the extensive preparation of the project's research aims, questions and method, the ability to extract the richest data will often come down to the relationships built and maintained, and the approaches a research student takes in interacting with the study participants. There is already extensive literature on the typical challenges associated with the data collection phase in both qualitative and quantitative research (Fontana and Frey 2000; Minichiello et al. 1995; Taylor and Bogdan 1998).

P. McKenzie (✉)
School of Education and the Arts, Central Queensland University,
Mackay, QLD, Australia
e-mail: p.mckenzie@cqu.edu.au

© The Author(s) 2019
D. L. Brien et al. (eds.), *The Doctoral Experience,*
https://doi.org/10.1007/978-3-030-18199-4_13

This chapter provides examples and discusses how to establish, build and maintain the relationships with the study participants. It affirms that the level of rapport a student can build with those study participants is a critical factor in developing an individual's research and subsequent work in that field in the future. With specific reference to Fontana and Frey (2000), I draw on my own PhD experience of undertaking a qualitative sociological study of music communities, which involves research into regional jazz communities using interviews with musicians and others involved in staging festivals and events.

Interviewing and Data Collection

According to Creswell et al. (2007, p. 129) there are many types of data in qualitative and quantitative research, but it all largely falls into four basic categories: "Observations, interviews, documents, and audiovisual materials". Jacob and Furgerson (2012, p. 1) state, "Researchers may use many different techniques, but at the heart of qualitative research is the desire to expose the human part of a story". One of the most useful ways to expose this 'story' is to interview participants. Yin (2014, p. 110) discusses two important tasks for the interviewer, namely: following one's own line of inquiry, and asking conversational questions in an unbiased manner. The predetermined open-ended questions allow for other questions to emerge from the dialogue between the interviewer and the interviewee (DiCicco-Bloom and Crabtree 2006, p. 315).

The examples provided in this chapter emerged from the use of semi-structured interviewing in my own PhD. One of the advantages of using semi-structured interviews is the ability to conduct individual in-depth inquiry, therefore delving into much deeper social and personal matters (DiCicco-Bloom and Crabtree 2006, p. 315). Researchers are often told to conduct their interviews in relaxed settings agreed upon by the interviewee. In most cases, this can either be done at their home residence, or an industry setting or even at a local café (DiCicco-Bloom and Crabtree 2006; Taylor and Bogdan 1998). Fontana and Frey (2000) have provided some of the key areas researchers should consider when engaging with participants. These include:

- Accessing the setting
- Understanding culture/language
- Deciding on how to present oneself
- Locating the informant
- Gaining trust
- Establishing rapport

The examples I provide emerge from a combination of an insider and outsider research approach. Insider research is conducted when the researcher is a member of the population in which they are investigating. This includes shared identity, language and shared experiences (Dwyer and Buckle 2009; Kanuha 2000). While this occurred in the music community case, I also interviewed musicians in an outside community. Although common and shared beliefs were evident, being an outside musician and academic created many challenges in conducting thorough and fruitful data collection. It is for this reason that this case was chosen, as it demonstrated the insider and outsider perspectives.

Pull Over, Take a Break, and Talk with the Locals

When I was first invited to play with the band, I sensed a disconnect with the guys side stage. We all talked and that was fine, but there was something missing in our interactions. It felt clinical. I felt like an outsider but once I started to play with the guys on the bandstand that night at the Casino, I sensed a different level of appreciation from them. After playing and taking on some improvisations, I could feel the group relax. I was no longer an outside musician. Even better, I wasn't seen as an academic. I was one of them. The on-stage energy and side stage banter from then on allowed for much deeper conversations and more meaningful interactions.

Research students can be heavily focused on the outcomes and deadlines of their study. Often, they forget some of the more enjoyable and fruitful aspects such as interacting and engaging in the field. Time taken to 'get to know' and engage with the study participants is an important component of the research journey (Miller 1952). Interacting with the participants can bring a range of benefits including:

* Deeper understanding of the field
* A more relaxed interviewing experience
* Acceptance in their field/community
* Richer data to be shared
* Future collaborations and networking

If possible, time taken to interact and engage with the participants prior to any data collection is ideal to strengthen the research relationship. It is important, however, to not over-do rapport building which could hinder the study (Miller 1952). In the case of my study, I was required to travel to a city in which I was not part of the music community. My biggest challenge was being accepted by the musicians in order to gather quality data. Although friendly and keen to contribute to the research project, I could feel a disconnect with the participants.

Firstly, being an academic and approaching people in an industry can be loaded with preconceptions from the participant's perspective. Breaking down these barriers by spending time with participants may help reduce this feeling and warrant a better understanding between the researcher and participant. One of the most effective ways to connect is to participate within their industry/community. Fontana and Frey (2000) describe this as 'accessing the setting'. In the case of the music community project, an academic that can perform with the musicians holds much value for both. This approach also follows the recommendations of Fontana and Frey who state: "He or she must be able to put him or herself in the role of the respondents and attempt to see the situation from their perspective, rather than impose the world of academia and preconceptions upon them" (1994, p. 367).

In relation to the personal vignette above, as a researcher I was able to be accepted in the field and build mutual respect via my performing/participation. The flow-on effects from this one encounter resulted in an increased level of networking with other musicians that I had not considered or anticipated. I was invited to other performances and commenced a new relationship with this music community based on a mutual respect gained from an acceptable quality of music performance. As a researcher, I was able to access the community, locate more participants and delve deeper into the participants' networks. When the data collection phase occurred later, I was also able to connect with more people and further concepts, which greatly benefited my study.

Get Comfortable on the Road: Attire and Location

Wow! That was a failure. As soon as I got back in the car, I realised what I had done. Sure, the interview went OK and I asked the right questions, but I think the way I was dressed was way too formal for a conversation in his backyard in North Queensland. I could tell he looked me up and down and sensed 'an academic type'. He even mentioned it in the interview about academics and their approach to performing. I made a mental note: next time, I'm wearing sandals and much more casual clothes.

The way research students present themselves can affect the interviewing experience and quality of the data (Fontana and Frey 2000). Choosing formal attire may be appropriate for a medical conference or industry environment, but it really does depend on the situation. In the case of my music community study, I chose to wear formal work clothes to an interview at a musician's house as this was part of my doctoral work. Although the interview was generally a success, the attire created a divide between us. It created a 'musician versus academic' situation where the musician appeared guarded with their information. Although being both a musician and academic, the clothing made it hard for me—as researcher—to establish a sense of rapport and connection. The divide was noticeable in the comments from the participant.

Upon reflection after this first interview, I adjusted my attire according to the situation and felt this positively impacted the interviewing experiences. Fontana and Frey (2000) list gaining an understanding of the culture and language of a participant's world as an important aspect of research training. In the case of the attire in my situation, this impacted on my ability to share the culture and language of the music community with which I was familiar. That incorrectly pitched attire was enough to project the different set of cultural values of my persona as a research student, despite our shared background in music.

The location or venue a research student chooses to interact with a study participant is also important in having a positive interviewing experience. Allowing the participant to choose the location may be a good idea to ensure they feel safe and relaxed. However, the researcher needs to be mindful that public places with too much noise may be distracting or limit the ability of the participant to discuss private matters. Noise may also affect recording (Jacob and Furgerson 2012). Developing participant trust is paramount in relation to the location. Intimidating environments such as workplaces may impact how the participant responds.

Going Off Road: Common Interests Outside the Research Area

I gathered some great insights in the one-hour interview but it wasn't until we walked outside past his boat that I was able to gain a deeper insight into this musician, and more importantly, this person. I commented on his boat and mentioned that I had a boat, and also fished. We then talked fishing for about an hour. This was great, but more surprisingly, interspersed in this conversation was the mention of musicians, experiences and further insights in my study area. I could never have foreseen or gathered this information in the earlier, more structured interview environment. It was such a random, but important, way of gathering data and having a conversation. The way our common interest in fishing linked to the study of music was accidental, but essential in the end for a successful data gathering experience; and, additionally, a stronger relationship.

One of the advantages of semi-structured interviews is the ability to be conversational. This includes being flexible and adapting to topics of conversation that may stray from the original interview guide. Providing the topics are appropriate and linked to the study, this can be a useful guide to building a meaningful conversation. During the process, researchers often use recording devices for the interviews. These recordings are then analysed at a later date. Research students need to be aware of the potential information/data that is missed before and after the recording. It is often these open conversations after, during or before an interview that can shed new light on a topic. Some researchers believe this is due to the way semi-structured interviewing can invoke a relaxed conversational approach which also "enables interviewees to provide responses in their own terms and in the way that they think and use language" (Qu and Dumay 2011, p. 246).

The research student must stay focused and aware of potential information at all times when interacting with a research participant (Jacob and Furgerson 2012). In my case, I was able to glean key information through the seemingly unrelated topic of fishing. In our conversation after the interview, we discussed a range of topics about fishing, but the participants also mentioned musicians and events. These connections further linked back to the study topic and provided a richer understanding of the people and the environment in which the study was being undertaken. I did not foresee this connection, but adjusted accordingly and was able to gather this new information. What followed from this experience was a deeper relationship through shared experiences. The participant and I established a stronger rapport and trust.

Continuing the Journey and Making Long Lasting Relationships

I couldn't believe my luck when I got off the phone! A week residency for my students was such a great opportunity. I could tell when talking to the venue owners that we got on really well. There was a good sense of mateship and trust. This happened after the gigs we did together of course, so I think it all added up. But to be invited to host a residency was completely out of the blue. The students loved being there and meeting the local jazz community. They gained so much from this real-world experience.

You just never know how an interaction may reap rewards in the future. As they have to delve deeply into their topics, research students who only look at the small picture potentially close doors for other opportunities once the research project is complete. Building a professional network can start with your research participants, which might then continue through your academic career.

As a result of my research, I was also invited to deliver clinics at schools associated with my participants. These occurred both during and after the research project was completed. This strengthened my relationship with the teachers, built connections with school musicians and, more importantly, contributed to the music community through providing an educational intervention. I was also able to build off this initial relationship and forge strong industry partnerships with these schools and their teachers.

Another example of developing relationships from my study arose when I volunteered to perform with the local jazz club. Giving back to the community I was interacting with was highly appreciated by the community, and I feel my participation showed a sense of respect for them. As part of these sessions, I also delivered masterclasses for the club's members. Fontana and Frey (2000) discuss that it may take a long time for participants to trust the researcher. In many cases, research students may be required to re-visit communities to gather further data, so it is important to build these long-term relationships. And this is what I did.

After the project, the maintenance of trust should still be a priority, especially if research papers are generated after the thesis is completed. If participants trust the researcher and see the long-term benefits for them of the study, the relationship may bring further rewards for the researcher's career. In the case of my study, the jazz club members donated an incredible collection of jazz memorabilia and music to my university. This, I feel, was evidence of a great deal of respect for the study and the way I conducted it. This has continued, and we are forging a very special relationship with the members with successive performances and collaboration. In another example, the owners of a private jazz venue invited me, and my students, to undertake a one-week performance residency at their venue. This residency was highly valued by both the students and myself, as it provided an industry-level opportunity for everyone. The week of performances was also beneficial for local businesses and the jazz community, as it attracted many patrons and publicity. This type of collaboration was made possible by the strong relationship forged through my research study.

Conclusion

This chapter has demonstrated the value of establishing and developing strong relationships with study participants, where possible. The example of my music community study has highlighted how to manage insider and outsider research approaches. Although there are many types of interviewing technique, my study used semi-structured interviewing which allowed for a more conversational approach to gaining access to participants' worlds (Qu and Dumay 2011), and fostered this relationship building.

Taking time out of the research to develop relationships was highly valuable to my research project, and yielded long-term benefits for both my study and my career. Spending time with, and engaging in, the participants' industry and professional practice assisted in developing the participant relationship and later helped with data collection. Fontana and Frey describe this as "accessing the setting" (2000, p. 654). Often overlooked details when interacting with participants include an awareness of attire and the selection of an appropriate location for interacting with participants. These aspects can greatly influence how the research student is perceived, and subsequently how participants might respond in interviews. The examples in this chapter show how I was able to be flexible and adapt the situation to suit each participant.

The ability to relate to and find connections between themes, in conversations that may initially appear unrelated to the interview plan, is also important. The benefits of connecting with participants on a range of topics in my study enabled a better rapport and what Fontana and Frey describe as "understanding the culture and language" (2000, p. 654). This was especially important for me coming into the community with an 'outsider' perspective.

Lastly, this chapter explored some of the benefits in continuing to develop the relationships beyond a research study. This may open up potential collaborative opportunities that will strengthen the research student's career, including future research and teaching opportunities. It is also important to be mindful of how these interactions can benefit the people and communities that are assisting in the research project. This will ensure a fruitful and enjoyable research journey for both the research student and their participants.

References

Creswell, J. W., W. E. Hanson, V. L. C. Plano, and A. Morales. 2007, "Qualitative research designs: Selection and implementation." *The Counseling Psychologist* 35 (2): 236–264.

DiCicco-Bloom, B., and B. F. Crabtree. 2006. "The qualitative research interview." *Medical Education* 40 (4): 314–321.

Dwyer, S. C., and J. L. Buckle. 2009. "The space between: On being an insider-outsider in qualitative research." *International Journal of Qualitative Methods* 8 (1): 54–63.

Fontana, A., and J. Frey. 1994. "The art of science."In *The Handbook of Qualitative Research*, edited by N. K. Denzin, 361–376. Thousand Oaks: SAGE.

Fontana, A., and J. Frey. 2000. "The interview: From structured questions to negotiated text."In *The Handbook of Qualitative Research*, edited by N. K. Denzin and Y. S. Lincoln, 2nd ed., 645–672. London: SAGE.

Jacob, S. A., and S. P. Furgerson. 2012. "Writing interview protocols and conducting interviews: Tips for students new to the field of qualitative research." *The Qualitative Report* 17 (42): 1–10.

Kanuha, V. K. 2000. "Being native versus going native: Conducting social work research as an insider." *Social Work* 45 (5): 439–447.

Miller, S. M. 1952. "The participant observer and over-rapport." *American Sociological Review* 17 (1): 97–99.

Minichiello, V., R. Aroni, E. Timewell, and L. Alexander. 1995. *In-depth Interviewing: Principles, Techniques, Analysis*. 2nd ed. Melbourne: Longman Cheshire.

Qu, S. Q., and J. Dumay. 2011. "The qualitative research interview." *Qualitative Research in Accounting and Management* 8 (3): 238–264.

Taylor, S. J., and R. Bogdan. 1998. *Introduction to Qualitative Research Methods: A Guidebook and Resource*. 3rd ed. New York: John Wiley & Sons.

Yin, R. K. 2014. *Case Study Research: Design and Methods*. 5th ed.. Thousand Oaks: SAGE.

14

Interrogating the Research Student-Supervisor Relationship

Susan Currie

Introduction

With all the focus on the intellectual and procedural work of the doctorate, it is easy for a doctoral student to overlook the importance of the interpersonal relationship between themselves and their supervisors. Although students are advised to carefully choose their supervisory team, the relationships between these individuals, how these relationships are managed and how they can then evolve into life-long research partnerships, is less often articulated or made an explicit part of research planning. Research students come to these relationships under different conditions. In the creative arts and humanities, it is common for a supervisor to be selected due to their area of expertise, research track record and public profile. At the other extreme, a student might have been invited to be involved in a particular academic's research project. Another student might not know even where to start in finding a supervisor. However, when the supervisory arrangement has been arrived at,

S. Currie (✉)
Brisbane, QLD, Australia

© The Author(s) 2019
D. L. Brien et al. (eds.), *The Doctoral Experience*,
https://doi.org/10.1007/978-3-030-18199-4_14

developing a positive and productive relationship is integral to the successful completion of a doctorate.

This chapter outlines why, once the appropriate person or persons willing to be doctoral supervisors have been chosen, it is important that a student clarifies their respective expectations to ensure that these are mutual, reasonable and flexible (Holbrook et al. 2013, 2014). This chapter also provides strategies for how this might best be achieved, as well as approaches for managing potential problems within the supervisory relationship, including what to do if a supervisor attempts to breach the boundaries of the relationship, fails to provide appropriate supervision, or sacrifices a student's interest to their own.

Choosing and Working with a Supervisor

As the doctoral student proceeds down the path of choosing, or working with, a supervisor or supervisory team, it is important that they understand they are entering a somewhat 'closed community' and establishing a long-term relationship with one or more of its members. While it is important that the department and supervisors have expertise in a student's area of interest, the culture of the community and the interpersonal skills of the supervisors are equally intrinsic to a student's future success. As Holbrook et al. note in their study of research student expectations and the potential for 'mismatch' with supervisors:

> Given the significant changes in cognitive development and the accompanying emotional experiences that candidates undergo, there needs to be an emphasis on how candidates can be supported in their learning to detect and address problematic expectations. Supervisors can play an important role here and need to be better informed about how these expectations manifest. (2014, pp. 242–243)

For my PhD, I planned to write a biography of a woman doctor who was an activist on women's health and social justice issues. I wanted a supervisor who would value my researching and writing this woman's story; who would appreciate that it was a form of activism on my own part and support that.

I wanted a supervisor with experience supervising in the area of creative non-fiction and preferably one who had also written a biography. But above all, as a mature student with an established career record, I wanted mutual respect between my supervisor and me, and to feel comfortable engaging with them. I wanted a supervisor who was reliable and supportive. I also wanted to be studying in an environment where I would be encouraged to engage with other PhD students and be given plenty of opportunities to share and discuss our work.

A top priority for a doctoral student in choosing supervisors is to become familiar with potential academic communities and to meet with potential supervisors. While Phillips and Pugh (2005, p. 102) assert that it is wiser to select a research topic to match a supervisor of choice than to select a topic and then be allocated to the relevant academic specialist, it is also important that the topic is one to which the student is committed, and not just one undertaken because it is an area in which a preferred supervisor is currently working. Online staff profiles can reveal a great deal about potential supervisors. As well as their research interests and publications, these online professional biographies can include how many students a potential supervisor is currently supervising and how many they have successfully supervised to completion. Be careful here though.

I was surprised to find that an academic was claiming online to have supervised my Master's thesis when he was only an associate supervisor, and I had in fact never met with him to discuss my thesis. When I raised this matter with the university involved, the response was that he was officially my associate supervisor and so could make a claim of this nature. As well as being disappointed with this outcome, this experience made me very wary about whom I would choose to supervise my PhD, and to make sure I met them in person first to get a good sense of how they might operate.

Seek recommendations from other researchers and academics. Advice on choosing supervisors is available not only from individual university websites but also from general websites set up for university research students, such as http://www.postgradaustralia.com.au (see, for example, Aborde 2018).

Students should seek to meet with potential supervisors, and ask them about their approach to supervision and how they prefer to work with their students. The most important aspect of this introductory meeting is for a student to get a feel for the supervisors as people. Research suggests that the characteristics of effective supervisors are: approachability and friendliness; being supportive and positive; being open-minded and willing to acknowledge errors; being organised and stimulating; and transmitting enthusiasm (Cullen, et al. 1994, cited in Orellana et al. 2016, p. 89). These academics can also be asked about their own doctoral experiences, and about what aspects of their work they are the most enthusiastic or passionate about. If there is a rapport between you, and you feel you could work well together, be encouraged. But also be careful. Make sure you feel comfortable that your relationship will be a professional one.

There is great benefit to be had in asking questions, not only of supervisors, but also of their current or former research students. Finding out whether these students are (or have been) treated with respect is obviously important, as is whether the supervisors are good listeners and if student work is commented on in a constructive and timely manner. Whether supervisors can identify when their students need help, and offer appropriate support, is another aspect of the equation. If potential supervisors are hesitant about the idea of a new student discussing such issues with their current (or past) students, that should sound a warning regarding their possible supervision style and even their competency.

Expectations

Effective research supervision involves: direction and leadership; participation in regular meetings; making time to enable students to develop original ideas; flexibility about project choice; encouraging ideas and individuality; and promoting close interaction with other academics, including attendance at conferences and publishing before completion of the research project (Cullen, et al., cited in Orellana, et al. 2016). It is important that students know what their university or department expects of the supervisory relationship. Most institutions formalise research supervisor and student rights, responsibilities and expected duties in various policy documents—some of which are published online (see, for example, University of Reading 2018). Not only should universities have documented policies and procedures in this regard, many also regularly carry out confidential surveys of the supervisory experience. Some even have students and supervisors jointly work through and sign a memorandum of understanding to clarify their roles and expectations. Such measures help to ensure a mutually understood working relationship between student and supervisor, and provide a reference framework in case of difficulties.

It takes time to develop a working relationship where both student and supervisor are comfortable, and students are clear about what is required of them. From the start however, students need to establish a way of working with supervisors that is not only productive but also respectful of both parties and their other commitments. It is essential, for instance, to establish what will be the best form of contact between student and supervisor. The times that are most convenient for meetings should also be discussed. Agreeing on the frequency of meetings and what is expected of each prior to, during and following those meetings, is another factor that should be negotiated and agreed. Once the student and their supervisors have reached a mutual agreement about these matters, and any others that are of significance to them, it is important that these are put in writing, and that everyone they affect has a copy. This agreement may need to be renegotiated and revised if unforeseen circumstances arise. Mutual agreement is again necessary, as is the documentation of any changes.

I knew my supervisor before she supervised my PhD. I had been an academic myself in a different disciplinary area. I thought this was potentially problematic in that she might assume I was more competent than I was, and I might hesitate to acknowledge my limitations. This issue was compounded by the fact that I was an external (distance) student. This potential issue was resolved by our honesty with each other about these matters and by our organisation of regular meetings—sometimes on Skype and even, on occasions, at the airport when my supervisor was enroute to somewhere else. We were flexible about how contact was to be made, and in agreement about the need for it to be regular and productive, and that the outcomes of that contact be recorded.

Student Responsibilities

Students should be comfortable in taking responsibility, not only for selecting an appropriate topic and ensuring that their research topics and approaches fit with their own interests and ethics, but also for maintaining a productive and successful working relationship with their supervisor or supervisory team. While obviously requiring guidance from their supervisors, students need to demonstrate a capacity to undertake their research independently. A supervisor is not, for instance, an editor of a student's work, meaning that students should carefully proofread any work before presenting it, to ensure that the supervisor sees work in the best light.

Some guidelines in relation to students' responsibilities are:

- If you are not clear exactly what is required of you, make sure you ask.
- Be respectful of your supervisor.
- At the same time, however, stand up for yourself in a positive yet not aggressive manner.
- A diary is essential. Make sure you include a record of contact with your supervisors and what was agreed upon in each meeting.

In summary, students should behave towards their supervisors as they expect their supervisors to behave towards them.

The Supervisory Relationship

Like Margaret Cook's Chap. 5, which suggests that the doctoral student should be seen as an apprentice, Susanna Chamberlin proposes that the supervisory relationship works best where the research student is treated as a 'colleague in training'. In this schema, the relationship is always on a professional basis and the student and their work is held in respect. She suggests that a good supervisor:

> recognises that their role is to guide through the morass of regulations and requirements, offer suggestions and do some teaching around issues such as

methodology, research practice and process, and be sensitive to the life-cycle of the PhD process. The experience for both the supervisor and student should be one of acknowledgement of each other, recognizing the power differential but emphasizing the support at this time. (2016)

In my own case, I was very fortunate to have a supervisor who was enthusiastic, supportive and constructive in her criticism. I was definitely not a model PhD student and kept changing my approach to my topic. My supervisor suggested I start writing the biography in conventional narrative form. However, I could not resist adding a fictional diary in one chapter and, at different stages, proposing a series of essays instead of a narrative, and incorporating my own life story in the text. When I emailed my supervisor to inform her that I was no longer writing a biography and providing details of the play I intended to write instead, she kindly suggested that this was a great idea for a future project, but that, given the research I had already done, the limitations of the play format, and my own lack of experience in the genre, I might be wise to stick to the biography. Thanks to her skills in listening to my ideas, and not dismissing them, but—instead—suggesting that I make notes of them in my diary for experimentation at a later point in time, I actually completed the biography. She also encouraged me from the beginning to attend conferences and present papers, and to submit my work for publication. We worked together on an article about an issue I had raised about statistics on the publishing of biography, and I was given credit as first author.

Potential Problems in the Supervisory Relationship

Gina Wisker reports that, unfortunately, some supervisors are less than satisfactory. These supervisors "do not see students regularly, show little interest in their work, make unrealistic demands on their progress, don't put them in touch with other students or networks, and provide harsh, confusing or no feedback" (2014). Ton Dietz raises a series of potential supervision problems. Most of these lie with the supervisor who changes position, and is no longer interested in their student's work or no longer interested in the student's research area more generally; or goes off the rails and "has a major dip [and is] ill, mad, worn-out, crazy, overwhelmed by work, personal dramas" (2009). He also notes that it is a major problem for satisfactory supervision if the student falls in love with their supervisor and/or vice versa.

Chamberlin (2016) goes further to categorise nine types of problematic supervisory relationships that can occur. It is important for potential students to be aware of these issues so that they both have a mind to them when choosing a supervisor, and also know that such behaviour is unacceptable should they be subjected to it during their doctoral candidature. These are the:

1. *Clone*: where the student's research is carried out solely to support the supervisor's reputation.
2. *Cheap labour*: where the student becomes a research assistant to the supervisor's projects.
3. *Ghost supervisor*: where the supervisor is mostly absent or missing.
4. *Chum*: where the student is expected to help out the supervisor domestically.
5. *Collateral damage*: where the supervisor is a high-powered researcher and the student has to take on their teaching, marking and administrative functions at the cost of the student's own research.
6. *Combatant*: where "each piece of research is interrogated rigorously, every meeting is an inquisition and every piece of writing is edited into oblivion" (Chamberlin 2016).
7. *Creepy crawler/s*: where the supervisor (or student) develops unhealthy and unrequited sexual obsessions with the other.
8. *Captivate and Con*: where supervisor and student enter into a sexual relationship.
9. *Counsellor*: where the supervisor operates in this way, over and above their professional role.

Universities have formal complaint and grievance processes available to research students should they be unfortunate enough to encounter problems with supervisors. Students should also remember that supervisors do not work in isolation, there are often department-based Research Deans or university-level Deans of Graduate Research who can assist and often mediate concerns with supervision before these become intractable. It is vitally important in all the situations mentioned above, and in any other similarly serious situations, that students have the option to change their supervisor or entire supervisory team.

Support Outside Your Supervisors

It is important, as has been noted in a number of the chapters in this book, that students do not depend on just one person for mentorship and guidance throughout their candidatures. A supportive 'team' or group of individuals can be of great assistance during problematic supervisory relationships. Various online communities can also provide support for graduate students. Suzanne Morris analysed eight blogs which reported bullying by supervisors and found common themes of confusion, unrealistic work demands, criticism, anger and rage, inappropriate attention and abuse of power. Her analysis points to the need for staff and student training sessions to encourage appropriate behaviour and reinforce the message that bullying is unacceptable (Morris 2011). Posts on the well-known *The Thesis Whisperer* website, on topics such as "How I broke up with my supervisor" (Anon 2013), received considerable response from other graduate students and provides an archive of possible actions.

Sexual Harassment

In carrying out research on an appropriate supervisor, one of the issues students should not overlook is a supervisor's reputation for behaving (or not behaving) appropriately in that role. Students do report this, and one published example—not my own story—follows.

When I did my PhD I quickly learned that my male supervisor had a long-standing reputation as a womanizer. On an early occasion, he asked me to meet him for a coffee outside the campus. During that meeting, I felt like he wanted to appear to be out with an attractive, young female student in public. Also, the conversation was very personal. I made a point not to meet him that way again. In the last year of my PhD, he started to carry out an affair with another student fairly obviously, and at the same time completely stopped reading my work and constantly postponed supervision. (Weale and Bannock 2017)

For an international student, this issue may be complicated by cultural issues, as can be seen in another published example:

Sukhon is an international PhD student and is new to Australia. In her first few meetings with her supervisor, he kissed her on the lips. Sukhon is unsure of whether this is a part of Australian culture or inappropriate of her supervisor. (Australian Human Rights Commission (AHRC) 2017, p. 179)

Such inappropriate behaviour negatively impacts the doctoral process. Research carried out by the University of Oregon found that, "for both men and women, sexual harassment by faculty or staff predicted symptoms like anxiety, dissociation, sleep problems and sexual problems" (Rosenthal et al. 2016). If, notwithstanding preliminary research in this regard, a student experiences sexual harassment from their supervisor (or another member of the university staff), it is vitally important that everything that happens is recorded. Jen Dylan advises students clearly in this:

Write. It. All. Down. Write down times, locations and whether anyone else was present. If you have text or email correspondences, save them. Even if you do not think that you want to do anything about it, you might change your mind months down the road. There is a greater likelihood that your claim will be taken seriously if the harassment or abuse is documented in detail. Or your experience might provide crucial supporting evidence to help move someone else's claim forward. (2017)

Sexual harassment is a workplace health and safety issue. Unfortunately, the 2017 Australian Human Rights Commission report on sexual assault and sexual harassment indicated that the issue was "far too prevalent", significantly underreported, and that universities "need to do more to prevent such abuse from occurring in the first place, to build a culture of respect and to respond appropriately by supporting victims of abuse and sanctioning perpetrators" (AHRC 2017). Before lodging a complaint through university processes, it is also important to find out what independent complaint processes are available. Seeking legal advice about the most appropriate course of action is empowering.

Conclusion

When making the decision about what to research and under whose supervision, it is easy to overlook the importance of the interpersonal relationship between student and potential supervisor. Research students come to that point in the path from different directions. A student might not know where to start in deciding on a topic or finding a supervisor. At the other extreme, a student might have been invited to be involved in a particular academic's research. This chapter has outlined a different kind of 'research' for all potential research students to carry out before committing to a particular field of research and a particular supervisor. Once the appropriate person willing to be a supervisor has been chosen, this chapter has presented why it is important that a student and a supervisor clarify their respective expectations to ensure that these are mutual, reasonable and flexible.

This chapter has also provided strategies for how this might best be achieved, as well as approaches for managing problems with the supervisory relationship. It has also outlined what to do if a supervisor attempts to breach the boundaries of the relationship, or fails to provide appropriate supervision, or sacrifices a student's interest to their own. Possibly because of my own legal background, I have explored at length the potential problems that might arise in the research student/supervisor relationship, how to avoid them, and what to do if they arise. The last thing I would want to do, however, is to discourage potential students by making the process sound like a minefield. My own experience was a very positive one, as it has been for most research students I know. And, as I have indicated, without the support of my supervisor, my biography would never have been completed and, soon after I completed my PhD, published (Currie 2016).

References

Aborde, N. 2018. "How to select a winning PhD supervisor." *Postgraduate Australia.* http://www.postgradaustralia.com.au/advice/study-advice-how-to-select-a-winning-phd-supervisor.

Anon. 2013. "How I broke up with my supervisor." *The Thesis Whisperer.* http://www.thesiswhisperer.com/2013/10/02/how-i-broke-up-with-my-supervisor.

Australian Human Rights Commission (ARHC). 2017. *Change the Course: National Report on Sexual Assault and Sexual Harassment at Australian Universities.* http://www.humanrights.gov.au/our-work/sex-discrimination/publications/change-course-national-report-sexual-assault-and-sexual.

Chamberlin, S. 2016. "Ten types of PhD supervisor relationship—which is yours?" *The Conversation.* http://www.theconversation.com/ten-types-of-phd-relationships-which-is-yours-52967.

Cullen, D., M. Pearson, L. J. Saha, and R. H. Spear. 1994. Cited in Orellana et al. (2016).

Currie, S. 2016. *A Prescription for Action: The Life of Dr Janet Irwin.* Melbourne: Australian Scholarly Publishing.

Dietz, T. 2009. "PhD students/candidates and supervisors." CERES Café, Wageningen, 13 February. slideplayer.com/slide/10323926.

Dylan, J. 2017. "7 steps you can take." *Inside Higher Ed.* http://www.insidehighered.com/advice/2017/05/12/advice-graduate-students-dealing-sexual-assault-and-harassment-essay.

Holbrook, A., B. Simmons, J. Scevak, and J. Budd. 2013. "Higher degree research candidates' initial expectations in fine art." *TEXT: Journal of Writing and Writing Courses,* special issue 22: 1–16. http://www.textjournal.com.au/speciss/issue22/Holbrook_et_al.pdf.

Holbrook, A., K. Shaw, J. Scevak, S. Bourke, R. Cantwell, and J. Budd. 2014. "PhD candidate expectations: Exploring mismatch with experience." *International Journal of Doctoral Studies* 9: 329–346. http://ijds.org/Volume9/IJDSv9p329-346Holbrook0575.pdf.

Morris, S. 2011. "Doctoral students' experience of supervisory bullying." *Pertanika Journal of Social Sciences & Humanities* 19 (2). http://www.espace.library.uq.edu.au/data/UQ_247499/UQ247499_OA.pdf.

Orellana, M. L., A. Darder, A. Pérez, and J. Salinas. 2016. "Improving doctoral success by matching PhD students with supervisors." *International Journal of Doctoral Studies* 11: 87–103.

Phillips, E., and D. S. Pugh. 2005. *How to Get a PhD: A Handbook for Students and Their Supervisors.* 4th ed. Maidenhead, UK: Open University Press.

Rosenthal, M., A. Smidt, and J. J. Freyd. 2016. "Sexual harassment compromises graduate students' safety." *The Conversation,* 18 May. http://www.theconversation.com/sexual-harassment-compromises-graduate-students-safety-58694.

University of Reading. 2018. Code of Practice on Research Students. http://www.reading.ac.uk/web/files/qualitysupport/Code_of_Practice_Sept2018.pdf.

Weale, S., and C. Bannock. 2017. "We felt inferior and degraded: Reporting sexual harassment at university." *The Guardian.* http://www.theguardian.com/education/2017/Mar/05.

Wisker, G. 2014. "PhD students: What to do if you don't work well with your supervisor." *The Guardian.* https://www.theguardian.com/higher-education-network/2014/dec/29/phd-supervisor-university-research-tips-relationship-work.

15

Recovering from a (Research) Disaster Using Resilience

Carmen Gray

Introduction

Students expect the doctoral journey to be long and difficult, but are they prepared for disaster? What happens if, for example, someone else publishes an (almost) identical project, making the student's research obsolete? While many outside of the academy might not see this as a 'disaster'—after all, nobody has died—for the researcher in training this is a major catastrophe, and it can result in a feeling that there is nothing left but to throw in the towel. This is what happened to me.

History is filled with tales of resilience. A newspaper advertisement taken out by Ernest Shackleton before his fateful journey to Antarctica on the *Endurance* reads: "MEN WANTED. For hazardous journey, small wages, bitter cold, long months of complete darkness, constant danger, safe return doubtful, honour and recognition in case of success" (Watkins 1993). Shackleton certainly did not exaggerate in his newspaper

C. Gray (✉)
School of Education and the Arts, Central Queensland University,
Rockhampton, QLD, Australia
e-mail: c.gray@cqu.edu.au

© The Author(s) 2019
D. L. Brien et al. (eds.), *The Doctoral Experience*,
https://doi.org/10.1007/978-3-030-18199-4_15

advertisement: the journey *was* long and perilous, and several of the men did not survive. Similarly, there were the luckless passengers aboard Uruguayan Air Force Flight 571 that, in 1972, crashed in the Andes. Those that survived the initial impact were forced to eat their dead comrades in order to remain alive, and as if that was not enough, they then learned that the search for their missing plane had been abandoned. They had to climb to safety themselves—a death-defying scramble across a mountain range—but they did it.

Less dramatic, although perhaps more relatable, are tales of resilience in the face of persistent failure: individuals trying and trying, and trying again until their goal is achieved. Such people display what we might refer to as 'grit', and the list of those who seem to embody this characteristic is filled with familiar names: Thomas Edison, Nelson Mandela, Oprah Winfrey, J. K. Rowling, to name but a few. Why is it that some are able to rally against failure time and time again, while others cannot? What innate quality do these people possess that gives them the ability to keep trying until they eventually arrive at success? Why are some people more resilient than others, and can resilience be learned?

This chapter considers how, from childhood adversity (Comas-Diaz et al. 2017) to 'antifragility' (Taleb 2012), it is important to consider how our environment shapes our ability to cope with misfortune. For doctoral students, the journey will inevitably be different; one where some will survive and even thrive, others will want to give up. What are the strategies that might be employed, by students and supervisors, to facilitate success? Drawing on my own tale of experiencing disaster, I will describe how I learnt to be resilient in the wake of a seemingly insurmountable situation, with the hope that others can prepare ahead for any potentially unfortunate turn of events.

On Resilience

The *Oxford Dictionary* defines resilience as: "1. The capacity to recover quickly from difficulties; toughness. 2. The ability of a substance or object to spring back into shape; elasticity" (2018). According to this definition, being resilient requires meeting difficulties, or some sort of abrasion, head on. This seems obvious, for without a setback of some sort, there would be no need to recover. We all face setbacks daily, but these are usually small and manageable: it is no great feat to bounce back from a cold coffee, a broken nail or a missed bus. But it takes resilience to recover from a great loss—whether a literal loss, such as a person or something precious, or a psychological loss, such as pride or confidence.

My own experience of 'abrasion' arrived in the form of a book, published while I was preparing my Confirmation of Candidature document, which fictionalised the same historical story I had begun to write for my research degree. It was a stunning blow. Not only was it the same story, based on the same historical events (albeit in a different writer's 'voice'), but also my research was intimately tied to an examination of these events. As such, both my creative work and the underpinning exegetical research were suddenly, horrifyingly, obsolete. The research I had conducted, the characters I had created, the drafts I had written—all were no longer relevant or usable. Worry gnawed away at me: I had difficulty sleeping as my thoughts raced in circles, leaping from one idea to the next but settling on none. I was left exhausted despite my lack of productive output.

As part of the process of recovering from this disaster, over the months that followed I began to examine how and why certain people are better able to recover from setbacks such as these. Research on the topic of resilience is extensive and varied, but can be loosely categorised into two schools of thought: those who believe traumatic or difficult events cause those affected to become psychologically weaker (Engle and Black 2008); and those who believe these same situations can result in greater psychological strength, or resilience (Taleb 2012). Along with these seemingly contradictory findings, research indicates that temperament plays a role in the levels of resilience we possess. For example, Elliot and Thrash (2010) consider 'approach motivated' and 'avoidant motivated' ways of processing, which can, according to Yeager and Dweck (2012), be improved with training. There is also research that suggests engaging in creative pursuits, such as music or dance, can increase levels of resilience (Harris 2007). Nicholas Taleb explores the topic of resilience from a different perspective in his book *Antifragile: Things that Gain from Disorder* (2012). In this book, he describes a state of being "beyond resilience or robustness" (1), where systems or living organisms thrive on dysfunctional environments and, in fact, are able to evolve to benefit from them.

Researching resilience provided a welcome diversion in the months that followed my own research disaster. At first, I was plunged into a state of despair; the story's characters, scenes and structure were already developed, and I had begun writing a first draft in which the voice of the main character leapt off the page, filling me with excitement and an eagerness to continue. I had planned for the exegetical research component of my project to include a visit to the town where these historical events took place, and in preparation I had joined various online community groups and forums and had begun interacting with the other members. All of this work made it more difficult to let go of the idea when I stumbled across the recently published book, which was so similar to my own idea and planning. My first strategy was to convince myself that my own version of the story would be so different from the published work, it would not matter that they both dealt with the same historical events. I telephoned my literary agent, hoping to get her agreement and support. But she barked down the phone at me: "Give it another decade, then it won't matter what you write!"

A decade? Perhaps she thought this was encouraging, but for me it was a death-knell for the piece. If my agent—a straight talking woman with an extremely cavalier attitude—was suggesting caution, I could only assume that caution was warranted. I accepted the inevitable. I knew I needed to rethink my research topic and the creative work that was at its core, but the problem was that I found this incredibly difficult to do. In retrospect, I now know that the reason I found it so hard to accept may have been because of my temperament.

Impact of Temperament on Responses to Stress

As highlighted above, Elliot and Thrash (2010) describe two different personality types: 'approach motivated' and 'avoidant motivated'. This translates as those who may be inclined to attempt a difficult task, and those who are more likely to avoid it, or give up. There is a certain degree of inevitability in our approach to challenges, and our innate personality can dictate our levels of resilience. This sense of inevitability is further emphasised in Folkman's book, *Stress: Appraisal and Coping* (2013). Here, the author concludes that there are two ways of coping in stressful situations—"emotion focused" and "problem focused"—and that we are likely to naturally gravitate towards one or the other. Those that are problem focused usually zero in on how to resolve the issue, while those unlucky enough to be emotion focused tend to become fixated on how the problem makes them feel, and in so doing fail to solve it. There are also those who would rather avoid the problem altogether, often by pretending it does not exist. It is hardly worth mentioning that research indicates this approach is ineffective. Those in these last two categories would no doubt find it disheartening to learn that our response to stress may, in part, be inherited: that our innate level of resilience is determined by our genes (Wu et al. 2013).

In trying to avoid dealing with the issues that arose for me, I had toppled into the 'emotion focussed' trap. By dwelling on how the problem made me feel, I had avoided dealing with it. While this approach prevented me from confronting the issue directly, perhaps resulting in me feeling even worse, the problem remained unsolved. Applying the information about temperament to my own situation, I realised I needed to move beyond feeling emotional about the loss of my creative work and research topic, and instead accept the problem. This left me with two choices: to quit or defer my studies, or to continue with a new research topic. This sounds simple enough but, in reality, just thinking about either of these choices left me feeling very pressured. I was stuck.

Changing Responses to Stress

Fortunately, we have the power to change our genetic response to stressful situations. Happiness and positive emotions, even transient ones, have an impact on our ability to manage stress (Cohn et al. 2009). If we tend to get caught up in how challenging situations make us feel, we can consciously try to adopt the 'problem focussed' approach and concentrate instead on finding a solution. This might be by applying creative thinking skills to the problem, managing our time better or by obtaining psychological support. Even the belief that we can increase our resilience is actually said to increase it (Yeager and Dweck 2012). Using a problem focussed approach rather than an emotion focussed approach allows us to redirect our energy, making us more likely to resolve the issue. This can result in a powerful feedback loop: when we succeed after working hard towards a resolution, our brains experience a rush of dopamine. This chemical reward encourages us to work hard next time we face a problem, eventually leading us to habitually persist when faced with challenging situations; or, to develop what we call resilience (Bromberg-Martin et al. 2010).

Approaching my problem as clinically as possible, I considered other research topics that interested me. As a creative writer, I usually have plenty of ideas floating around, albeit in various states of development. Most of these are notes or drawings (I am also an illustrator) scrawled in hardcopy and scanned into my computer. I scrolled through them with a critical eye, examining their potential for something—anything—and discarding them one by one until I had narrowed the options down to two, very different, ideas. One of these seemed to be more fully resolved than the other, with lots of character sketches and a few dozen pages of notes. But the underpinning research that aligned with the other, less-developed work interested me more. I saw a glimmer of hope: was this the way forward?

Other Ways to Increase Resilience

Hope, self-efficacy and optimism are important qualities to foster when developing resilience, and they too can be improved with training (Avey et al. 2009). Increased 'psychological capital'—a term used to collectively describe the three qualities—is also shown to improve productivity in the workplace by reducing sick leave, staff turnover and compensation claims (Avey et al. 2009). Psychological capital, in particular hope and optimism, are vital when writing any lengthy work. Whether it is a thesis or a novel, the psychological hurdle of creating a first draft is always difficult. The sheer volume of words and the number of days, weeks and months it takes to write them can be overwhelming. It is also stressful because until that first, second or perhaps even third draft is complete, it is difficult to assess the value of the work. This makes investing such a vast amount of time a huge risk. In fact, a friend and fellow writer once likened the mindset of a fiction writer to that of a gambler, speculating during the drafting process for potentially little, or even, no return. Knowing that all the time and energy poured into a creative work may result in a piece that is, for whatever reason, unpublishable, requires a willingness to take these same sorts of risks. This is particularly true for those of us who cannot afford to spend a year or more on a project that results in little or no return, whether in the form of financial remuneration and/or career advancement.

To counter the negative thought patterns that can emerge during this process, focussing on building psychological capital in the form of self-efficacy, hope and optimism can be helpful. In his book, *How to Fail at Almost Everything and Still Win Big*, Scott Adams describes how, prior to developing his now beloved character Dilbert, he would spend time each day writing, "I, Scott Adams, will become a syndicated cartoonist" (2013). This positive affirmation may not have been directly responsible for his successes, but he claims it was one of the habits that helped him remain optimistic, despite the numerous rejections and criticisms he received, until he achieved his goal.

I knew that starting my research again would require a positive mindset. Not only did I need to approach my studies feeling confident I could complete the work in the (now diminished) time remaining, I also needed to believe the new research topic was important and interesting enough for me to invest the necessary time and energy into it. At first, it was difficult for me not to focus on the seemingly insurmountable amount to work I needed to do, but after reading through my notes and immersing myself in the characters and their various situations, I began to feel genuinely interested and excited again. Suddenly I really wanted to write this new creative work and conduct the underpinning research. Although on a larger scale I realised the process of working through the problem was similar to the process I applied to many of the creative problems encountered daily in my work, I needed to see this sudden change of plan as a challenge, and examine it from a different point of view.

Applying Creative Thinking to Challenges

Edward de Bono's classic book, *Six Thinking Hats* (1985), outlines a method of applying creative thinking techniques to problem solving. In this work, de Bono cites the benefits of examining a problem in various ways—ways that perhaps we would not normally consider—to eventually arrive at a solution. He uses the analogy of wearing a different hat to symbolise the different perspectives from which to view a problem. This approach once again directs our attention away from thinking emotionally, and towards finding a solution, just as I had done when forcing myself out of my 'emotion focussed' approach and towards a 'problem focussed' way of tackling my challenge. This required much effort, and it made me wonder: was there a way to make it easier to be resilient? Could robustness become my default state, instead of one that could only be reached through considerable effort?

Benefiting from Stress

In his book *Antifragile: Things that Gain from Disorder*, Nassim Taleb (2012) describes the ability to withstand stressors as being 'antifragile', which he argues is *beyond* resilience or robustness. It is easy to determine if something is antifragile according to his simple test: if something becomes stronger when exposed to random events and shocks, it is antifragile; if it becomes weaker, it is fragile. Over time, things that are antifragile become more robust due to the adaptations caused by these stressors. Examples include bacteria that have been exposed to antibiotics; the highly evolved human brain; and certain financial and political systems. It stands to reason, then, that humans also require a certain amount of stress to become resilient (Taleb 2012).

In seeming contrast to these findings, there is a commonly held belief that a dysfunctional, stressful childhood is more likely to result in a dysfunctional, stressful adulthood. In other words, those people who suffer stressors during their formative years are *less* functional than their more sheltered counterparts, because they are more fragile. This hypothesis has been verified by multiple studies, each examining the impact of stressful events on the developing individual (for example, Engle and Black 2008; Kwong and Hayes 2017). These studies reveal that (certain) stressors weaken us and cause us to be less able to manage challenges, making us less resilient. This raises the question: how can we have, on the one hand, organisms and systems that become more robust when exposed to shocks; and on the other hand, multiple studies pointing to the opposite when applied to human beings?

A closer examination of such studies reveals that those who exhibited lower coping abilities after exposure to stressors in childhood had faced what we might call 'catastrophic stressors' early in life, for example grinding poverty, abuse or abandonment. In contrast, systems classified as anti-fragile—those that become stronger when stressed—faced smaller stressors across a longer timeframe. Bacteria do not transform to become resistant to antibiotics; rather, a resilient bacterium survives longer than the bacteria around it, and is able to reproduce while the more suscepti-ble bacteria cannot. The human brain has evolved due to stressors because, as they encountered difficult situations, some humans faced, and learned from the experience. In other words, they developed resilience towards those particular stressors, giving them an advantage over less resilient or experienced people, and also the chance to pass on these traits to the next generation. From this, it is logical to conclude that resilience is built over time, by stressors that are not overwhelming. Then, as resilience increases, more challenging stressors can be managed. In short, if we want to be antifragile we must develop in an environment that conditions us to minor stressors before hitting us with a catastrophic, life-altering disaster.

So how do these ideas help us to face a challenge that is, for us person-ally, immense? What if we did not experience a childhood in which chal-lenges of exactly the right difficulty were encountered at exactly the right time? What if we had a childhood that was *too* challenging, causing us to become *less* resilient? Resilient or not, our behaviour—our ability to cope with stressors—has been learned. An athlete does not spend their life on the couch only to run forty-two kilometres on marathon day. Likewise, we cannot expect a huge challenge not to derail us if we have no experi-ence in managing smaller challenges. Assuming we have not yet built up the resilience levels necessary to cope with a major problem, we can instead learn the steps that a resilient person takes when faced with a great challenge and apply that process to our own situation.

According to the American Psychological Association (Comas-Diaz et al. 2017), dealing with disasters—research or otherwise—can be assisted by:

- Letting yourself experience strong emotions, and also recognising the times when you may need to avoid experiencing them in order to continue functioning.
- Stepping forward and taking action to deal with your problems and meet the demands of daily living, and also by stepping back to rest and re-energise yourself.
- Spending time with loved ones to gain support and encouragement, and also nurturing yourself.
- Relying on others, and also relying on yourself.

Increasing resilience does not need to be especially difficult or complicated. According to Harris (2007), even something as simple and accessible as listening to music can have a marked effect on resilience levels. The same goes for dance and other forms of creative exercise too, as illustrated by Harris's research into its effects on young men who survived a war into which they had been recruited as child soldiers. Participants reported a drop in their symptoms of "anxiety, depression, intrusive recollection, elevated arousal and aggression" after gatherings in which they performed traditional dancing and drumming (Harris 2007).

Conclusion

After Shackleton's ship, the *Endurance*, became trapped in pack ice miles from its destination, the crew were forced to abandon her. They camped on the ice for two months until it too broke up, then they braved the wild Atlantic Ocean in lifeboats. After five days, they landed on an inhospitable island from which rescue was unlikely. Undaunted, Shackleton selected several of his crew and together they set out on a seemingly suicidal voyage—seven hundred and twenty nautical miles—to a whaling station. After miraculously surviving for several weeks thanks to their nautical skills, they landed safely only to discover that the beach where they had washed up was deserted. The whaling station was over fifty kilometres away, on the other side of a mountain range. After a brief respite, Shackleton and his men set off once more, taking with them only a length of rope and an axe. After climbing for two days and a night, they arrived at the station where Shackleton organised for ships to return and rescue the remainder of his men. This incredible journey is one of the most noteworthy examples of resilience ever documented. As one of Shackleton's acquaintances, Sir Raymond Priestley, once famously stated, "Scott for scientific method, Amundsen for speed and efficiency, but when disaster strikes and all hope is gone, get down on your knees and pray for Shackleton" (quoted in Brennan 2003, p. 1079).

While I conducted this research to help me overcome my own disaster, I came to understand that being resilient was a mental game and it was one that I could not lose—provided I kept getting up—no matter how many times fate knocked me down. 'Just keep going' became my mantra, and it worked: most of the first draft of my new creative work is complete, and my work on the exegetical research is proceeding well. By thinking longer and harder about the best topic to study, I arrived at a solution that was, in many ways, better than my original idea. The biggest challenge of the whole process was the struggle to keep going; to find hope when the situation seemed hopeless; to face the problem and actively search for a solution. In other words, to be resilient, just like Shackleton.

References

Adams, S. 2013. *How to Fail at Almost Everything and Still Win Big*. New York, NY: Penguin.

Avey, J. B., F. Luthans, and S. M. Jensen. 2009. "Psychological capital: A positive resource for combating employee stress and turnover." *Human Resource Management* 48 (5): 677–693. https://doi.org/10.1002/hrm.20294.

Brennan, M. G. 2003. "Shackleton, Ernest (1874–1992)." In *Literature of Travel and Exploration: An Encyclopedia, vol. 3 R to Z*, 1078–1079. New York and London: Fitzroy Dearborn.

Bromberg-Martin, E. S., M. Matsumoto, and O. Hikosaka. 2010. "Dopamine in motivational control: Rewarding, aversive, and alerting." *Neuron* 68 (5): 815–834. https://doi.org/10.1016/j.neuron.2010.11.022.

Cohn, M. A., B. L. Fredrickson, S. L. Brown, J. A. Mikels, and A. M. Conway. 2009. "Happiness unpacked: Positive emotions increase life satisfaction by building resilience." *Emotion* 9 (3): 361–368. https://doi.org/10.1037/a0015952.

Comas-Diaz, L., S. S. Luthar, S. R. Maddi, H. K. O'Neill, K. W. Saakvitne, and R. G. Tedeschi. 2017. "The road to resilience." *American Psychological Association (APA)*, brochure. http://www.apa.org/helpcenter/road-resilience.aspx.

De Bono, E. 1985. *Six Thinking Hats*. Boston: Little, Brown.

Elliot, A. J., and T. M. Thrash. 2010. "Approach and avoidance temperament as basic dimensions of personality." *Journal of Personality* 78 (3): 865–906. https://doi.org/10.1111/j.1467-6494.2010.00636.x.

Engle, P. L., and M. M. Black. 2008. "The effect of poverty on child development and educational outcomes." *Annals of the New York Academy of Sciences* 1136 (1): 243–256. https://doi.org/10.1196/annals.1425.023.

Folkman, S. 2013. "Stress: Appraisal and coping." In *Encyclopedia of Behavioral Medicine*, edited by M. D. Gellman and J. R. Turner. New York, NY: Springer.

Harris, D. A. 2007. "Dance/movement therapy approaches to fostering resilience and recovery among African adolescent torture survivors." *Torture* 17 (2): 134–155.

Kwong, T., and D. Hayes. 2017. "Adverse family experiences and flourishing amongst children ages 6–17 years: 2011/12 National Survey of Children's Health." *Child Abuse & Neglect* 70: 240.

Oxford Dictionary [online]. 2018. https://en.oxforddictionaries.com/definition/resilience.

Taleb, N. N. 2012. *Antifragile: Things That Gain From Disorder*. New York: Random House.

Watkins, J. 1993. *The 100 Greatest Advertisements 1852–1958: Who Wrote Them and What They Did*. New York: Dover Publications.

Wu, G., A. Feder, H. Cohen, J. Kim, S. Calderon, D. Charney, and A. Mathé. 2013. "Understanding resilience." *Frontiers in Behavioral Neuroscience* 7 (10). https://doi.org/10.3389/fnbeh.2013.00010.

Yeager, D. S., and C. S. Dweck. 2012. "Mindsets that promote resilience: When students believe that personal characteristics can be developed." *Educational Psychologist* 47 (4): 302–314. https://doi.org/10.1080/00461520.2012.722805.

Part V

Completing the Doctoral Journey: Introduction to Part

Donna Lee Brien, Craig Batty, Elizabeth Ellison, and Alison Owens

While undertaking the considerable task of contemplating, beginning and completing a doctoral program, doctoral students will constantly be challenged. They must build advanced thinking skills, subject matter expertise and communication competencies. In this process, they will constantly and continually, over many years, confront a myriad of influences that are direct and indirect, positive and negative. This part of this volume asserts that the process will necessarily engender significant

D. L. Brien (✉) • E. Ellison
Noosaville, QLD, Australia
e-mail: d.brien@cqu.edu.au; l.ellison@cqu.edu.au

C. Batty
Sydney, NSW, Australia
e-mail: Craig.Batty@uts.edu.au

A. Owens
North Sydney, NSW, Australia
e-mail: Alison.Owens@acu.edu.au

change in a student, and that this will simultaneously incite creativity. This part of the book summarises some of the significant transformations that are encountered during a research project, and discusses the effects of struggling with shadows and restructuring the self through cognitive alteration. The chapters provide vital insights for other students to assist their encounters with change and changing, and alert them to some of the expectations on this creative research journey.

In Chap. 16, Gail Pittaway works from the idea that the prospect of meeting one major deadline, and writing the thesis that is necessary for doctoral completion, can be a problematic hurdle for many students. Her proposed solution is to break the writing of the thesis into a series of deadlines and to then find opportunities to publish work-in-progress as the work proceeds. This, Pittaway suggests, can become an empowering and rewarding aspect of the research journey, which can also serve to diffuse feelings of isolation that many students report feeling as, via this process, the student makes connections with others, forms communities of practice (as described by Colleen Ryan in Chap. 7), and gains confidence with the various aspects of their long and challenging project. Pittaway also comments on the personal—as well as scholarly and professional—benefits of taking up various opportunities for the wider dissemination of thesis work-in-progress, with reference to supportive publications, styles of public presentations, and participation in postgraduate seminars, external conferences and suitable public events such as cultural festivals and events.

Bernadette Ryan discusses the thinking skills she developed that assisted her doctoral project in terms of understanding what was needed in order to conduct systematic and rigorous research throughout her PhD study. Different modes of thinking are described as basic tools for achieving the required rigour of research and, therefore, producing a study that contains both quality knowledge with the high degree of excellence required to attain this capstone degree. Outlining the modes of objective, subjective, reflective and reflexive thinking she used, Ryan not only came up with creative solutions to overcome major obstacles in her fieldwork, but describes how these continue to support her decision-making in her life after the study was complete and the degree awarded.

Charmaine O'Brien brings the volume to a close by discussing how the doctoral journey necessarily engenders change. In this, the significant developments and alterations in cognitive and creative capabilities do not transpire in isolation; restructuring one's thinking also shifts emotional and social aspects of meaning making. Indeed, the doctoral journey can stimulate a profound shift in understanding of self, during which the students' identity is often transformed. By shifting focus to the post-doctoral individual, O'Brien discusses how completed PhD students might understand their journey as transformative; recognise their possibilities as a creative individual; and consider the advantages of their distinctive capacities for thriving in a state that can be described as 'liquid modernity'.

Of course, the end of the doctoral journey can signal different things for different students. For some, it will be another step in their already established career; for others, it might mark the beginning of their quest for academic employment. Regardless, in the current era that is prioritising research impact and the applied nature of research to communities and sectors outside of the university setting, it is important for students to find ways of making their research meaningful. Students, like their supervisors, would be remiss to ignore the trend towards linking research impact to employability, workload allocation, and potential promotion. And while peer-reviewed academic publications remain the gold standard, there are other non-traditional methods for students to engage with sources outside of academia.

Most importantly, perhaps, is understanding how it can be really rewarding to recognise that the completed doctoral research has a real impact. Seeing that work—that has been so consuming for so long—resonate with others is another aspect of life post-doctorate that can assist in the transformation from student to researcher. Engaging with mainstream or independent media can be a useful way of sharing student stories; and students can also use social media to tell part of their own journey as they go. After all, some of the most supportive research networks for doctoral students and early career researchers can be found online in blogs (see, for instance, *The Thesis Whisperer*, a popular blog run by Australian academic Inger Mewburn) or through platform hashtags like #phdchat. While there still remains some stigma about social media being unnecessary or trivial because it does not contribute to scholarly citations, it might generate collaborations, invitations and interest in a student's research. It is worth noting that some of the authors in this book have already applied their doctoral research to opportunities beyond academia, for example, running workshops teaching creative writing in the wider community or freelance coaching. Of course, this speaks to the necessity for doctoral students to identify a strong set of transferrable and generic capabilities (such as in professional communication and career self-management, see Bridgstock 2016) that are not linked purely to their areas of expertise, considering the limited employment opportunities in academic positions alone. Of course, finally, all the relationships and networks that have been built during the doctoral journey—and discussed in various chapters of this book—can also be drawn upon to assist in this reorientation. The personal and interpersonal knowledge, skills and strengths that have also been developed during the doctorate will also be of considerable use at this next stage of the scholarly journey.

References

Bridgstock, R. 2016. "The university and the knowledge network: A new educational model for twenty-first century learning and employability." In *Graduate Employability in Context: Theory, Research and Debate*, edited by M. Tomlinson and L. Holmes, 339–358. London: Palgrave Macmillan.

Mewburn, I. *The Thesis Whisperer*. https://thesiswhisperer.com.

16

Meeting Milestones and Refining, Presenting and Publishing Doctoral Work

Gail Pittaway

Introduction

While there are now opportunities to complete research degrees by publication across a wide range of tertiary institutions, the prospect of one major deadline—the completion of the thesis—is usually enough for most students to manage. However, the concept of breaking the thesis into a series of deadlines and finding opportunities to publish work in progress can be an empowering and rewarding aspect of the doctoral journey. This can also break the tendency for research students to work in isolation, as the student makes connections with others, forming communities of practice, and gains confidence with the various aspects of their long and challenging project. Furthermore, by developing confidence in sharing ideas, seeking peer review feedback and editorial advice from a wider range of readers as some of these sections are submitted for publication, the writing

G. Pittaway (✉)
School of Media Arts, Waikato Institute of Technology (Wintec),
Hamilton, New Zealand
e-mail: Gail.Pittaway@wintec.ac.nz

© The Author(s) 2019
D. L. Brien et al. (eds.), *The Doctoral Experience*,
https://doi.org/10.1007/978-3-030-18199-4_16

of the thesis is encouraged and energised. In this chapter, such opportunities for the wider dissemination of thesis work-in-progress will be explored, with reference to locating and working with supportive publications, styles of public presentations, and participation in postgraduate seminars, external conferences and suitable public events such as cultural festivals.

In this chapter I draw attention to the benefits of extending the circle of connection beyond the immediate research area or discipline to the wider realm of academic life, as observed through publication, peer review and dissemination of ideas, and through such public events as conferences, symposia and conventions. In addition, I promote students' engagement with cultural and related events in the wider community, both as ways of providing opportunities to deepen their own awareness of the thesis, and to find ways to explain and share with others from outside the academy. The advantages of stepping out beyond the limits of the known world are great, if the place to land is well chosen and receptive to the work of emerging researchers.

Rather than consider these as excursions away from the linear thread of the original thesis, it is better to think of them as stopovers on the doctoral journey, the effects of which can enhance students' awareness of the literature in the field, deepen and enhance their writing skills and style, and create a stronger sense of direction in their own thinking and arguments. As Boyer (1990) points out, there are several more aspects to the nature of academic research beyond the pursuit of an original concept: the scholarship of discovery. There is also the scholarship of integration, the scholarship of application and the scholarship of teaching. This chapter stresses the value of these other forms of scholarship for the doctoral student.

The Scholarship of Integration

My doctorate began with a conference. I had already taught creative writing at secondary and tertiary levels for nearly two decades when I was challenged by the theme of an upcoming writing conference organised by The Tertiary Writing Network in New Zealand. This was themed as 'The Future of Writing'. It is always my inclination to consider the past as influencing the future. I began reflecting on what kinds of writing had survived through centuries, even millennia, and came up with shop signs, wax or clay tablets as coins, and domestic lists or documents, all reaching back into the ancient world and preceding storytelling—especially in the form of rudimentary book-keeping and household writing, and recipes. The latter interested me the most and, by tracing the history of food writing from its earliest occurrences, I began a chain of research that has resulted in my undertaking a PhD in the field of creative nonfiction, writing a food memoir and discussing examples of this emerging genre in contemporary literature, while acknowledging the historical precedents from which this arose.

Participating in conferences and symposia is particularly beneficial for doctoral students, as these academic events provide opportunities for students to extend their networks, reflect on theories, or simply widen the scope of their literature reviews, even if they do not present a paper. Conferences tend to be larger affairs than symposia in terms of the numbers of attendees, and may have several sessions of speakers running concurrently. There are several ways that students can present or discuss work at such events without adding to their scholarship burden by writing a full new piece of research. They can form panels with others in similar areas of investigation or research to present sections of their theses, for instance. Many larger conferences also invite poster presentations, in which a research idea is distilled into a visual form and the student explains the poster in a shorter presentation to a small audience, or even simply explains it as people walk by. Students can interview experts, or even form panels with those from completely contrasting discipline areas for greater depth of exploration of ideas.

Symposia are usually one- or two-day events in which all attendees have an interest in one theme, which could be as varied as, for instance, food, palliative care, volcanoes or town planning. Attendees often come from very diverse discipline areas, and such meetings can include scholars and experts as diverse as archaeologists, scientists, poets and historians. The effect of this variety on both experts and emerging experts is to broaden the range and extent of each person's research and this can lead to future cross-disciplinary collaborations.

The informal and social aspects of both these types of organised gatherings, whether conferences or symposia—the book launches, coffee breaks, dinners and field trips—are where significant networking also occurs and where ideas can be tested in a conversational mode. The experience of attending such events enhances the student's academic range and fosters the development of ideas and theories through explication and discussion.

The selection of such events needs to be judicious and, here, the wider community of colleagues, supervisors or post-graduate groups can recommend safe and supportive events for students to attend and gain confidence. Some conferences even have specific sessions designed for postgraduate researchers, while seminars and even symposia and conferences designed specifically for postgraduate researchers are becoming increasingly common. The advantages of taking up such opportunities are immense, for the stimulation they provide to the researcher and the boost to the energy and enthusiasm they bring. While registration costs to attend can be prohibitive, let alone those of travel and accommodation, conference convenors can be approached to request one-day or half-day rates, student discounts and even billeting support.

The Scholarship of Application

In addition to the opportunities that conferences, symposia and more informal university-based gatherings offer to present work-in-progress, students will also benefit from writing up sections of their work to disseminate in published form. Getting published in both academic and non-academic forums is another tactic to enhance the quality of any thesis, as well as developing a portfolio of publications, which are essential for any research graduate who wishes to make a career in academia. Journal articles and papers in published conference proceedings usually employ double blind review processes, where neither the author nor the reviewer knows the other's identity. Anonymity gives the student a chance to focus upon an unknown audience and on the need for clarity of explication of a section of their research.

Whether taken from the literature review, methodological or theoretical challenges, case studies, interviews or findings section of the thesis, or representing entire polished thesis chapters, what the student submits for publication must be clear and follow a strong line of argument. Although taken from the thesis, the piece must stand alone and not summarise a larger part of the thesis. The reviewer's role is effectively an editorial function. Firstly, they advise the publication of the quality of the work reviewed and offer advice on whether to publish, or not. Secondly, they give direction to the author regarding suggestions for improvements that are appropriate to the nature of the publication and its remit. Providing an ancillary to the judgement of the student's supervisors, these anonymous reviews are useful indicators of progress on the scholarly path. A reviewer is usually an academic with a publication history or, if a newcomer to this role (which is another valuable activity for the doctoral student as considering the writing of others in the field can provide valuable models for how—and how not—to write) is likely to be given clear guidelines from the publication's editor, regarding what to comment on.

These reviewers are also known as 'peer reviewers' and, for the highest quality assurance, there are often at least two peer reviewers in addition to the editor and the publisher's copy editors. The collective work of writers and readers in this practice is what Thomson and Kamler call a "discourse community" (2013, p. 17). This book is, in fact, written by such a group. Each chapter was shared with at least two peers and the editors, to refine the writing and define each topic more accurately. The volume arose out of a two-day symposium of doctoral students; a true discourse community of peers.

Reviewers can call for improvements on every aspect of the work from the content to its presentation. In terms of the content, it must be situated in the field, correct, backed up by evidence and well argued. The reviewer will also want to be engaged with the article, and so the writing style and how the argument is expressed are important factors. No matter the topic, genre or publication platform, considering the reader is paramount and the content should be structured clearly rather than lose its way in detail and contradiction. Matters of presentation include attention to spelling, grammar, punctuation, agreement between singular and plural components, sentence and paragraph structure and how the work follows the publication's style in terms of layout, referencing, use of subtitles, capitalisation and so forth. An assiduous peer reviewer may even indicate specific minor errors in the piece if they believe it has sufficient merit to be recommended for publication. A reviewer, however, rather like a thesis examiner, is likely to be distracted and even annoyed by technical errors, so doctoral students, like all would-be published authors, should assiduously follow any guidelines set for publication.

Although critical feedback is often confronting to receive, as Golding states in an article for research students, "Use any feedback to figure out how to make your writing more reader-friendly. This is the gift of feedback—it gives you ways to improve your writing, and helps you to write like a reader" (2017, p. 52).

During my candidature, I have had several articles published which have added to my understanding of food writing as culturally significant. My own experience of receiving feedback from peer reviewers has been invaluable. There is always a little trepidation as I see a message from the editor with my feedback attached, as I dread the prospect of having to rewrite something I have spent a long time creating. However, invariably, even with quite stringent—and even the most strident—feedback, the effect is to make my writing more effective, to clarify my thinking and, in my case, to assist with what is my main failing as an academic writer, to create a stronger structure for my argument, leading to a more fulsome conclusion.

James Arvanitakis encourages students to think of themselves as 'citizen scholars' (2017), to extend their role beyond the thesis and the solely academic and investigate opportunities to write in popular forms such as blogs, online forums, social media such as Facebook and Twitter, and even in YouTube and Instagram postings. The less restrained style of such musings can generate discussion, empathy and above all, energy for the writer, when, in such long-term projects, enthusiasm can wane. Arvanitakis also encourages doctoral students to participate in radio, newspaper and television interviews and other discussions as means to promote their work to the public, and find new ways to express their ideas—the latter suggestion which will be expanded in the next section. All of these opportunities should not be seen as unwelcome diversions or distractions from the main work of the thesis, but as ways to ultimately enhance the experience.

The Scholarship of Teaching

Cultural or community events such as festivals, expositions or similar public occasions may seem distant from scholarship but, increasingly, the worlds of public information and entertainment, industry and culture intersect with the work of the academy. A century ago, it would have been unheard of to take university studies in tourism, marketing and communication, let alone media studies, but today, so-called 'town and gown' are partners, and universities and tertiary providers are no longer remote institutions like the seminaries they derive from, which kept their scholars separate from the outside world. This is strongly evident in the sciences, where products are developed and tested, and also in architecture and engineering, business, communication and the creative arts where 'live' clients and situations are analysed and problems solved.

As Margaret Cook points out in Chap. 5, the doctoral student is an apprentice in the academic world. In the Middle Ages, an apprentice was called a 'journeyman' (from the French word *journée*, meaning 'day') a name given to qualified or trained tradesmen who were only employed by the day and worked as itinerant labourers, developing their skills before establishing themselves as independent tradespeople (Emms 2005). Ignoring the gender bias of the Middle Ages' nomenclature, this connection between apprenticeship and the community can be further explored in terms of contemporary scholarship. The various trades belonged to guilds (effectively communities of practice) that participated, and even competed, in annual religious or civic festivals, such as Easter, May Day, Christmas pageants and fairs all across Europe (Styan 1996, pp. 23–27). Modern Christmas pantomimes and Santa parades, with gaudy floats, crossdressing and spectacle, are the last vestiges of this tradition when, in the past, guild members would build sets, perform dances and songs and wear ornate and symbolic costumes. Shakespeare's play, *A Midsummer Night's Dream*, reflects this tradition, when a group of tradesmen compete with other local groups to perform an entertainment for the wedding of King Theseus and Queen Hippolyta (Act V Sc. 1, ll. 45ff.).

While it is unlikely that contemporary scholars will be building floats or stitching sequins onto costumes for anything other than diversion and entertainment, there are many other activities that serve to link the academy with the community, and in which the student can participate and benefit. Science fairs, arts festivals, home shows, sporting events, expositions and open days are all occasions wherein doctoral students can demonstrate, discuss and develop the ideas inherent in their theses. By having to explain concepts to non-specialists, ideas can crystalise, phrasing be refined, the order of the argument and the logic of methodology tested. In explaining the thesis to others, the student is exploring the knowledge to greater levels of understanding for both parties; this can be classed as the "alchemy of learning" (Nashashibi 2004, p. 41).

My friend Cate's thesis is in the discipline of education and she is testing theories of educational leadership, using a small focus group of an intermediate school classroom and their teacher. The New Zealand school she has selected is linked to the local university's School of Education and training college for teachers, so cooperation between scholars and classroom are as much a part of the school life as are the student teachers learning their craft through application. Cate's methodology is to work with the classroom teacher to develop classroom practices and activities based on the ideas of three theorists of leadership in education, observe these in action, and describe, then analyse the results. She maintains a journal of the process, films the activities in action and also interviews the children and teacher for their feedback.

The school administration hosts several open nights for current and prospective families and the wider community, and for one, Cate was invited along with a few of the other trainee teachers, to present an account of their activities and projects to this new audience. Cate decided to make a large poster along one wall of the classroom, dividing it into three sections: one column for the three theorists and their theories of educational leadership; one for some of the ideas and activities which Cate and the teacher developed to reflect these theories; and one final column for responses from the students and teacher, with photographs and student work displayed.

Cate reported, "It was so helpful for me to explain my thesis to the parents and wider community. I feel that my participants understand what I'm doing quite well, but it was important to talk about the educational theory to non-academics and people who are not closely involved in my research. By sharing my ideas and methods with them I felt I learnt even more about the concepts themselves and it was so inspiring to be able to share the classroom work that my thesis had generated".

Conclusion

Across a wide range of tertiary institutions, the prospect of one major deadline—completion—is usually enough for most students to manage. However, breaking the thesis into a series of deadlines and finding opportunities to publish work in progress (as opposed to the doctorate by publication), can be an empowering and rewarding part of the research journey. This can also disrupt research students' tendency towards isolation, as the student makes connections with others, forming communities of practice, and gains confidence with the various aspects of this long and challenging project.

Furthermore, by developing confidence in sharing ideas, and seeking peer review feedback and editorial advice from a wider range of readers as some of these sections are submitted for publication, the writing of the thesis can be encouraged and energised. In addition to the scholarship of discovery, which is the most widely held expectation of postgraduate research, Boyer's three additional forms of scholarship—the scholarship of integration, the scholarship of application and the scholarship of teaching—can also be a useful part of the doctoral journey, enriching the work, life and thinking of the student. Lastly, while the writing of the thesis will be enhanced, building up connections from within and outside the academy will also lay the foundations for future careers and for life once the doctorate is completed.

References

Arvanitakis, J. 2017. "How to survive a PhD: 22 tips from the Dean of Graduate Studies." Blog website. http://www.jamesarvanitakis.net/how-to-survive-a-phd-22-tips-from-the-dean-of-graduate-studies/?portfolioCats=5%2C14%2C13%2C15%2C16%2C18.

Boyer, E. L. 1990. *Scholarship Reconsidered*. San Francisco, CA: Jossey-Bass.

Emms, S. M. 2005. "The modern journeyman: Influences and controls of apprentice-style learning in culinary education." https://aut.researchgateway. ac.nz/bitstream/handle/10292/85/EmmsS.pdf

Golding, C. 2017. "Advice for writing a thesis (based on what examiners do)." *Open Review of Educational Research* 4 (1): 46–60.

Nashashibi, P. 2004. *The Alchemy of Learning: Impact and Progression in Adult Learning*. Shaftesbury, Dorset, UK: Learning and Skills Development Agency, Blackmore Ltd.

Styan, J. L. 1996. *The English Stage: A History of Drama and Performance*. Cambridge, UK: Cambridge University Press.

Thomson, P., and B. Kamler. 2013. *Writing for Peer Reviewed Journals*. London: Routledge.

17

Transforming from Naïve Research Student to Confident Critical Thinker

Bernadette Ryan

Introduction

Universities now encourage research students to develop a set of skills beyond the academic—communication abilities, time management skills and the ability to work under pressure. Academic demands add pressure for a student to demonstrate an understanding of, and compliance with, the ways of working in, their field of study. However, it is also imperative to become a competent critical thinker—that is, to raise a level of mindfulness to a higher level in terms of making judgements about complex situations. The research process requires a conscious examination of a large quantity of material, including the new or empirical data related to the research topic. Doctoral study, therefore, necessitates a dual intellectual challenge for research students. On a personal level, they need to open their mindful capacity to receive, absorb and hold information, form opinions, produce discussions, and create bountiful and clear writing. In relation to

B. Ryan (✉)
Blayney, NSW, Australia
e-mail: bernadette.ryan@cqumail.com

© The Author(s) 2019
D. L. Brien et al. (eds.), *The Doctoral Experience*,
https://doi.org/10.1007/978-3-030-18199-4_17

197

institutional expectations, students need to refine academic ways of thinking and making judgements, employing rigour in how they portray information, produce interpretations and make critical appraisals of that material, in order to produce an accomplished, competent and transparent study. Ultimately, beyond the thesis, the process of completing a research degree produces an intellectual.

Reflecting on my own research degree experience, in this chapter I discuss what I believe was my most significant post-doctoral transformation—how completing my doctoral degree changed the way I know, and think about, the world. The chapter charts my journey of objective and subjective thinking, revealing how these modes of thinking are tools for providing a student with awareness about how they know what they know, and simultaneously for achieving a high level of rigour in their research. It is by way of understanding the kinds of work that these modes of thinking do that gives shape to the idea of 'systematic' rigour.

Reflective and reflexive thinking skills are also important, as they are called on to function simultaneously with objective and subjective thinking, and make a considerable contribution to the development of intellectual abilities. Reflection, a concept developed by American philosopher John Dewey (1933), assists a student's thought processes for making appropriate decisions in planning and processing the internal and external dimensions of their study. Modes of how reflectivity is utilised during the research process are outlined in this chapter. Pierre Bourdieu's (2008) reflexive sociology is introduced in the second part of this chapter to describe modes of thinking that can assist a student while conducting a study in the social sciences. As social science is the study of human behaviour, the discussion outlines modes of thinking for reflexively connecting the many different levels of human behaviour involved in producing PhD projects across a range of disciplines. It summarises *how* social structures occur, and *why* they change. Importantly, reflexive sociology describes the social conditions under which a student will call on their capacity for adaptation in order to turn to creativity and innovation as a means for overcoming challenges, and successfully completing a quality program of study.

Doctoral Thinking

It is not easy to quickly grasp the meaning of the term 'new knowledge'. However, in their thesis, a doctoral student will be required to not only produce new knowledge, but also demonstrate how they have produced it. The theories and methods used for 'proving' and validating such knowledge statements are called epistemologies (epistemology in the field of philosophy). Epistemologies are used in the research process for proving 'how you know what you know'. They are ways of thinking that are used for 'knowing' whether something is true or false. Comprehension of these theories can be difficult, as a research student is not necessarily going to be an expert in such philosophical thinking. Nonetheless, the thinking required to complete a PhD—a Doctor of *Philosophy*—needs to be complex, critical and reflexive. As they decipher their appropriate future doctoral path, amidst layers of intersecting concerns, doctoral students will, as I demonstrate below, be participating in advanced intellectual thinking. When they become a research student they will be required, however, by the demands of producing rigorous research, to practice a higher level of intellectual thinking. This is essential for producing the required new knowledge.

When deciding to enrol in my PhD, I was already thinking subjectively and objectively about both the personal and institutional factors that would affect my candidature. For example: full-time or part-time study? Which university would best support my focus area? How would I go about refining a study idea? What possibilities were there concerning supervisors, or what if that relationship became fraught? My evaluation and resolution of these questions more or less fell onto the objective side of my thinking—in so far as my consideration necessitated dealing with institutional requirements, which largely relied on the objective advice of established academics and/or PhD administrators. My private consideration during this planning stage, however, largely involved subjective thinking in terms of evaluating the suitability of a particular program to my own personal preferences and dislikes, and taking into consideration aspects such as my family, friends and health, as well as my ability to travel, the time I had available, where I wanted to study, and any potential economic support.

In these early stages, intellectual thinking—that is, both objective and subjective thinking—was used for processing the relevant information. For example, while consciously assessing the requirements of a doctoral program, it was necessary to 'stand back' mentally to conceptualise which choices would be the most suitable for my imagined future study. In this process, using reflective thinking skills, those which we commonly use for making plans for future actions, I—like other prospective students—questioned my reasoning and logic. I questioned why I thought a particular set of choices for my future doctorate was better suited to me than others. While doing this, I found that I was thoughtfully re-inspecting the foundations upon which I grounded my opinions that any particular set of ideas was the most suitable.

Assessing Knowledge Claims

Across each and every phase of a research project, objective thinking is essential for understanding and processing the grounds for making knowledge claims (Usher 1996). Objective thinking is necessary for demonstrating in a dissertation how one knows the knowledge claimed is true or false; that is, valid. A doctoral student will also be required to explain what steps were taken to verify their knowledge claims are valid, as Robin Usher (1996) affirms, to verify that the claims are "based on observation and measurement, systematically and methodically carried out" (p. 12). Important aspects of producing valid statements are that "the researcher was 'objective', that is, that he or she was unbiased, value neutral and took care to ensure that personal considerations did not intrude into the research process" (Usher 1996, p. 12).

The cognitive tasks are plentiful for maintaining a systematic and consistent mindfulness regarding objective and subjective concerns while processing all tasks for a study. Usher describes that this "is necessary in order to become an 'ideal universal knower', interchangeable with all other researchers" (Usher 1996, p. 12). While this is an essential aspect of undertaking research, it can be taken for granted while performing research procedures. However, a student will become aware of this aspect of their thinking as it becomes necessary to produce valid statements in their dissertation. Despite this, the philosophical literature on theories for proving 'how you know what you know'—that is, proving the validity of what you know—can be difficult to comprehend. These procedures are not formulaic, and they need to be made effective for each new study's specific set of conditions and dimensions.

Colin Lankshear and Michele Knobel (2005) introduce the idea of 'objective reflexive thinking' for clarifying the internal and external dimensions of a study (pp. 40–53). On the one hand, the internal dimensions of a study relate to the assumptions of a study, that is, the information the study aims to achieve. For instance, a study assumption could be something like: *Sixteen-year old females in Sydney are more interested in social networks than sixteen-year old males.* For that kind of study, the aim would be to deliver information and valid knowledge that will provide an answer of true or false to the question lying behind this assumption. External dimensions, on the other hand, involve the procedures for conducting the study, such as reviewing the literature, and using various methodologies to plan strategies for collecting and analysing the data collected. These procedures need to clearly connect both the external and internal aspects.

As such, a student would need to engage reflexive and reflective thinking to evaluate the most suitable strategies for collecting and processing data in order to produce the necessary information to answer the study assumption (Lankshear and Knobel 2005, p. 40). If they fail to do this, a student may—using the above example—head to Melbourne to gather data from twenty-year old individuals, which would not resolve the study assumption. This is, of course, a greatly oversimplified example of a failure to connect internal and external aspects. In a real study the two dimensions can present quite complex conditions that can be difficult to ascertain. Mindfully retaining all aspects of both dimensions of a real study while, at the same time, reflexively processing the study's various partial concerns, is intellectually challenging. In many instances, perplexing problems can arise, and a suitable marriage between the internal and external dimensions cannot be fulfilled. In this situation, adjustments will need to be made and/or new approaches to the study will have to be created.

I learned about this first hand while completing an assignment about the research process in the first year of my PhD, which was to critique a study conducted by Purdie et al. (2000) titled *Positive Self-identity for Indigenous Students and its Relationship to School Outcomes*. The authors of this study had evidence indicating that Indigenous Australian students have markedly lower school participation, retention and success rates than their non-Indigenous counterparts. These authors formulated an assumption that there was a link between the student's sense of self-identity (positive or negative), and the outcomes from their schooling (high or low). During their planning phase, the research team objectively evaluated theories and methods for surveying respondent's 'self-concept'. They anticipated adopting an available self-concept measuring instrument for the fieldwork questionnaire, however they found no specific instrument available for young Indigenous Australians. They reviewed literature on Indigenous Australians' self-concept, endeavouring to find shared meanings they could then use to create a new self-concept questionnaire, but they found scant information on the topic. Another constraint they faced was the large variation of age and literacy skills of children they planned to survey. In other words, these researchers experienced difficulties connecting the internal and external dimensions of their study. Their thesis clearly described these problems, and it provided their reasoning for simplifying an existing 'self-concept' to use in their study. The outcomes found the study assumption to be false; results revealed that Indigenous students had a higher family and school 'self-concept' than their non-Indigenous counterparts.

Adjustments made to the methods used are expected to be clearly explained in a doctoral thesis. This intellectualising procedure, known as the transparency of a study, demonstrates a framework through which universality and neutrality may be scrutinised by other researchers. Other aspects that affect a student's study, either positively or negatively, are their own predisposed and embedded social perspectives and practices. These are ways of thinking developed by the student's exposure to their family and educational background, as well as cultural differences in religion, nationality and politics, and natural differences of gender and age. Reflexive sociology, discussed below, is a process that encourages a student's self-critical evaluation of their perspectives and practices during the research process; it is a process that provides an important link to becoming a deeply critical thinker.

Reflexive Sociology: Thinking Through Social Relationships

Given that sociology is the study of human practices within a web of social relations, it would be natural to assume that the practice of sociology would be seriously concerned with the image of itself as a science of social thinking and action. In this reflexive sense, sociology includes student's critical thinking about their own relational perspectives and practices while conducting a study. Reflexive sociology rejects the conception of a value-neutral thinking. It rejects the assumption of a totally objective worldview, which is more often than not perceived as external to the observer and devoid of subjective social relations, practices and values. Reflexive sociology, instead, encourages a student to be reflexive while conducting their study, and to evaluate the power relations operating within it, especially at the end when findings are being arrived at.

This mode of thinking has been significantly influenced by French sociologist Pierre Bourdieu (2008), through his reflexive study entitled *Distinction: A Social Critique of the Judgment of Taste* (original work published in 1984). Bourdieu found judgments of taste generated and reinforced power relations in society. Some judgments of taste were, for example, perceived as socially cultivated and sophisticated human practices, while other judgments were viewed as gauche and unrefined. Bourdieu's important contribution to the social sciences was his model of human practices (Bourdieu 2008, p. 170). The model has three relational human aspects: habitus, capital and field, which are briefly outlined below. In social contexts, these three aspects intersect and interplay to create, reinforce and generate the human perspectives and practices that Bourdieu found represented power relations in human relationships (Bourdieu 1990, 2008).

'Habitus' contains socially deposited human ways of behaviour and thinking, opinions and attitudes (also called dispositions). These dispositions of habitus develop out of, and within, a student's conditions of existence, such as their family, class, education and cultural background. These dispositions become embedded, and are carried by a student from one context to another. In a new context, a student will use their embedded dispositions to inform their ways of thinking and acting, and if the new context is particularly different and imposes constraints, it may become necessary for a student's habitus to change in order to adapt to the new context. This is the creative aspect of habitus.

Given that the doctoral context is new, different and challenging for students, it is likely to change their dispositions of habitus. In these new conditions, there are also significant pressures: large quantities of information to evaluate, unpredictable levels of social structures to negotiate, and innumerable unexpected restraining conditions. Fortunately for a student, these are the kinds of conditions that necessitate an urgent need for adaptation, and the need to turn to creativity as a course of action.

You may ask why a student would want their habitus to endure all the pressures of the doctoral context. The answer, suggested by Bourdieu's model of human relations, is 'capital'. Capital can be the reward of a struggle to achieve, and it also can be the cause of struggle. There are countless forms of capital: economic, symbolic, cultural, religious, political, and law/legal, for instance. The interplay between the law and a student's practices in a doctoral study affects their reflexive thinking about issues such as ethics in research, and intellectual property rights. This idea of the law can also produce other serious concerns for a doctoral student, and the success of a study can even be placed in jeopardy.

My doctoral study (Ryan 2016) was to explore the meaning of 'protest' in Thai phleng phuea chiwit (songs for a better life) music. The study was designed to compare musicians' ideas about a better life with the ideologies of the Thai 'Sufficiency' philosophy, which provided guiding ideologies for Thailand's national economic and social development, and was bestowed upon Thailand by decree of His Majesty, the late King Bhumibol Adulyadej (Rama IX), in 1999. Under Thai Lése Majesté law, it is a crime to insult, defame or criticise the King, or any member of the royal family, or any royal development projects, such as this 'Sufficiency' initiative. Lése Majesté charges beget mandatory gaol sentences, and the number and duration of incarcerations for this crime have increased since 2006.

Given this, it was critically important for me to consistently engage reflexively with Thai law across all phases of my study. This was necessary for the participants' safety, my safety, and the success of my study. Lése Majesté law made it impossible, for instance, for me to ask the project participants direct questions about 'Sufficiency'. To circumvent problems of inference with regard to Lèse Majesté, open-ended questions were asked in the study survey and interviews, such as: How do you think your phleng phuea chiwit songs can offer 'a path to a better future' for Thai people? What do you want to communicate when you sing your songs? What do you think is important to know about phleng phuea chiwit music? From musician responses to these questions, I contrasted their meanings of 'a better life' in Thailand with the Sufficiency's ideologies of a better life for Thais.

In terms of 'capital', a student's desire to conduct a doctoral study reveals their desire to gain educational and cultural capital. Cultural capital, and other forms of capital, can be viewed as rewards for overcoming the myriad challenges of completing a research study. These can also be financial, as David Swartz (2002) claims, that "expectations generated by habitus depend on capital holdings ... on average, people with greater capital holdings will have higher expectations for career outcomes than those with less capital" (p. 655).

'Field', the other aspect in Bourdieu's model of human practice, interplays with 'habitus' and 'capital' to create, reinforce and generate human power relations. In any context, there are many different fields in which an individual will generate perspectives and practices for creating and reinforcing relations of distinction in the struggle for capital (Bourdieu 2008, pp. 226–257). The field of a PhD provides and affirms a world of distinctive social perspectives and practices. It is actually a 'field of fields' functioning as a social system for expressing social differences. Within it there are numerous field-specific programs offering a world of social relations, such as Arts, Social Science, Business, Dentistry, Medicine, Engineering, Music and many more, in which a doctoral student interplays with habitus and capital, theirs and others, to discover and produce new human relations, for themselves and others. In recent years, countless new fields have emerged because of the rise of digital technologies and globalisation. These fields have changed many social perspectives and practices. For example, the music industry has opened the way for: MP3 markets; world beat popularity; power shifts between audience and artist; changes in perspectives of key popular music concepts, such as 'authenticity', 'identity', 'musicianship', and 'audience'; and new ways that people relate to music, such as sampling, re-mixing, and creating videos for

YouTube or Facebook (Longhurst and Bogdanovic 2014). The cross-pollination of music styles, resulting from globalisation, has inspired an increase in cross-cultural popular music studies. New international virtual fields, such as The International Association for the Study of Popular Music (IASPM), have become a hub for transcultural networking to assist students conducting studies in a foreign field.

A foreign field of fields can impose additional demands on a student's reflexive and reflective thinking skills while conducting the study, and this was one I had to negotiate.

Thailand was the field of my study to explore the social meaning of 'protest' in phleng phuea chiwit songs. In the first year of my PhD, I prepared the strategies for the Thai fieldwork. However, during my pilot study trip to Thailand, I realised significant differences between Thai culture and my Australian culture that I had not anticipated.

Within a short time of arriving in Thailand, it became apparent that I would have to make major adjustments to my study fieldwork strategies in order to adapt the study to the significant difference between Thai participants' first language of Thai, and my language, English. I knew that my level of proficiency in the Thai language would not suffice for conducting in-depth comprehensive interviews with musician participants in a specialised field such as music in Thailand and its social meanings. I also realised that the participants would have similar difficulty in comfortably conversing in English on these specialised music matters.

To overcome this momentous social relational barrier to conducting my study, I had to change my planned fieldwork strategies and create more effective communication for the study goals. All participant contact information was translated from English into the participant's first language, Thai. This included: the study information letter explaining the aim of the research to Thai musicians, the consent form for musicians to sign if they chose to become a participant of the study, and the survey questionnaire. I organised a Thai translator interpreter for every participant contact meeting and interview. Following this stratagem in the field, I was satisfied that the time-consuming procedures had generated rich data for the study, as the participants answered questions with ease in their language giving abundant detail.

For my better understanding of the Thai data, before beginning analysis, I arranged for it to be translated into my first language, English. However, while thinking about the PhD field, its power relations and requirements, a deeply important question arose: How authentic was the English translated data compared to the Thai participant's original source data? As a paramount aim of any research study is to create accurate reliable knowledge, and reinforce PhD standards by demonstrating clearly how that knowledge was gained, it became imperative to employ a verification strategy. For this, independent translators crosschecked the accuracy of meanings generated by Thai participants with those generated after translation into English transcripts.

Without doubt, the particular intermix of fields related to my study, Thailand and a PhD, brought unforeseen obstacles to the interplay with habitus and capital. For generating perspectives and practices of distinction in Thai phleng phuea chiwit, I had to create a balance of strategies to reinforce the habitus and capital of Thai musicians (support their cultural differences) and PhD requisites (support academic expectations). This was necessary to generate in-depth, accurate information upon which I could confidently verify valid thesis outcomes.

While conducting a study in a foreign context, a student will most likely find it necessary to adapt creatively, and adjust their strategies to successfully complete the study. Nonetheless, all adaptive procedures will require intellectualising in accord with established institutional expectations. This means that a student's implemented creative changes for conducting the study will need to find harmony with the regard for systematic rigour by providing a written account of *why*, *how* and *what* adjustments were made. This is necessary in the production of the quality, new knowledge expected in a doctorate.

Given the significance of intellectualising all procedures of a research higher degree process in order to produce a rigorous study, a student's function in a PhD field can be regarded as extremely important. Their production of knowledge with a high degree of rigour is vital and key to the sustainability and reputation of a PhD field. In this regard, layers of autonomously operating contexts with differing levels of social practices, including the student's, come together under a shared homologous goal, which is to produce a PhD project that will contribute new knowledge to an academic field. In this sense, a PhD field of fields can be viewed as a highly supportive social system in a struggle for various forms of capital to be gained from producing a quality PhD project.

Conclusion

In a doctoral graduate's post-completion everyday life, when only memories of the PhD work and its struggles remain, it is difficult to take information for granted, as the consistent practice of critically evaluating relational perspectives and practices relevant to information has become an embedded habit. This kind of intellectual capital can be viewed as one of the enduring rewards of completing a PhD. After conducting a reflexive social science study, as was the case for me, the world of social relations is likely to be perceived as a world of humans generating power and value relations. This knowledge can have an emancipating effect on one's thinking for evaluating their own values in society, and for clearly determining what values they wish to act upon, support and/or generate.

References

Bourdieu, P. [1984] 2008. *Distinction: A Social Critique of the Judgment of Taste.* 14th ed. Translated by R. Nice. New York and London: Routledge.

Bourdieu, P. 1990. *The Logic of Practice.* Stanford, CA: Stanford University Press.

Dewey, J. [1910] 1933. *How We Think: A Restatement of the Relation of Reflective Thinking to the Educative Process.* Revised ed. Boston, New York, and Chicago: D.C. Heath & Co.

Lankshear, C., and M. Knobel. 2005. *A Handbook for Teacher Research: From Design to Implementation.* 2nd ed. Maidenhead, UK: Open University Press and McGraw Hill House.

Longhurst, B. and D. Bogdanovic. 2014. *Popular Music & Society.* 3rd ed. Cambridge, UK: Polity Press.

Purdie, N., P. Tripcony, G. Boulton-Lewis, J. Fanshawe, and A. Gunstone. 2000. *Positive Self-identity for Indigenous Students and Its Relationship to School Outcomes: A Project Funded by the Commonwealth Department of Education Training and Youth Affairs.* Brisbane, Australia: Queensland University of Technology. http://www.voced.edu.au/content/ngv%3A35756.

Ryan, B. 2016. "The roles of phleng phuea chiwit music (songs for life) in forming identities within the forces of globalisation in Thailand: Individuated perspectives similar to 'sufficiency' philosophies." PhD diss., Central Queensland University.

Swartz, D. L. 2002. "The sociology of habit: The perspective of Pierre Bourdieu." *The Occupational Therapy Journal of Research* 22: 625–655. http://d.org/10.1 177/153944920202205108.

Usher, R. 1996. "A critique of the neglected epistemological assumptions of educational research." In *Understanding Educational Research*, edited by D. Scott and R. Usher, 9–32. London and New York: Routledge.

18

Who Am I Now?: The Doctorate as a Process of Transformative Learning

Charmaine O'Brien

Introduction

Over many decades, the eminent psychotherapist Carl Rogers listened to many hundreds of people talk about their darkest fears and most discomforting desires. He noticed what they had in common and used what he learnt to inform his profound theories of human psychology (Rogers 1969, p. 184), including an assertion that our most peculiar concerns about self are common amongst people. With this in mind, I want to make a confession about my initial motivation for enrolling in a PhD in creative writing: I did so because I hoped it would provide me with the resources to write a book through the acquisition of a financial scholarship. I feel somewhat ashamed of my mercenary intentions towards a process intended to foster noble intellectual ambitions, but, if Rogers is the reliable guide I hold him to be, I expect I am not the only soldier of fortune to have enrolled in a creative doctoral program. While I did not

C. O'Brien (✉)
Sydney, NSW, Australia
e-mail: charmaine.obrien@cqumail.com

© The Author(s) 2019
D. L. Brien et al. (eds.), *The Doctoral Experience*,
https://doi.org/10.1007/978-3-030-18199-4_18

get that particular bursary, I still found myself determinedly committed to the doctoral journey despite the failure of my pecuniary hopes. At some point my motivation changed, as did my project, and it ended up quite differently to what I anticipated. As it turned out, I experienced the doctoral process as personally transformative. Frankly, I am not sure if this self-identified 'transformation' has been a good thing or not.

It has been five months since I submitted my thesis—and still awaiting my examination—and I feel bewildered still, as if I do not know who I am now, and I am concerned I may never again be able to focus on anything more challenging than television crime series. I wondered if my experience was unique, a sample of one, but typing the sentence "Why do I feel so strange after finishing my PhD?" into a search engine reveals that my persistent lack of focus and energy are commonly experienced by students who have finished their dissertations. Many hundreds of entries and comments on the post-PhD state describe struggling with fatigue, anxiety, stress and depression, as well as a measure of guilt at feeling this way. Such states are, hopefully, transitory and likely an equalising response to ending a long period of "consuming preoccupation" (Brooks 1988). However, they might also be a response to something similar to my sense of not being the same self as when I commenced my doctoral studies. One student has written, for instance:

> Six months later, I am beginning to come to terms with the fact that exiting the PhD is, in fact, a fairly significant life event in all sorts of ways … [it] led me to realize how profoundly the process of a PhD changes your life … you need to carve out a whole new identity. (The Thesis Whisperer 2015)

Perhaps then, my sense of myself as transformed post-PhD has some universality, and an exploration of the process and impact of such change might be useful to others. This chapter explores how a doctoral student might understand their journey as a transformative one, and considers the implications of such change and how it might be better prepared for and supported. It further considers the inherently creative nature of the PhD process, and suggests this offers distinctive advantages for thriving in the contemporary world.

Transformational Learning

My background as a psychological coach undoubtedly influenced my choice to conceive of my doctoral experience as 'transformative', as claims are often made for coaching as a modality to "transform your life" (Hanssmann 2014, p. 24). Exploring the idea of transformation as an outcome of the doctoral process led me to the concept of Transformative Learning (TL). TL is defined as learning that involves qualitative changes in our frames of reference and "habits of mind" (Illeris 2014, p. 574; Mezirow 2000). A "frame of reference is a 'meaning perspective', the [cognitive] structure through which we filter sense impressions" (Mezirow 2000, p. 16) and "fundamentally organize our understanding of ourselves and our life world" (Illeris 2014, p. 574). It is made up of 'habits of mind', or sets of assumptions, which act as the "filter for interpreting the meaning of experience" and subsequently shape our resulting "point of view" (Mezirow 2000, p. 16). How we interpret our experience will guide the actions we take in response to it. The need to understand and order our experience in this way, or make meaning of it, is a "defining condition of being human"; it is the process by which we integrate new experience with what we know to avoid the threat of "chaos" (Mezirow 2000, p. 3). Failure to make experience conform to what we already know is threatening because it destabilises a sense of how we know the world, and ourselves in it, resulting in psychological 'dis-ease' (Albertson 2014). Our instinctive tendency then is to try and fit our experience with what we already know. Mezirow (2000, p. 16) alternatively describes meaning perspectives as a "network of arguments" whereby we subject experience to an argument informed by value judgments and beliefs, in order to align it with our current perspective on self, others and the world. When we process new experience to "conform to existing knowledge structures" we "assimilate" it (Kegan 2000, p. 50). When we find ourselves with an experience that we cannot argue into our current way of knowing we might then change our meaning making processes to accommodate it (Kegan 2000, p. 50). The process of accommodation happens through critical discourse and reflection on assumptions and beliefs that lead to "reconstructing dominant narratives" and taking new action in the world in response to this (Mezirow 2000, p. 19). Of course, the proceeding description could be said to apply to any learning. Indeed, Newman (2012) claims the very concept of TL is void as all learning is by its nature "transformative". TL is also criticised for being "too cognitively orientated" (Illeris 2014, p. 574), conceiving of learning as an entirely rational and analytical process and not addressing its emotional aspect. Yet, TL has been described as leading to transformation in self-concept, and "all learning which implies change in the identity of the learner" has affective impact (Illeris 2014, p. 577; Mezirow 2000, p. 21).

Self-concept is what we believe we are and how we value ourselves; self-identity is how we define self through the groups we belong to. These interrelated psychological constructs are formed by our mental processes, including emotionality, and are of primary affective significance (Illeris 2014). If TL affects change in the way we conceive of ourselves and how we belong it can hardly be held to be an entirely cognitive and rational process. It is beyond the scope of this discussion to further review or argue the criticisms of the TL construct. I will therefore proceed on the assumption of the potential of TL as a process affecting transformational change.

The PhD as Transformational Learning

Kegan (2000, p. 48) describes two types of learning: informational and transformational. Informational learning extends our skills and "established cognitive capacities" by bringing "valuable new contents into the existing form [frame of reference] of our way of knowing". Informational learning changes what we know and is indisputably true of the doctoral process: acceptance into a doctoral degree, and especially a PhD, requires the student to possess understanding of the current state of knowledge in a chosen domain in order to propose a relevant project. Likewise, students need to have well-developed research skills to be considered capable of undertaking higher research. To produce a qualifying thesis, a student must advance their thinking skills, subject matter expertise and communication competencies, all of which could be considered informational learning. Transformational learning, on the other hand, changes how we know: putting the form [or our epistemology] itself at risk of change by pushing the learner to build their capacity for abstract thinking such that they "can ask more general thematic questions about the *facts* [of informational learning] and consider the perspectives and biases of those who wrote the historical account creating the facts" (Kegan 2000, p. 48).

Transformative learning thus reconstructs the frame of reference within which we construct meaning (Kegan 2000; Illeris 2014). Is it possible for a student to complete a PhD without 'changing their mind' in this way? It seems inherent to the doctoral process that a student becomes "critically aware of one's own tacit assumptions and expectations and those of others and [be able to assess] their relevance" and where necessary challenge and reconstruct these (Mezirow 2000, p. 21). Such significant alterations in cognitive capabilities do not occur in isolation; restructuring thinking also shifts emotional and social aspects of meaning making. "Numerous catalysts serve to set off transformational change ... personal crises, dissatisfaction with the status quo, insufficient capacity and cross-cultural exposure" (Hanssmann 2014, p. 30). I posit that the PhD process has significant potential to catalyse transformational change in students.

The criticism of TL as being too focused on its cognitive aspects and presented as a rational process draws further parallels with the doctoral process. Undertaking a PhD is constituted as a purely intellectual process that specifically demands non-emotionality. Such cognitive reductionism suggests it as a "bloodless" process in which emotion has no role (Kegan 2000, p. 67). Yet, making the "cognitive shift [required]" for any significant learning, that catalyses a "qualitative evolution of mind" such that the way we make meaning changes, "entails a wrenching, no less, of self from cultural surround and into new sets of relationships, including with the symbolic order" (Kegan 2000, p. 67)—hardly an emotionless process. My doctoral journey has transformed my habits of mind and meaning perspectives and, therefore, the way I now make sense of my experience. Again, I think this is an integral aspect of the doctoral process, as it requires "adaptive challenges ... not [just] knowing more but knowing differently" (Kegan 2000, p. 52). The transformational potential in it needs to be acknowledged and, therefore, better prepared for and supported.

Perhaps my case is an unusual one: I deliberately set out to develop my creative capabilities through the production of a practice-led thesis comprising a creative work and exegesis. I chose to approach my creative development firstly by exploring psychology research on creativity to understand what might be limiting it in the first instance, subsequently coaching myself using my newly gained knowledge as a tool to try and shift these blocks (Grant and Greene 2001). It was a theory-driven discovery process that was simultaneously intensely personal. This process feels like it has resulted in a "fundamental shift", or transformation, in my perspective on self and how I engage with the world (Kegan 2000, p. 52). I expect this shift will settle in over time, but for now it has left me feeling wrenched, or as Nora declares in Ibsen's *A Doll's House* as she is "coming to a new set of ideas about her ideas and where they even come from … 'I don't know where I am in these matters'" (quoted in Kegan 2000, p. 57). In expressing all of this, I have been describing my experience of what I consider to be transformational change in psychological terms, but to truly be transformative it needs to move "beyond purely intellectual insight and [be] substantiated by a change in [my] behavioural choices and an enlarged internal and/or external capacity to engage with [the] world and pursue [my] goals" (Hanssmann 2014, p. 29). In other words, I have to take new action, and this is where I am particularly struggling.

It would be easy to make the case that my experience is a singular one, due to the unique method I designed and implemented for my project. However, a significant number of PhD students struggle with mental health issues such a depression and anxiety (Levecque et al. 2015) and doctoral studies can be "hazardous to marriage" (Brooks 1988). There are significant emotional and social factors involved when someone experiences mental health challenges or a relationship breakdown, suggesting that the doctoral journey is not an entirely rational experience for others as well. Yet, there is little acknowledgement of the considerable potential for personal transformation through the doctoral process and the emotional challenges arising from such change. This may be heightened in students undertaking a creative work as part of their doctorate, as the sustained effort necessary to produce creative work is widely considered

to be driven by intrinsic motivation linked to purpose and this fundamental impetus is largely emotionally fired (Gardner 1988).

Change as Part of the Process

The primary aim of the PhD is to make an original contribution to
knowledge, to add something to a specified domain. Therefore, when a
student sets out on a doctoral journey they are necessarily looking to create change. As this book outlines in many of the other chapters, what is
required to make a change in knowledge, even if it is incremental, is
enormous, which is why it takes years: a significant amount of change on
a number of fronts has to happen for this change in knowledge to be
brought about. That such a protracted and arduous intellectual undertaking might catalyse concomitant emotional and social transformation
seems obvious, however these changes are often unexpected—perhaps
because they are not discussed enough, or at all—and therefore unplanned
for (terms like 'relationship breakdown' or 'dealing with financial distress'
are not often included as items in a doctoral plan). The changes I have
experienced during the doctoral process that I identify as transformative
have been unexpected. On reflection, I was so busy 'making' the PhD
that it was only at the end of the process—when the work of it was no
longer there—that my emotion and confusion about 'who am I now?'
emerged into awareness.

Theoretically, I welcome the idea of personal change, after all I work as
a psychological coach supporting self-identified aspirations for growth
and development in others. Nonetheless, even when a person is in a state
of 'change readiness', the process of changing is often challenging (Grant
2010; Albertson 2014): "Change and fear, the findings confirmed, go
hand in hand" (Hanssmann 2014, p. 29). This "seems even more potent
in transformational change that might affect fundamental aspects of …
identity" because it asks us to change the "whole way [we] understand
[self], [the] world and the relationship between the two" (Hanssmann
2014, p. 29; Kegan 2000, p. 57). If the process of transformative learning
catalyses epistemological change as proposed, this change has to be

"accommodated" (Kegan 2000, p. 52). This causes a "break down or abandonment of elements of existing mental structures (cognitive as well as emotional and social) and an establishment of a basis for alternative assimilative rebuilding of a new understanding or new ways of thinking, feeling and behaving" (Illeris 2014, p. 575).

Changing the way the self is understood and how that self exists in the world can be "a long, often painful voyage, and one that much of the time, may feel more like a mutiny than a merely exhilarating voyage to discover new lands" (Kegan 2000, p. 67). Even when freely sought, change is often resisted, because the process not only requires "learning and enacting new [thinking and behavior], but the possibility of losing [your] very self" (Hanssmann 2014, p. 29). According to Hanssmann, those who work to affect transformational change have an ethical duty to alert clients to the "significant ramifications that the change they pursue might have" (2014, p. 30). When I set out on my doctoral journey, I was not expecting my identity to evolve, as there was no forewarning of that possibility on the PhD map. In this chapter I hope to sound that siren.

Support Needed

Transformational change requires emotional support (Kegan 2000; Hanssmann 2014; Albertson 2014). Doctoral students rightly look to their supervisor for support in learning to challenge and change the ways they think academically. Due to the potential concomitant challenges to self/identity, students might also find themselves looking to their supervisors for emotional and social support (Kearns et al. 2008). If students are fortunate, they might find themselves with supervisors who have the time and capability to provide such support. The question must then be asked about whether the possibility of receiving such support should be left to luck. And, moreover, should supervisors be expected to be able to respond usefully to the emotional turmoil and discomfort some students might undergo if the process of working on a doctorate sets off significant personal change? I only raise these questions here, but feel they need to be addressed more widely.

Support at Hand

Having shared my personal experience, I will consider how the doctoral journey might be better managed, such that students find themselves with a sense of positive forward motion during the process, including the period between submitting a thesis, examination and final completion. Transformational learning is challenging. The change it inspires can take an individual on a downward spiral as their meaning making structures re-form to accommodate new understandings of the self and the world (Albertson 2014). In order to survive what might initially be perceived as a threat to identity—where/how do I fit now?—an individual needs support. The right support, including guidance to develop a "map and destination", can ensure that transformational change eventually leads to flourishing—personally and professionally (Kegan 2000, p. 67). The academic trek for a doctoral student is well charted. Transformational change is an emergent process and it cannot be 'planned' for. Nevertheless, recalibrating the doctoral map such that personal change is considered from the outset can prompt the student, ideally with guidance from their university, to understand how they might manage the personal emotional and social aspects of their doctoral journey—such that these do not become impediments to their PhD success.

Doctoral students have traditionally aimed for an academic career. However, opportunities in academia are declining in number and quality, and the best laid plans for a scholarly career might fail to come to fruition (Levecque et al. 2015). Not all doctoral students aspire to be academics, others have different ambitions and some students, like myself, might find themselves struggling to come up with a coherent plan because of the detours and challenges faced on the journey. According to Levecque et al. (2015), devising a plan that considers various possibilities for life post-PhD can be useful in preventing mental health issues arising both during and after the process. In other words, students should give themselves a broader scope of how they make meaning of their doctorate, such that the perspective they take on it is one in which the future holds considerable positive possibility.

In his influential book, *The Rise of the Creative Class* (2002), Richard Florida identified scholars as members of the 'creative class'. The standard definition of creativity is to bring something new and useful, or original and effective, into being (Runco and Jaeger 2012). By its very nature, a doctorate therefore qualifies as creative: it has to add something new to knowledge and it has to be useful—useful in being a coherent argument for your original contribution, in a format that can be comprehended, or used, by others. The creative process requires the emergence of a novel idea in response to a problem: testing the potential usefulness of this idea to solve the problem in the first instance; a long period of hard work putting it to work to arrive at a solution; emerging the new idea in a useful format; and engaging external others in recognising and legitimising it (Gardner 1988). Anyone who has completed a doctorate will recognise this process.

Creativity requires curiosity, focus, cognitive and emotional flexibility and adaptiveness, and persistence, amongst other personal characteristics (Gardner 1988). The successful completion of a doctorate requires the same of a student. There is a prevailing global sentiment that declares future prosperity will be increasingly dependent on the generation of knowledge through innovation (Farmakis 2014; Goepel et al. 2012). Creativity is the prerequisite for innovation and creativity has been "co-opted as the driving force in the new economy" (Throsby and Hollister 2003, p. 11). Consequently, creative behaviour is highly prized and sought after (Runco and Abdullah 2014, p. 248), and "all sorts of creative people are seen as the ... source of innovative ideas in inventing the future" (Throsby and Hollister 2003, p. 11)—I suggest people such as those who have demonstrated their creative capabilities in completing a doctorate. Recognising oneself at the end of the doctoral journey to be a 'creative' offers a place to contain a transformed identity, and a point to set off on the post-doctoral journey armed with important skills for the future.

References

Albertson, S. 2014. "Deconstruction toward reconstruction: A constructive-developmental consideration of deconstructive necessities in transitions." *Behavioural Development Bulletin* 19: 76–82.

Brooks, A. 1988. "Health; For graduate students, marriage presents a special problem." http://www.nytimes.com/1988/11/03/us/health-for-graduate-students-marriage-presents-a-special-problem.html.

Farmakis, E. 2014. "Fostering the creative economy." *Standford Social Innovation Review*. https://ssir.org/articles/entry/fostering_the_creative_economy.

Florida, R. 2002. *The Rise of the Creative Class: And How It's Transforming Work, Leisure, Community and Everyday Life*. New York: Basic Books.

Gardner, H. 1988. "Creativity: An interdisciplinary perspective." *Creativity Research Journal* 1: 8–26.

Goepel, M., K. Hölzle, and D. Knyphausen-Aufseß. 2012. "Individuals' innovation response behaviour: A framework of antecedents and opportunities for future research." *Creativity and Innovation Management* 4: 412–426.

Grant, A. M. 2010. "It takes time: A stages of change perspective on the adoption of workplace coaching skills." *Journal of Change Management* 10 (1): 61–77.

Grant, A. M., and J. Greene. 2001. *Coach Yourself*. Great Britain: Pearson Education Limited.

Hanssmann, E. 2014. "Providing safe passage into larger life: Supporting clients' transformational change through coaching." *International Journal of Evidence Based Coaching and Mentoring* 8: 24–38.

Illeris, K. 2014. "Transformative learning re-defined: As changes in elements of the identity." *International Journal of Lifelong Education* 33 (5): 573–586. https://doi.org/10.1080/02601370.2014.917128.

Kearns, H., M. Gardiner, and K. Marshall. 2008. "Innovation in PhD completion: The hardy shall succeed (and be happy!)." *Higher Education Research & Development* 27 (1): 77–89.

Kegan, R. 2000. "What form transforms?" In *Learning as Transformation. Critical Perspectives on a Theory in Progress*, edited by J. Mezirow and Associates, 35–69. San Francisco: Jossey-Bass.

Levecque, K., A. Frederik, A. De Beuckelaer, J. Van der Heydan, and L. Gisle. 2015. "Work organization and mental health problems in PhD students." *Research Policy* 46: 868–879.

Mezirow, J. 2000. "Learning to think like an adult: Core concepts of transformative theory." In *Learning as Transformation. Critical Perspectives on a Theory in Progress*, edited by J. Mezirow and Associates, 3–33. San Francisco: Jossey-Bass.

Newman, M. 2012. "Calling transformative learning into question: Some mutinous thoughts." *Adult Education Quarterly* 62 (1): 36–55.

Rogers, C. 1969. *A Therapist's View of Psychotherapy: On Becoming a Person.* London: Constable & Co.

Runco, M., and A. M. Abdullah. 2014. "Why isn't creativity being supported? Distressing analyses of grants and awards for creativity research—Or lack thereof." *Creativity Research Journal* 26: 248–250.

Runco, M., and G. J. Jaeger. 2012. "The standard definition of creativity." *Creativity Research Journal* 24: 92–96.

The Thesis Whisperer. 2015. "What's it like to be 'finished'?" *The Thesis Whisperer*, 6 May. https://thesiswhisperer.com/2015/05/06/whats-it-like-to-be-finished.

Throsby, D., and V. Hollister. 2003. *Don't Give Up Your Day Job: An Economic Study of Professional Artists in Australia.* Surry Hills: Australia Council. http://www.australiacouncil.gov.au/workspace/uploads/files/research/entire_document-54325d2a02a3c8.pdf.

19

Conclusion to Volume

Donna Lee Brien, Craig Batty, Elizabeth Ellison, and Alison Owens

In this book, we have presented a wide variety of topics that characterise the doctoral experience from the vantage point of the usually largely 'invisible' work that underpins a research degree; that is, the human experience that can make or break a successful completion, and that can have a major influence on how the student approaches research after the doctorate. While the book has presented challenges and breakthroughs from the specific perspective

D. L. Brien (✉) • E. Ellison
School of Education and the Arts, Central Queensland University,
Noosaville, QLD, Australia
e-mail: d.brien@cqu.edu.au; l.ellison@cqu.edu.au

C. Batty
School of Communication, University of Technology Sydney,
Sydney, NSW, Australia
e-mail: Craig.Batty@uts.edu.au

A. Owens
Learning and Teaching Centre, Australian Catholic University,
North Sydney, NSW, Australia
e-mail: Alison.Owens@acu.edu.au

© The Author(s) 2019
D. L. Brien et al. (eds.), *The Doctoral Experience*,
https://doi.org/10.1007/978-3-030-18199-4_19

223

of creative arts and humanities students, we argue that many, if not most, of these experiences can be applied to students working in any discipline. As explained in the Introduction, the book arose from a research project that asked students to share and explore their doctoral challenges and breakthroughs in a collaborative setting, and it was during these two days that students identified with others' experiences, and began to understand the nature of doing a doctorate: of the cognitive (learning) and emotional (personal) underpinnings of what is essentially the highest level of formal learning. During this research project, and in speaking with the students involved, it became clear that while doctoral research and writing is different for every student and the specific challenges each faces in completing that research are also different, all students travel the same path to becoming fully-fledged researchers with skills and competencies that will carry them forward in their chosen career, academic or otherwise. This path is undoubtedly challenging—and it should be—but with the right attitude and mentorship, it can be truly transformational. This is the human, or invisible, journey necessary for all research students to follow if they are to fully experience the potential for higher learning. In other words, this is what makes undertaking a doctorate a journey.

Conceptualising the Doctoral Journey

As is apparent from the student-authored chapters that comprise this volume, the notion of undertaking a journey is common to the doctoral experience. Students prepare themselves for the terrain ahead; they meet and overcome obstacles, learning about themselves on the way; they meet allies (supervisors, peers) and possibly enemies (some supervisors, peer reviewers and others), who help them to make sense of what they are trying to achieve; and, at the end, they can look back on the journey and work out what it was all about, in relation to both the research project and the research process. The metaphor of the journey is well documented in education and, in particular, in doctoral education.

In their project on developing supervisory skills, Blass et al. note that metaphors became useful ways to understand how different supervisors approach the way they work with students, and here the journey meta-phor comes in: "One saw supervision like a string of pearls; with the supervisor helping the student thread the pearls together. Other meta-phors related to chains and links; or journeys and travellers" (Blass et al. 2012, p. 35). In their article on supervising creative writing students, Berry and Batty (2016) use the journey metaphor to structure their argu-ment, presenting fictional vignettes of student issues that arise along the journey, and how they as supervisors help their students to overcome them. As they argue of their role, "As mentors, sidekicks, wise old people and shape-shifters, supervisors occupy a variety of roles in service of the candidate's rite of passage into the academy" (2016, p. 5). Considering creative writing research degrees specifically, Jeri Kroll similarly acknowl-edges the multifarious role of the supervisor: as "academic, artist, mentor, disciplinarian, cheerleader [... and] creative scholar" (2009, p. 3).

While many scholars, critics and writing experts have written about the journey, it is Joseph Campbell who is heralded as the originator of the concept, in his book *The Hero with a Thousand Faces* ([1949] 1993), which features the monomythic story structure known as the Hero's Journey. Briefly, the Hero's Journey is comprised of a series of chronologi-cal stages through which the protagonist (hero) travels and, as a result, experiences both a physical and emotional transformation. It is struc-tured as such:

Stage 1: Departure, Separation
World of Common Day
Call to Adventure
Refusal of the Call
Supernatural Aid
Crossing the First Threshold
Belly of the Whale

Stage 2: Descent, Initiation, Penetration
Road of Trials
Approach to the Inmost Cave
Meeting with the Goddess
Woman as Temptress

Atonement with the Father
Apotheosis
The Ultimate Boon

Stage 3: Return
Refusal of the Return
The Magic Flight
Rescue from Within
Crossing the Threshold
Return
Master of the Two Worlds
Freedom to Live

The Hero's Journey has been popularised by Hollywood script consultant and story 'guru' Christopher Vogler (1999, p. 212), who offers the following summary:

> Heroes are introduced in the ORDINARY WORLD where they receive a CALL TO ADVENTURE. They are reluctant and at first REFUSE THE CALL, but are encouraged by a MENTOR to CROSS THE FIRST THRESHOLD and enter the Special World where they encounter TESTS, ALLIES AND ENEMIES. They APPROACH THE INMOST CAVE, crossing a second threshold where they endure the ORDEAL. They take possession of their REWARD and are pursued on THE ROAD BACK to the Ordinary World. They cross the third threshold, experience a RESURRECTION, and are transformed by the experience. They RETURN WITH ELIXIR, a boon or treasure to benefit the Ordinary World.

In the research project that underpinned this book, we also found that the model of the Hero's Journey was useful in understanding the experiences that the students had undergone. In particular, we were able to map their personal and cognitive turning points against the structure of a journey, as can be seen in the diagram below (Table 19.1):

This table clearly suggests a transformational journey that is akin to those associated with creative writing and film products. Not only this, if the structure is looked at through the lens of specific educational theory,

Table 19.1 Doctoral physical and emotional journey

Physical journey (learning hurdles)	Emotional journey (human response)
Getting the proposal together and shopping it around.	Excitement and enthusiasm.
Proposal questioned and altered on supervisor's recommendation—didn't understand implications but trusted supervisor.	Deflation and confusion.
Accept your dream is not very sophisticated after all and move on. First harsh lesson: you are a beginner in this project.	Stubbornness and perseverance. Frustration, despair depression.
Don't know if I want to go on in this direction but keep working on it as it seems like the best option. Research skills don't quite match the task yet.	Frustration/overwhelmed.
Brain started to make connections. Epiphanies/resilience.	Affirmed, confident.
Acceptance of proposal and enrolment. You finally get the project and realise you have made quite a lot of progress cognitively.	Relief and enthusiasm.
Ability to see room for improvement and that you have improved.	Fear of failure/criticism. Sense of achievement and energised.
Start working on research and gathering ideas. Every new paper you read stretches your mind and your skill as a researcher and thinker starts to make some forward progress.	Excitement.
Develop networking, presenting and writing skills. Recognise your tribe.	Desire for belonging.
Confirmation of Candidature feedback is savage and lots of re-writing.	Worry—I am not good enough to do a PhD. All confidence gone.
Rewrite. Forced to think more clearly as you recognise you have weak arguments.	Stressful, felt like last chance.
Project accepted and move into research and writing. Every day, skills and experience increases—conferences, speaking to peers, writing papers. Slow but sure progress as a researcher.	Peaceful, confident, excited, pride, acceptance.
Ability and confidence to review others' work.	Consolidation and practice of critical analysis skills

(continued)

Table 19.1 (continued)

Physical journey (learning hurdles)	Emotional journey (human response)
First draft.	Overjoyed.
Working through first draft with supervisors. Whoops, some things are not working! You don't know as much as you thought and find your research skills are useless if you cannot analyse well or form good conclusions about the evidence.	Anxiety, loss of confidence, overwhelmed Panic, wounded, gutted, anger.
Realised method needed to change. Got brave enough to change it and suddenly everything fell into place. Suddenly discover you did not know what you did not know but now, you get it!	Empowered and felt voice had been found. Excited. Racehorse seeing the final turn.
Develop time management skills and identify propensity for procrastination.	Worry.
Meticulous corrections, editing, more corrections. Realised far more work than I thought. Now understanding why the supervisor suggested changes.	Dig deep into stores of resilience and patience and focus on the end.
Started to doubt conclusions. My cognitive skills took a leap and I could see flaws in the argument better and figure out how to overcome them. The PhD process had worked! Developing expertise/becoming an expert.	Panic, low confidence, compromise and acceptance.
Recognising negative sequelae (anxiety, negative thoughts, emotional growth).	Acceptance.
Thesis off to examiner.	Overwhelming relief.
Process drags on.	Depressing, frustrating, anger sets in.
Minor corrections. I had developed the sophistication to know what was useful in the comments and to amend the work accordingly.	Elated, happy, relieved. What do I do now? I might have a PhD but I don't really belong to this tribe. Empowered, negativity, isolation.

we can see that successful transformation requires a bold, sustained spirit of inquiry that questions deeply held assumptions of the self, of the discipline and of the community to whom the problem matters (Mezirow and Taylor 2009). Such questioning must resist the urges to 'temporize', 'escape' or 'retreat' from the implications of relativism and contingency (Perry 1981).

Hence, transformation is necessarily prefigured by the disorientation depicted in Campbell's 'ordeal' ([1949] 1993), Mezirow's 'disorienting dilemma' (Mezirow and Taylor 2009) and Perry's 'unbearable disorientation' (1981). The implications of this necessary process of disorientation as a gateway to transformation are important, both for doctoral students and their supervisors. Transformative learning can deliver a profound reformulation of what can be known, or alternatively, an acute personal crisis (Roberts 2006). Responding to this risk, the importance of self-care and resilience, as well as facilitative, empathetic supervision, are emphasised in the chapters of this book. This is seen as the means to enable the sometimes uncomfortable learning journey that leads to personal commitment in a world of relative values and contingent truths (Perry 1981)—that is, Campbell's 'enlightenment'.

Indeed, a number of research studies have utilised the metaphor of a research journey to represent the process of doing a doctorate (for example, Batchelor and Di Napoli 2006; Lee et al. 2013) and for the process of research itself (McGowan et al. 2014). What this book does is draw together student perspectives and, in their own voices, provide a perspective on this journey from the student point of view. While not shying away from the difficulties and challenges, these student chapters chart their process of empowerment through their embrace of that journey's challenge.

References

Batchelor, D., and R. Di Napoli. 2006. "The doctoral journey: Perspectives." *Educate* 6 (1): 13–24.

Berry, M., and C. Batty. 2016. "The stories of supervision: Creative writing in a critical space." *New Writing: The International Journal for the Practice and Theory of Creative Writing* 13 (2): 247–260.

Blass, E., A. Jasman, and R. Levy. 2012. "Supervisor reflections on developing doctoralness in practice-based doctoral students." *Quality Assurance in Education* 20 (1): 31–41.

Campbell, J. [1949] 1993. *The Hero with a Thousand Faces*. London: Fontana.

Kroll, J. 2009 "The supervisor as practice-led coach and trainer: Getting creative writing doctoral candidates across the finish line." *TEXT: Journal of Writing and Writing Courses*, special issue 6: 1–21. http://www.textjournal.com.au/speciss/issue6/content.htm.

Lee, E., C. Blackmore, and M. Seal. 2013. *Research Journeys: A Collection of Narratives of the Doctoral Experience*. Newcastle upon Tyne: Cambridge Scholars Publishing.

McGowan, K. A., F. Westley, E. D. G. Fraser, P. A. Loring, K. C. Weathers, F. Avelino, J. Sendzimir, R. R. Chowdhury, and M. L. Moore. 2014. "The research journey: Travels across the idiomatic and axiomatic toward a better understanding of complexity." *Ecology and Society* 19 (3): article 37. https://doi.org/10.5751/ES-06518-190337.

Mezirow, J., and E. W. Taylor. 2009. *Transformative Learning in Practice: Insights from Community, Workplace, and Higher Education*. Jossey Bass.

Perry, W. J. 1981. "Cognitive and ethical growth: The making of meaning." In *The Modern American College*, edited by W. Chickering, 76–116. San Francisco: Jossey-Bass.

Roberts, N. 2006. "Disorienting dilemmas: Their effects on learners, impact on performance, and implications for adult educators." Paper presented at the Fifth Annual College of Education Research Conference: Urban and International Education Section, Miami, Florida. http://digitalcommons.fiu.edu/cgi/viewcontent.cgi?article=1249&context=sferc.

Vogler, C. 1999. *The Writer's Journey: Mythic Structure for Storytellers and Screenwriters*. 2nd ed. London: Pan Books.

Appendix: The Doctoral Journey Planner[1]

---

[1] This planner is by AK Milroy.

© The Author(s) 2019
D. L. Brien et al. (eds.), *The Doctoral Experience*,
https://doi.org/10.1007/978-3-030-18199-4

Destination	'To do' lists	Time allocated (days)	Time remaining (days)
1. Preparing for the journey Ontological, epistemological and axiological ruminations and discussions	□ select appropriate supervisors and draw up a Memorandum of Understanding (MOU) in order to establish ground rules and expectations □ discuss and confirm your research proposal with your supervisors □ check—does the proposal require ethics approval?	Preparing your travel documents: the PhD application and 'visa'	1460-day
2. The proposal Methodological considerations	□ decide on your research question and topic title (both may change during the course of candidature) □ prepare a literature review/state of the art review □ outline your research design (methodology), including what data you intend to collect and how you intend to analyse it □ apply for ethics approval □ prepare your chapter list, or Table of Contents, and create a directory structure to reflect the same, preferably using a cloud-based system, Save As versions, so that you have a backup (which can be accessed from any location). In an ideal world, you would keep three copies: one on your computer, one in the cloud and another on an external storage device in a fireproof safe. Save your documents as versions in case you delete an idea, but subsequently decide it is an important point to include □ detail the significance of the study, answering the 'so what?' question □ review with supervisors □ edit and proof-read, repeat □ submit □ wait for proposal to be accepted	365	1065

(continued)

(continued)

Destination	'To do' lists	Time allocated (days)	Time remaining (days)

3. Confirmation of candidature	□ prepare your oral presentation in defence of your proposed research
	   □ keep it simple, clear, concise
	   □ use visuals effectively
	   □ remember the five P's: Preparation Prevents a Predictably Poor Performance
		7	1058

4. Ethics approval Axiological considerations	□ confirm that you have approval from the ethics committee, adjust as required □ examine your relationship to your research based on your social and cultural identity, and how this may affect your research	2	1056

5. Collecting/ creating data	□ begin
	  ○ collecting your data based on your research design and/or
	  ○ making artefacts based on your research design and/or
	  ○ creative writing based on your research
		600	456

6. Coding data	□ the literature/state-of-the-art review from 2. above will assist you in making a list of categories/codes from the key terms of your research question/s	30	426
7. Analysing data	□ identify what you will use to analyse your data by choosing the coded data that is most relevant to answering your research question/s	30	396

(continued)

(continued)

Destination	'To do' lists	Time allocated (days)	Time remaining (days)

8. Explaining/ Interpreting the data	□ using your codes, to develop the units of analysis, develop an explanatory scheme in order to interpret the data (e.g. defining; compare and contrast; causes and effects)
	□ prepare 'show and tell' type research outputs
	   ○ traditional research outputs: papers, publications
	   ○ non-traditional research outputs (NTROs): exhibitions, performances, public readings etc.
		30	366

9. Final write up	□ be clear about what you want to say and the ideas you wish to communicate □ practice the art of fast writing (which is about getting your ideas down on paper—it is NOT about editing) and slow revising (to craft the words into clearer expressions) (Gardiner & Kearns 2018)	60	306
10. Review by supervisory team	□ incorporate changes into your final document	30	276
11. Edit and proof-read final document (repeating as required)	□ edit to reflect higher level concerns such as the flow of ideas and the presentation of evidence to back up your claims □ proof-read your work, focusing on mechanical errors and formatting (tip: edit the first proof on-screen, then print out a hard copy and read it aloud) □ check the university's requirements □ submit to a copyright checking site	30	244
12. Submit	□ ensure your digital copy is readable across both Mac and Windows operating systems by saving it as a Portable Document (PDF) file	3	240

(continued)

(continued)

Destination	'To do' lists	Time allocated (days)	Time remaining (days)
13. Thesis defence	☐ schedule a time ☐ invite committee members ☐ share and defend your ideas—remember that this is an 'open book' examination and you wrote the book! (Peters 1997)	14	0
Strategic side-trips	☐ peer reviewed papers (ask your supervisory team for minimum numbers) ☐ attend exhibitions, performances, readings and publish relevant blog posts etc. ☐ produce artefacts (how many are required to answer your research question/s?) ☐ attend domestic conferences ☐ attend international conferences ☐ ensure allowed holidays are taken (30 days per year over four years) ☐ practice self-care: daily nutrition and exercise	40 40 40 8 8 120 daily	

Index

© The Author(s) 2019
D. L. Brien et al. (eds.), *The Doctoral Experience*,
https://doi.org/10.1007/978-3-030-18199-4